IMAGES
of America

CLINTON

I0806488

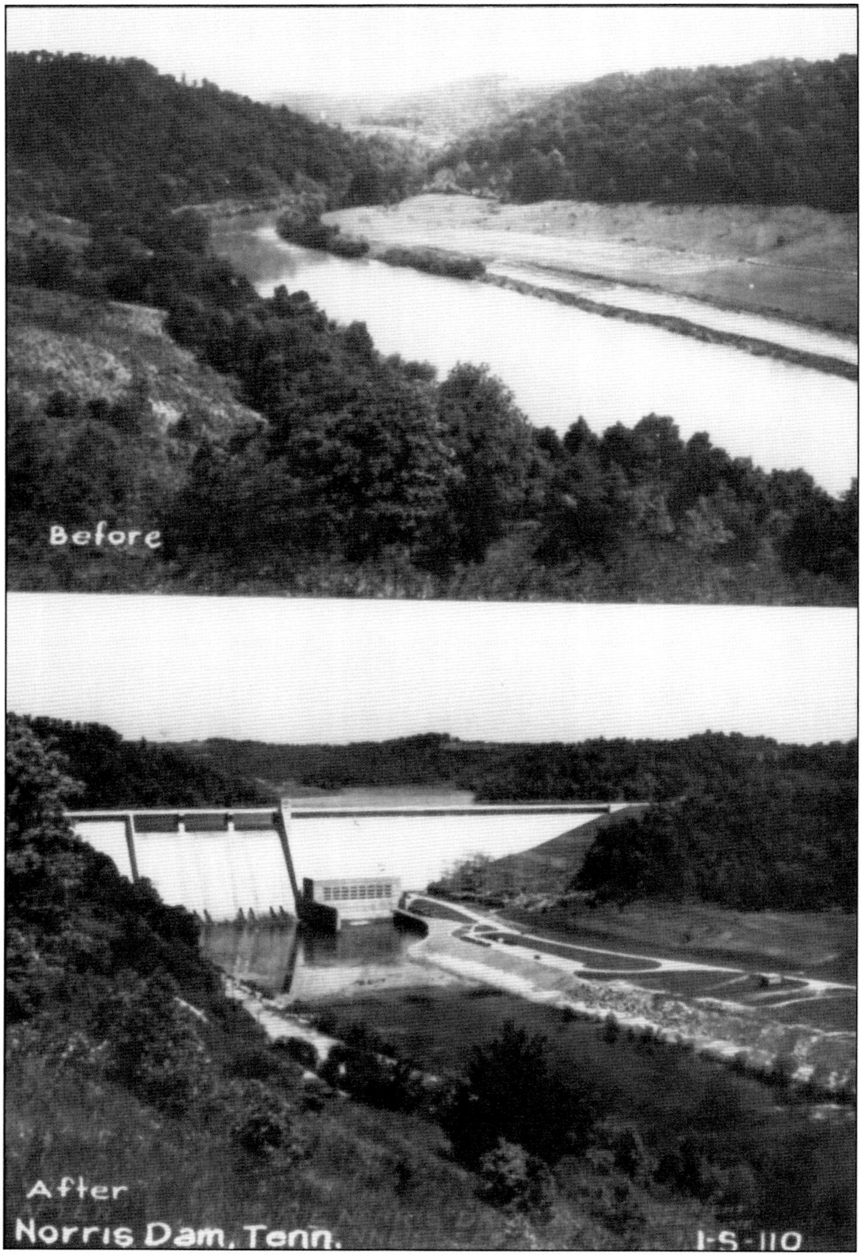

The completion of Norris Dam in 1936 irrevocably changed the future of Clinton. The removal of people from land that had been in their families for generations and the influx of workers from out of the area helped shift the county's focus from agriculture to industry. With flood control came the loss of river traffic and the end of the Clinch River pearl trade. (Courtesy of Mary Harris.)

On the Cover: The Strader Hotel stood on Depot (now Market) Street. Convenient to the Southern Railway depot, it catered to pearl buyers who frequented Clinton during the pearling season from May through October. This picture was taken in 1905 by Bernie H. Shinliver, owner of Clinton Art Studio. (Courtesy of the *Clinton Courier-News*.)

IMAGES
of America

CLINTON

Stephanie A. Hill

ARCADIA
PUBLISHING

ISBN 978-0-7385-8808-7

Published by Arcadia Publishing
Charleston, South Carolina

Printed in the United States of America

Library of Congress Control Number: 2011927631

For all general information, please contact Arcadia Publishing:
Telephone 843-853-2070
Fax 843-853-0044
E-mail sales@arcadiapublishing.com
For customer service and orders:
Toll-Free 1-888-313-2665

Visit us on the Internet at www.arcadiapublishing.com

This work is dedicated with love and affection to my husband, David Chris Hill, my son, Joseph Stephen Minter, and my grandson, Joseph Aaron Minter.

Contents

Acknowledgments

I wish to thank Bonnie Page, Mary Harris, the late Katherine Baker Hoskins, and the members, past and present, of the Pellissippi Genealogical and Historical Society for their dedication in helping to preserve the history of Clinton and Anderson County. Thanks also to Jerry and Ella Lynn Crossno of Norris, who educated me about the history of Norris Dam and the town of Norris and who saved a treasure trove of photographs and made them available to the public through the Norris Museum. Their work was my inspiration, and without all their efforts, my work would have been much harder.

I also wish to thank everyone who provided images for this book. I have given credit to contributors under individual photographs, but special thanks go to Mary Elkins Barker, Kay Crowell Davis, Elizabeth Thomason Bumgardner, and Susan Fowler for welcoming me into their homes, allowing me access to their family photographs and documents, and sharing with me their knowledge of the people and history of the communities in Anderson County. Special thanks also go to Judy Duncan Blakely for making an overnight trip from Kingsport to share her photographs and documents. I also want to express my appreciation to the husbands who graciously accepted a stranger's intrusion into their homes and family time.

Finally, I owe the biggest thank you to my husband, David Chris Hill, for his love, support, and encouragement, without which I would never have had the courage to undertake this project.

INTRODUCTION

Before Tennessee became a state, the area that became Anderson County had seen exploration by long hunters and had been surveyed by Daniel Boone for the partners of Richard Henderson & Co. Pioneers had already settled the area, many of them Revolutionary War veterans who had received land grants in what would become Tennessee for their service in other states.

Although it was never a large or profitable business in Anderson County, slavery did exist in the area, and the Civil War brought divided loyalties, making raids by both sides a frequent occurrence. Many homes and buildings were destroyed, and the land in many areas was stripped bare and laid waste. After the war, Clinton and Anderson County remained a rural area with timbering and agriculture as the primary industries until coal mining began to boom. Coal mining stimulated growth through an increased use of the railroad, which meant the building of the first depot in Clinton, the building of a junction line from Harriman to Clinton, and an influx of miners from as far away as Italy and Wales. National attention first focused on the area during the Coal Creek War of 1891–1892, a confrontation between coal miners and mine owners that ended the use of convict labor in the mines.

The building of Magnet Knitting Mill by six Clinton businessmen in 1906 brought the second influx of workers from outside the area and gave Clinton and Anderson County its next exposure to national attention. The building of Norris Dam by the Tennessee Valley Authority from 1934–1936 displaced many families, causing a shift in population from farm to town. Although it ended the Clinch River pearl industry, stopped barge traffic on the Clinch River between Clinton and Knoxville, and reduced the number of working farms, the construction project brought jobs and training to the local workforce and helped create the area's tourism industry.

More jobs and further population growth came with the federal government's building of Oak Ridge. Again, there was a shift from agriculture to factory jobs and with it an increase in education and skills. After World War II and the shift from war materiel production to scientific research, opportunities arose for new businesses and support personnel.

Clinton again received national media attention in 1957 with the bombing of Clinton High School during desegregation and once more in the 1970s with the renewed production in the coal mines of northern Anderson County and the efforts of members of Save Our Cumberland Mountains to stop strip mining. The completion of Interstate 75 from Lake City to Knoxville brought a further influx of population and growth and made the county's tourism and recreational resources available to more people. These factors combined to attract industries seeking to capitalize on a skilled labor force, access to markets, and low taxes.

Clinton now boasts three industrial parks, two major tourist attractions, two state parks, and recreational opportunities for hunters, fishermen, boaters, and off-highway vehicle (OHV) enthusiasts.

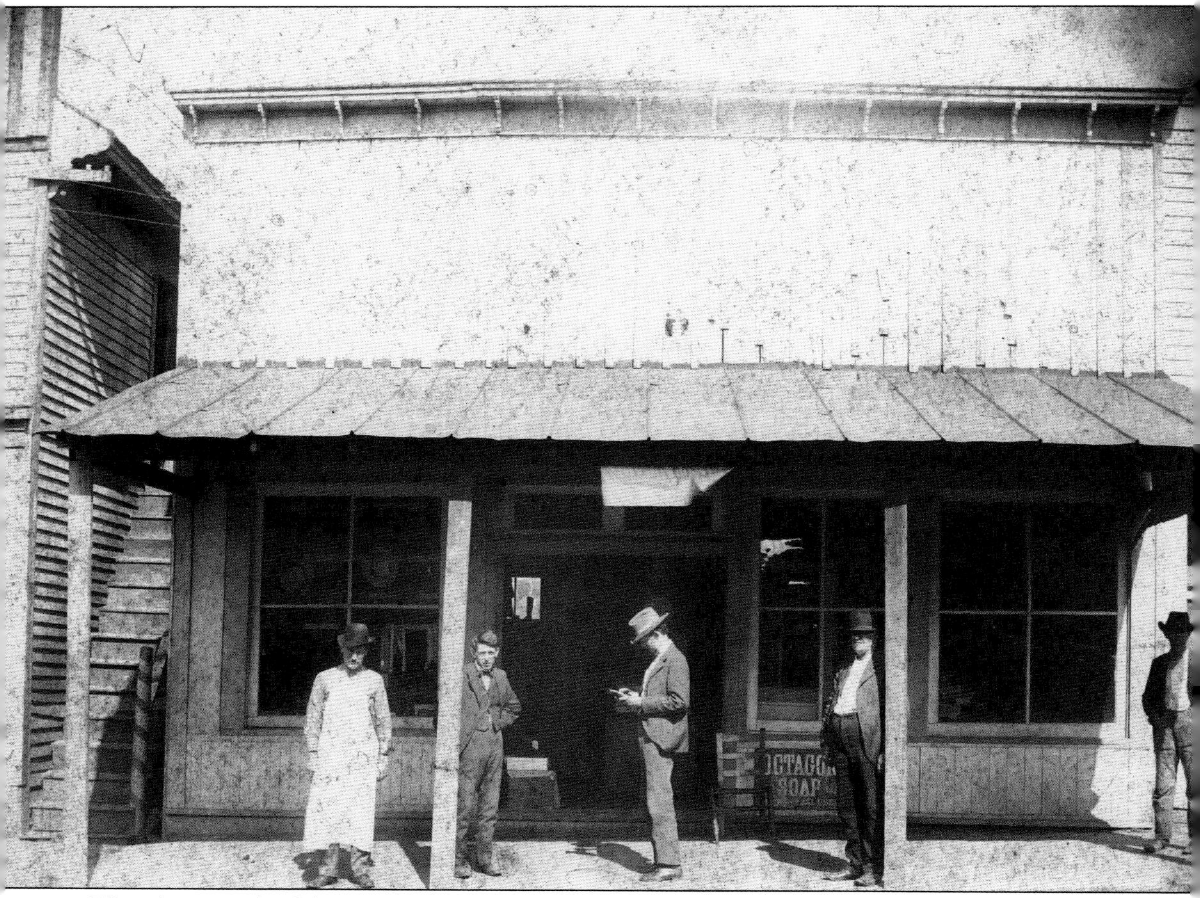

This photograph of the W.N. Foster dry goods store was taken in 1905. The store, its warehouse, and the Foster residence were destroyed in Clinton's great fire of 1908. The Fosters moved to Courthouse Square and opened a hotel and store there. Clinton suffered two devastating fires in the early 1900s. The first fire occurred on June 20, 1905, and burned an entire block at Depot (now Market) and Commercial (now Cullom) Streets. Destroyed in the blaze were R.P. Crowder & Co. grocery store, John F. Miller & Co. furniture and casket store, R.B. Bohanon's Hotel, Keebler's, and the Virginia Bottling Works. Built of brick, Union Bank stopped the spread of the fire, although a residence behind it burned. Several brick businesses on the opposite side of the street were heavily damaged. The great fire broke out on January 25, 1908, and destroyed 27 businesses and four residences. The city later passed an ordinance requiring that all new construction be brick. (Photograph by Bernie Shinliver; courtesy of the *Clinton Courier-News*.)

One

PEOPLE

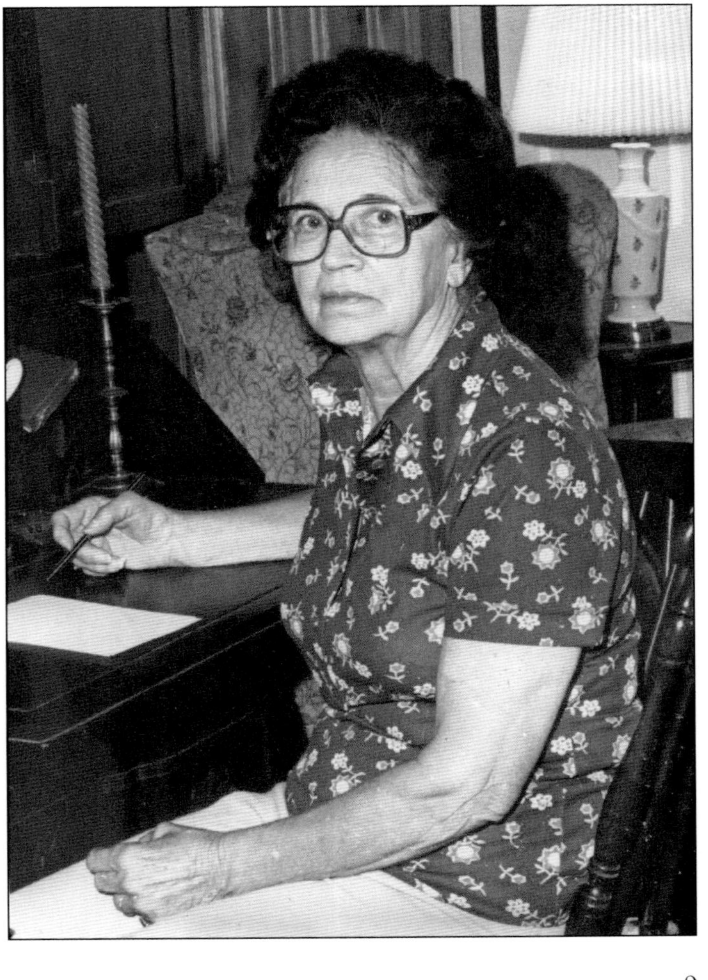

Katherine Baker Hoskins served as the county director of budgets and accounts, circuit court clerk, acting county court clerk, county administrator, and Anderson County historian. In addition to working 25 years at Magnet Mills, where she was editor of the plant publication the *Magnet*, she wrote many articles on local history for the *Clinton Courier-News* that were later published as *Historical Sketches*. (Courtesy of the *Clinton Courier-News*.)

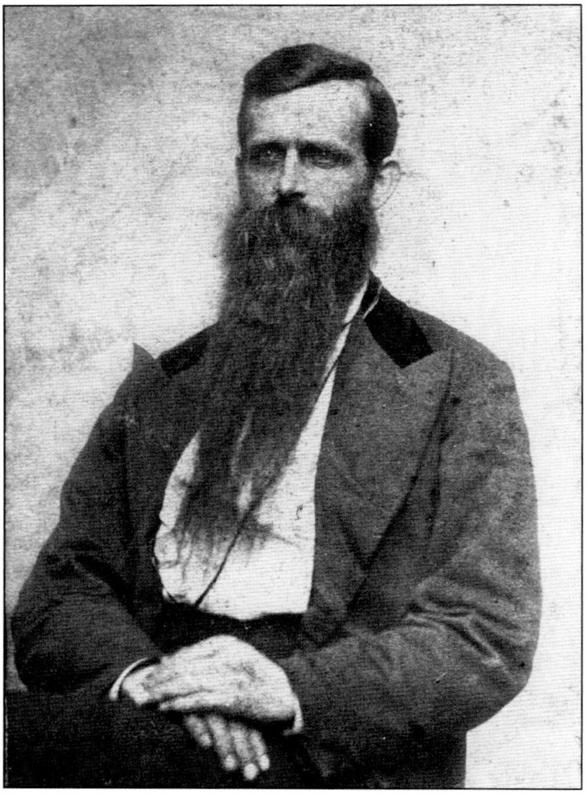

Dr. Peterson M. Liles was a physician who practiced medicine in Clinton for more than 20 years at the turn of the century. He was also a druggist with his own drugstore, located on Depot (now Market) Street next door to Dr. Sam B. Hall. He married Mary Peltier, and they had two children, Blanche and David. (Courtesy of Elizabeth Thomason Bumgardner.)

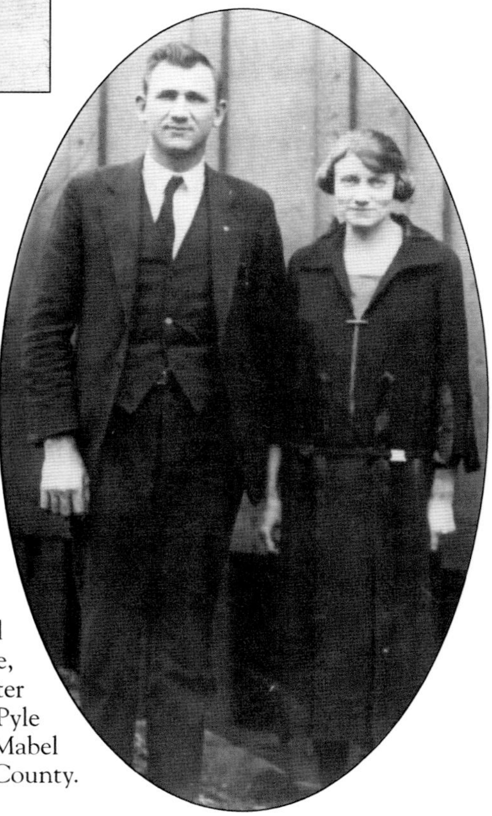

Harry Elmer Pyle, who was born in 1896 and died in 1969, was the son of James Edward Pyle and Hiley Ann Bell. He married Mabel Claire Stone, who was born in 1896 and died in 1947, the daughter of Charles Lee and Mary Lou Jett Stone. Elmer Pyle is buried at Pine Hill Baptist Church Cemetery. Mabel Pyle is buried in Lynnhurst Cemetery in Knox County. (Courtesy of Mary Harris.)

Walter Scott Thomason, who was born in 1868 and died in 1932, inherited the David Hall cabin from Nancy Arnold in 1902. Thomason traveled with the railroad and boarded with Arnold, helping to take care of her and the property during the last years of her life. He and his wife, Nannie, raised 10 children in the home. (Courtesy of Elizabeth Thomason Bumgardner.)

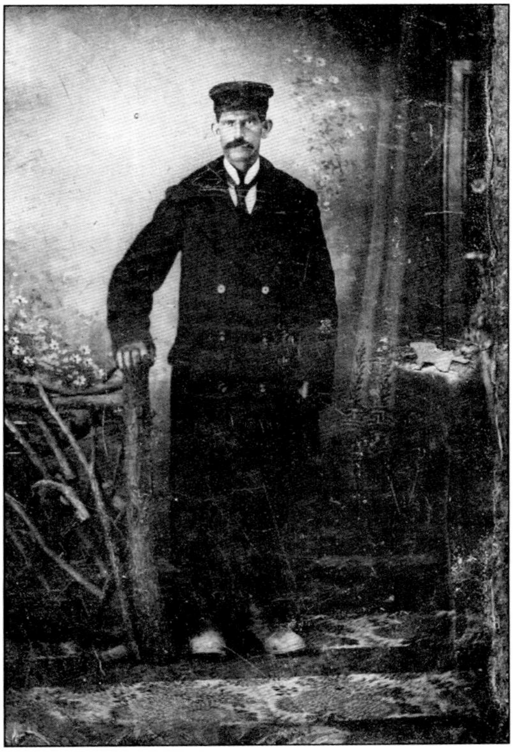

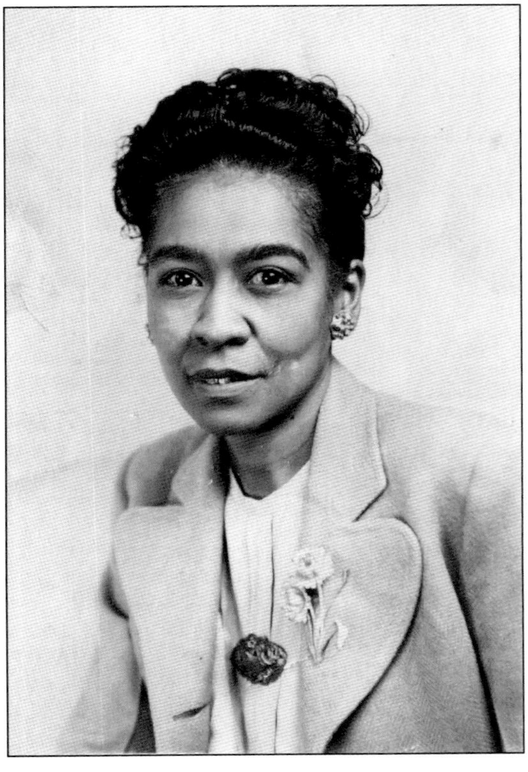

Theresa Blair taught first through fourth grades at the Green McAdoo School from the 1940s through its closure in 1965. Green McAdoo was a two-room schoolhouse for African American children, with the first through fourth grades in one room and fifth through eighth grades in the other. (Courtesy of Jo Ann Allen Boyce.)

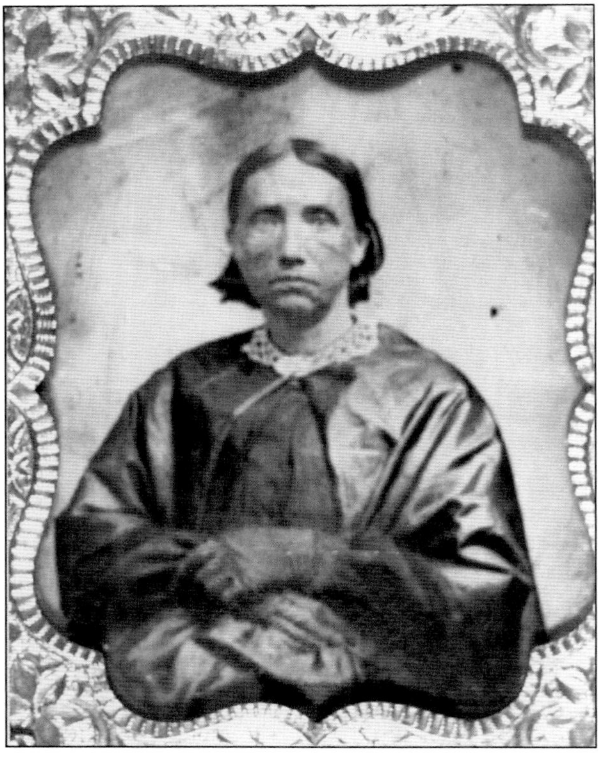

Sarah Tunnell, who was born in 1813 and died in 1893, was the daughter of William Tunnell and Elizabeth Worthington. She married William Peak, who was born in 1812 and died in 1864, the son of Jacob Peak and Mary Jones. Sarah Tunnell Peak is buried on Jacob Peak's farm in the Robertsville area of Oak Ridge. (Courtesy of Judy Duncan Blakely.)

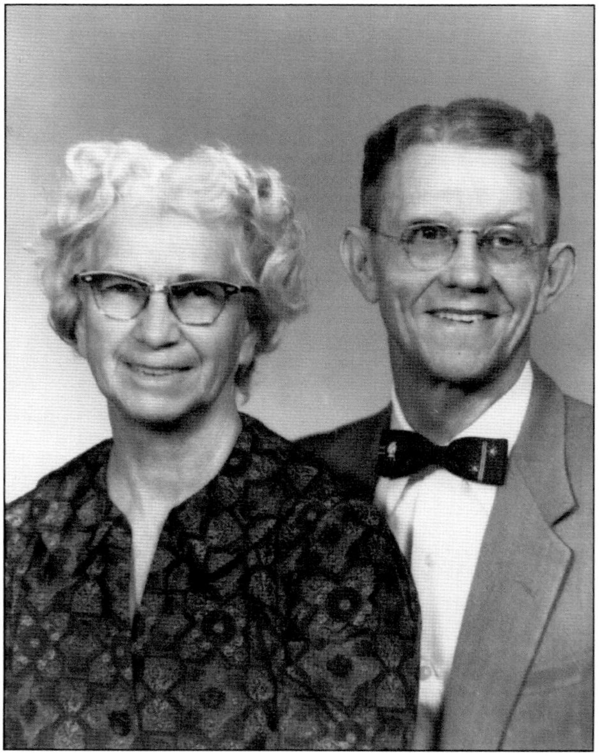

Buel Abner was born in 1905 and died in 1992. He was the son of Elihu Abner and Martha Jane Willoughby. He married Bertha Alice Hatmaker, who was born in 1904 and died in 1985. Buel and Bertha Hatmaker Abner were the parents of Charles Hugh Abner. (Courtesy of Charles Hugh Abner.)

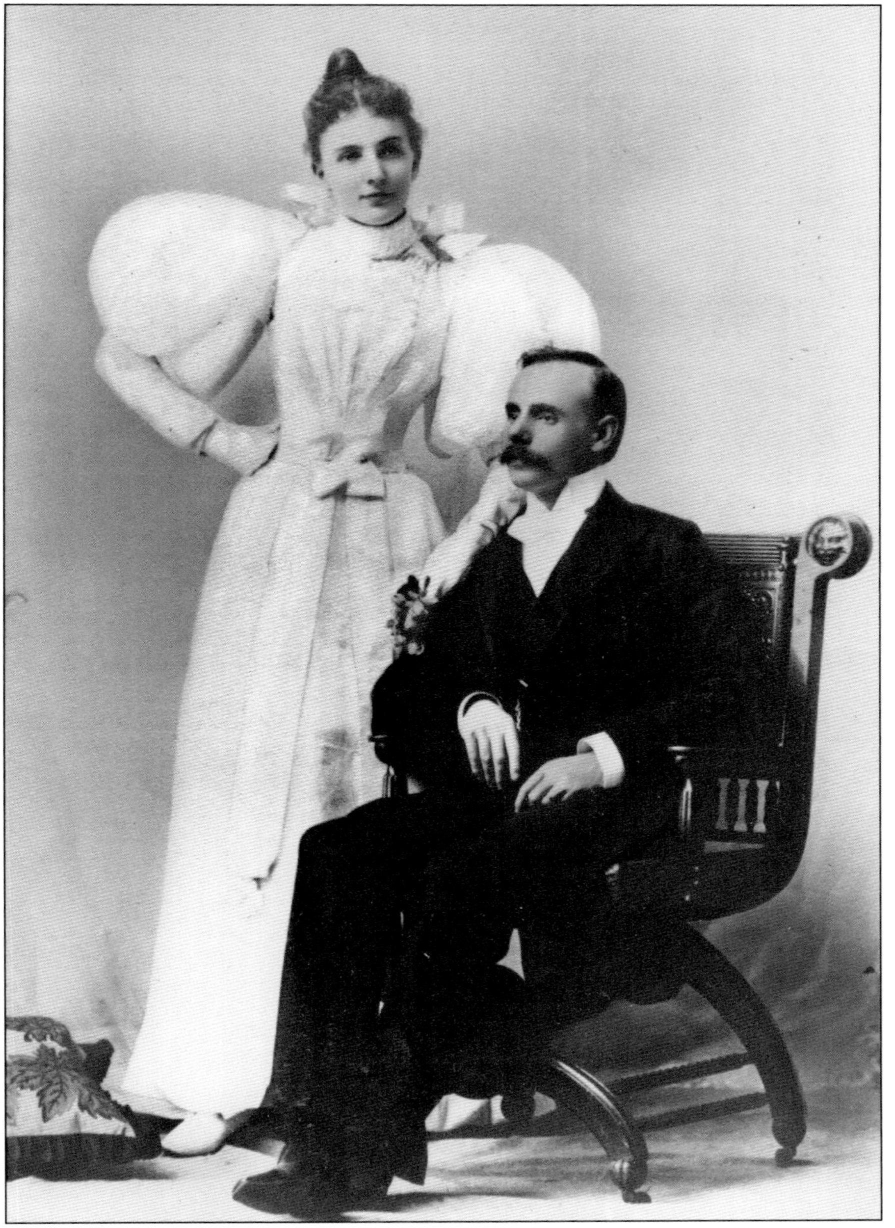

Samuel Patton Fowler and his wife, Mary Lee Robertson, were natives of Knox County, where they married in 1895. They moved to the Dutch Valley area of Clinton when Mr. Fowler assumed management of the East Tennessee Nursery Co., which had been incorporated in 1902 by his brother James A. Fowler and two partners. He became a partner in the business in 1906 and bought the old Edwards home, called The Hemlocks, located at the intersection of Old Dutch Valley Road and Old Lake City Highway. The home was built in the 1830s in what was then called the Ross community. After Sam Fowler built a one-room school and began teaching the local children, the community and school became known as Fowlers. After the nursery was dissolved, he opened a law practice in Clinton. Samuel and Mary Lee Fowler had six children. (Courtesy of Susan Fowler.)

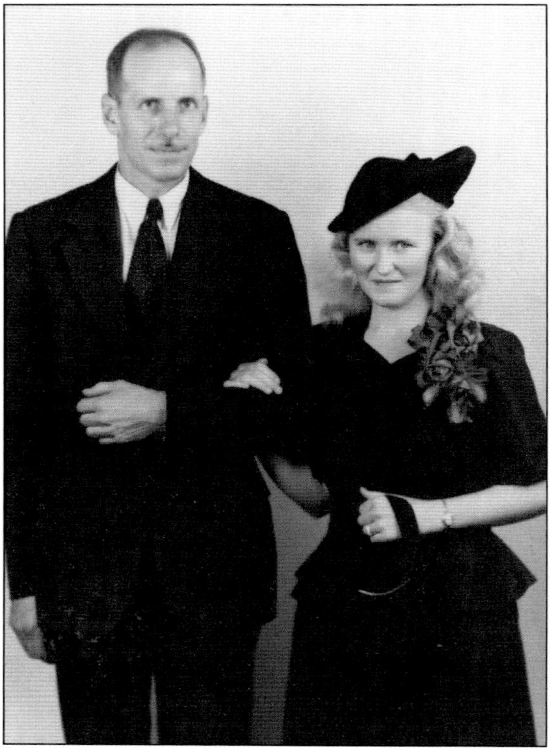

Samuel W. Fowler was the son of Samuel Patton and Mary Lee Robertson Fowler. He was a World War II veteran and worked at Morris-Bolling Ford in Clinton. He married Bertha Rucker, and they lived in The Hemlocks after his parents' deaths. Samuel W. Fowler passed away in 1993, and Bertha Fowler passed away in 2010. (Courtesy of Susan Fowler.)

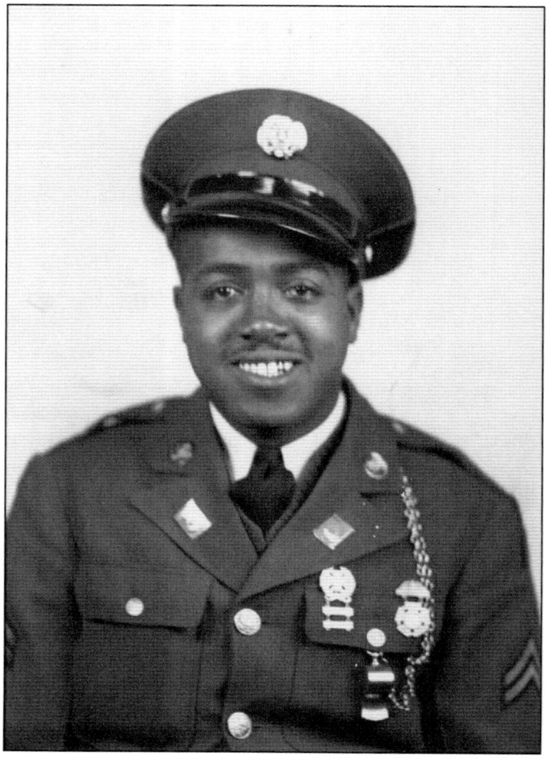

With the post–World War II layoffs in Oak Ridge, employment opportunities for unskilled labor outside the coal mines became hard to find. Opportunities opened in the automobile industry up north, which meant moving away from family and friends or making weekly commutes. Military service offered an alternative opportunity to many. Raymond Moore joined the military along with many other young Anderson County men. (Courtesy of Jo Ann Allen Boyce.)

Frank W. Wallace, who was born in 1894 and died in 1951, was a son of J. Shields and Nora Murray Wallace. A lifelong bachelor and a veteran of World War II, Wallace lived and worked on the family farm near Andersonville and is buried in Andersonville Cemetery. (Courtesy of Kay Crowell Davis.)

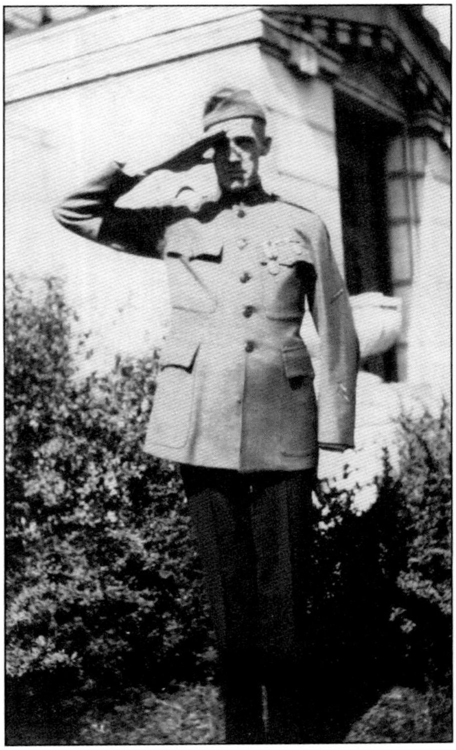

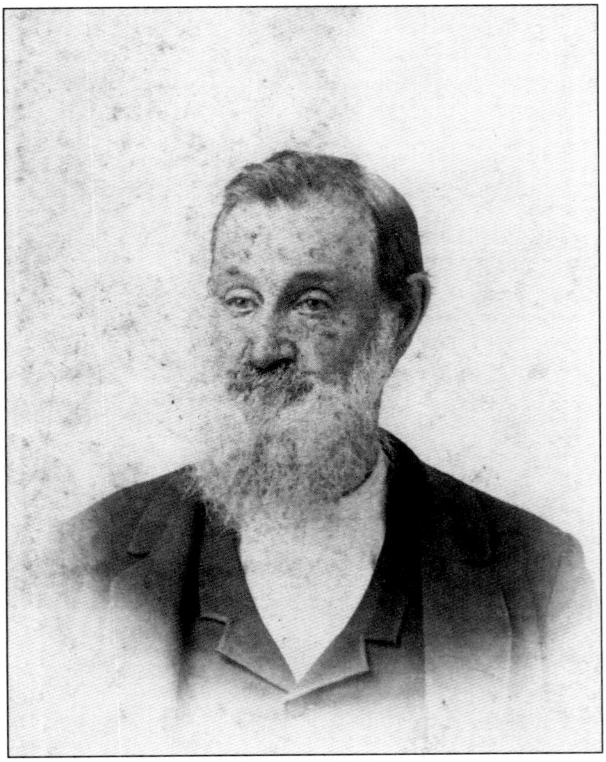

Col. John Coffee Chiles was born in 1820 and was an early settler in the Edgemoor area of Anderson County. He was a Union veteran of the Civil War, having served in the 3rd Regiment, Tennessee Infantry. After his wife's death, he made his home with Robert and Obedience Ann Moore, his son-in-law and daughter, until his death in 1902. (Courtesy of Mary Elkins Barker.)

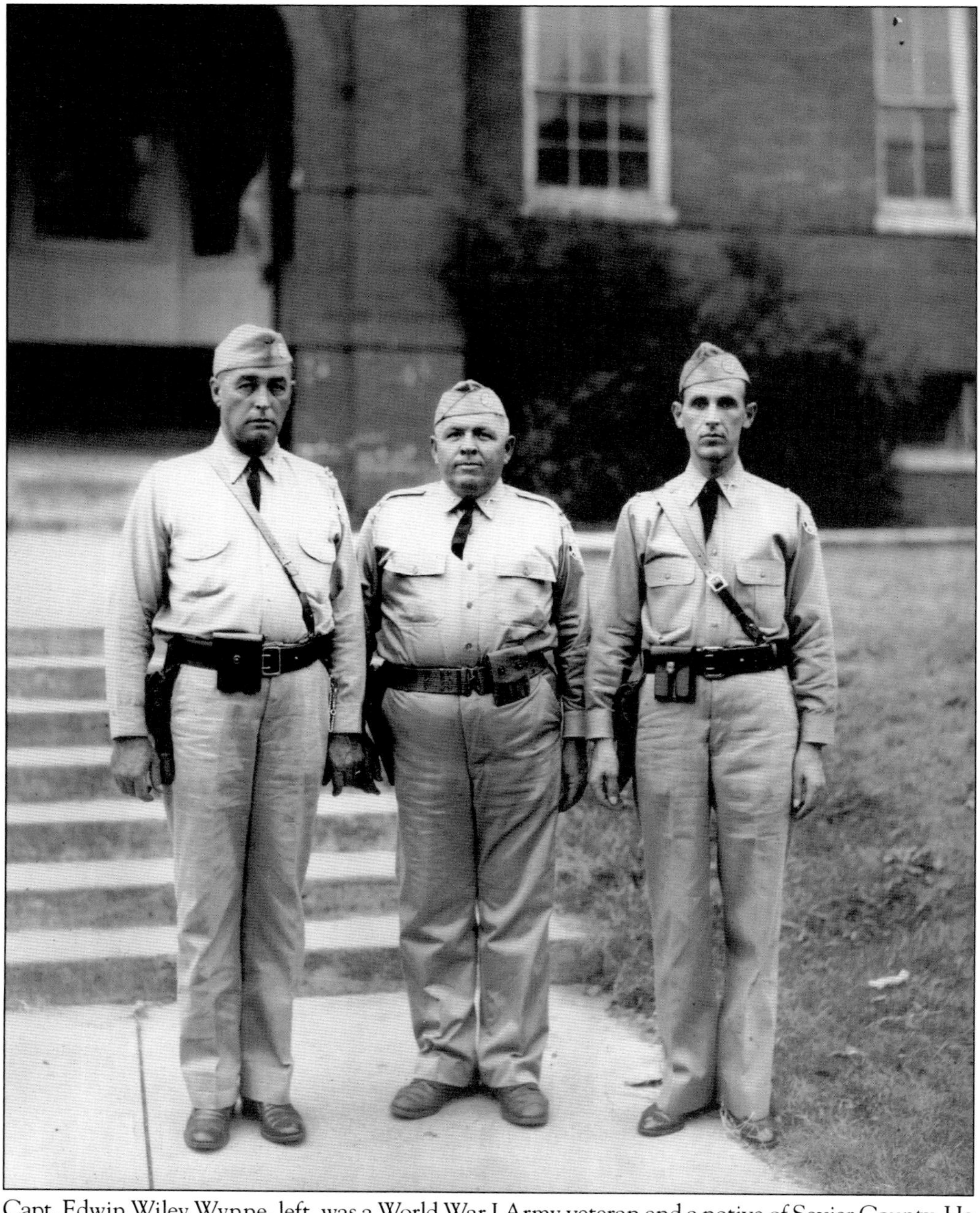

Capt. Edwin Wiley Wynne, left, was a World War I Army veteran and a native of Sevier County. He moved with his family from Alcoa to Clinton in 1926, when he accepted a position as compensation agent with the coal mines. In 1927, he established the first unit of the Tennessee National Guard to be based in Clinton since before the turn of the century. After it was activated during World War II, he organized a Home Guard unit in Clinton and served as its commander. In 1920, he had established a National Guard unit in Blount County. He served 18 years on Anderson County's Selective Service Board and was one of the organizers of the Clinton American Legion Post, where he served as post commander for three years. He died in 1959. (Courtesy of the Pellissippi Genealogical and Historical Society.)

Paul Rogers enlisted in the US Marine Corps and was a veteran of World War II. He was the son of Minnie Abner, who was born in 1896 and died in 1985, and Roscoe Rodgers, who was born in 1889 and died in 1967, both of Anderson County. (Courtesy of Charles Hugh Abner.)

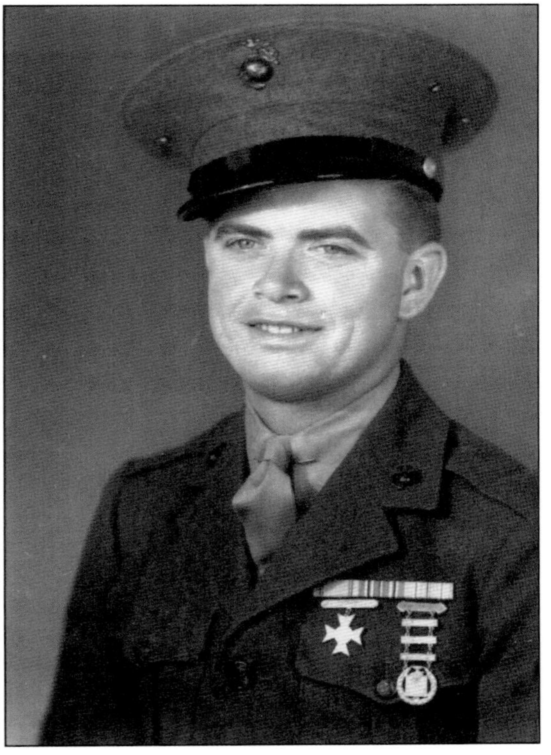

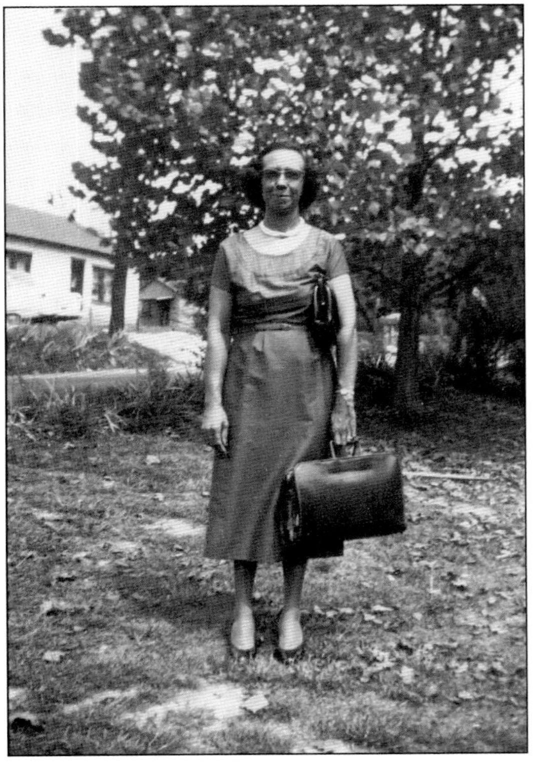

Alice Josephine Hopper Allen was the wife of Herbert Allen. A native of Roane County, she served as pianist for Mount Sinai Baptist Church, where she was a member of the choir. In the photograph at left from about 1950, she is pictured carrying her music case to church for choir practice. (Courtesy of Jo Ann Allen Boyce.)

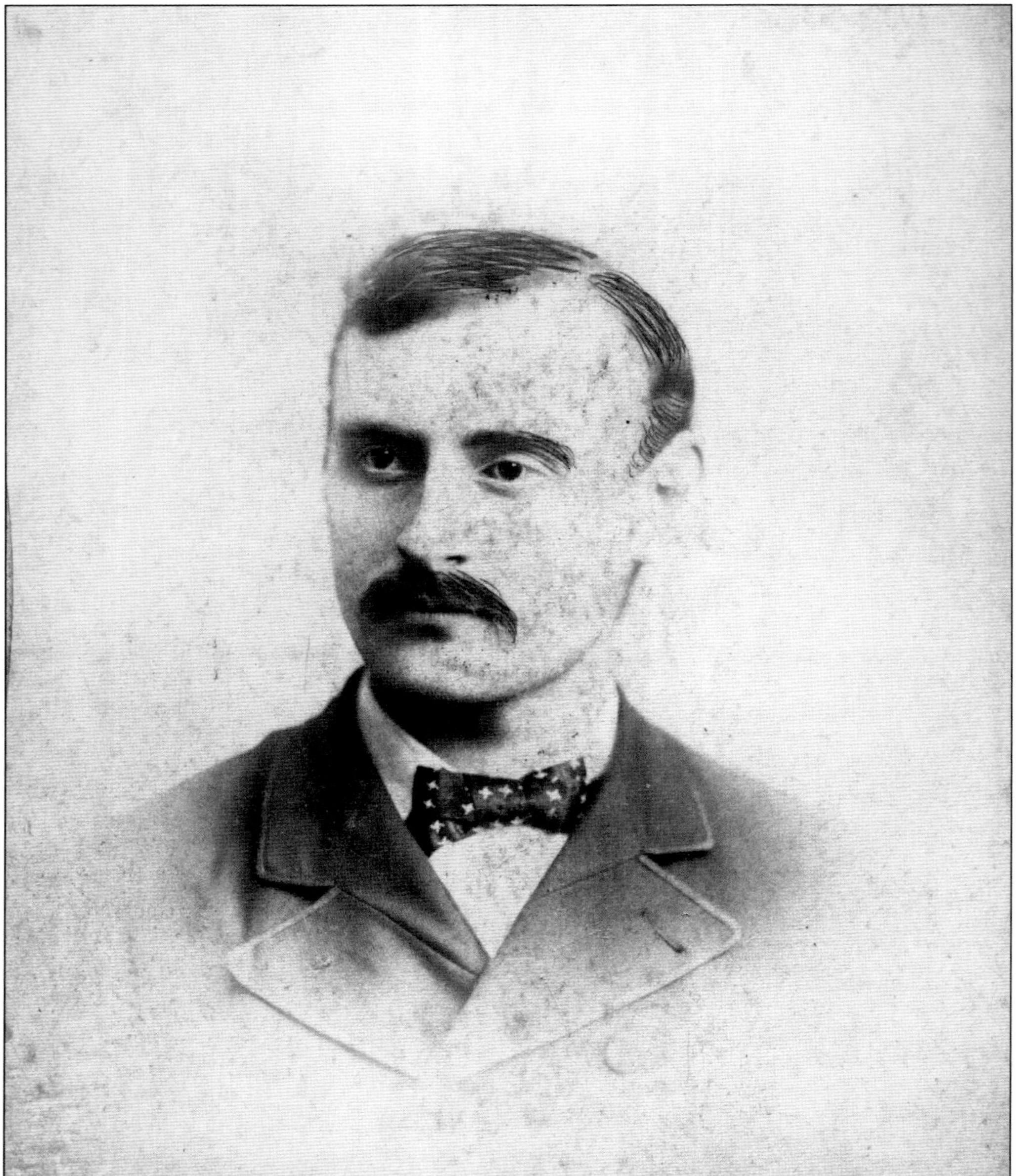

James Alexander Fowler, the son of Joseph Wesley and Mary Conner Fowler, was the brother of Samuel Patton Fowler and a partner with him in the East Tennessee Nursery Co., which he had incorporated in 1902. He graduated from Athens University, taught at Clinton Academy, read law under Judge W.R. Hicks, and was licensed to practice law in 1886. He clerked for circuit court clerk Clay Slover while building his practice. He was secretary of the Anderson County Republican Executive Committee and an organizer of the Union Bank of Clinton, which he served as its attorney. He became the assistant US attorney general in 1908 and served under the Harding administration. He married Lucy Hornsby of Athens. The Fowlers built a home at the corner of Medaris Street and Maire Avenue in Clinton before moving back to Knoxville. (Courtesy of Susan Fowler.)

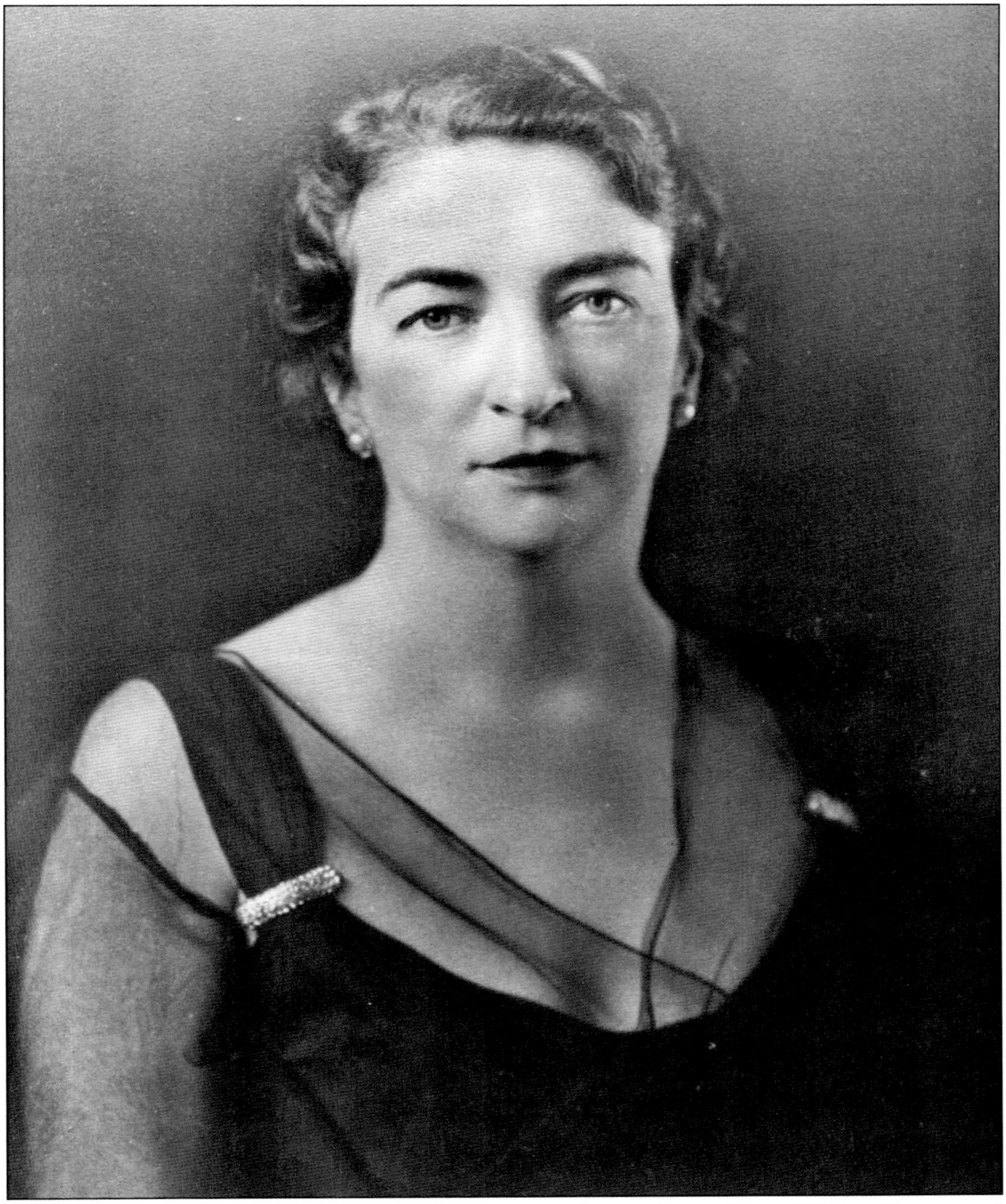

Eloise Jaudon Harris Wynne was a native of Virginia, the daughter of Rev. William Francis and Polly Payne Harris, and the wife of Edwin Wiley Wynne. She graduated from Richmond College in Virginia and received her master's degree in education from the University of Tennessee. She was chief chemist for Aluminum Company of America (ALCOA) before moving to Clinton in 1926. She taught chemistry and biology at Clinton High School, was a charter member of the Anderson County Chapter of the National Foundation for Infantile Paralysis, and organized the Clinton, Lake City, Norris, Oak Ridge, and Oliver Springs units of the American Legion Ladies Auxiliary. She served as executive secretary of the Red Cross and was a member of the James White Chapter of the Daughters of the American Revolution (DAR). The Wynnes had two daughters, Edwina and Mary Frances. (Courtesy of the Pellissippi Genealogical and Historical Society.)

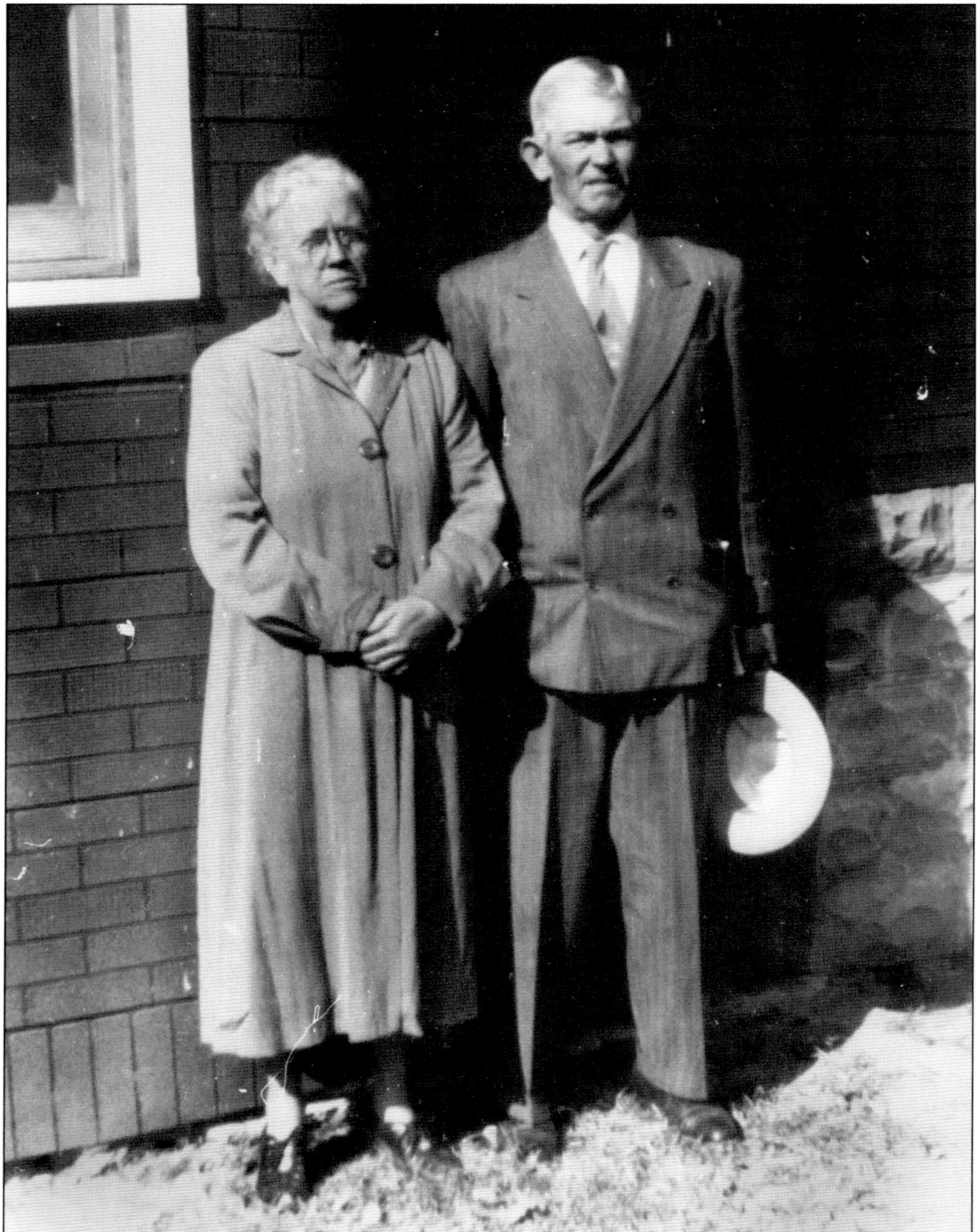

Hubert Arthur Foust, the son of James Lewis and Minerva A. Foust, was born in 1898 and died in 1977. His wife, Martha Tennessee Lindsay, was the daughter of Isaac Thomas Lindsay and Nancy Arminda Bullock. She was born in 1896 and died in 1982. They lived in the Clear Branch area of Anderson County and are buried in Leach Cemetery, behind Clear Branch Baptist Church. Harry Monroe Foust, who was born in 1905 and died in 1992, and Abraham Lincoln Foust, who was born in 1903 and died in 1974, were two of Hubert Arthur Foust's brothers. Harry Monroe Foust left Tennessee and settled in California. (Courtesy of Charles Hugh Abner.)

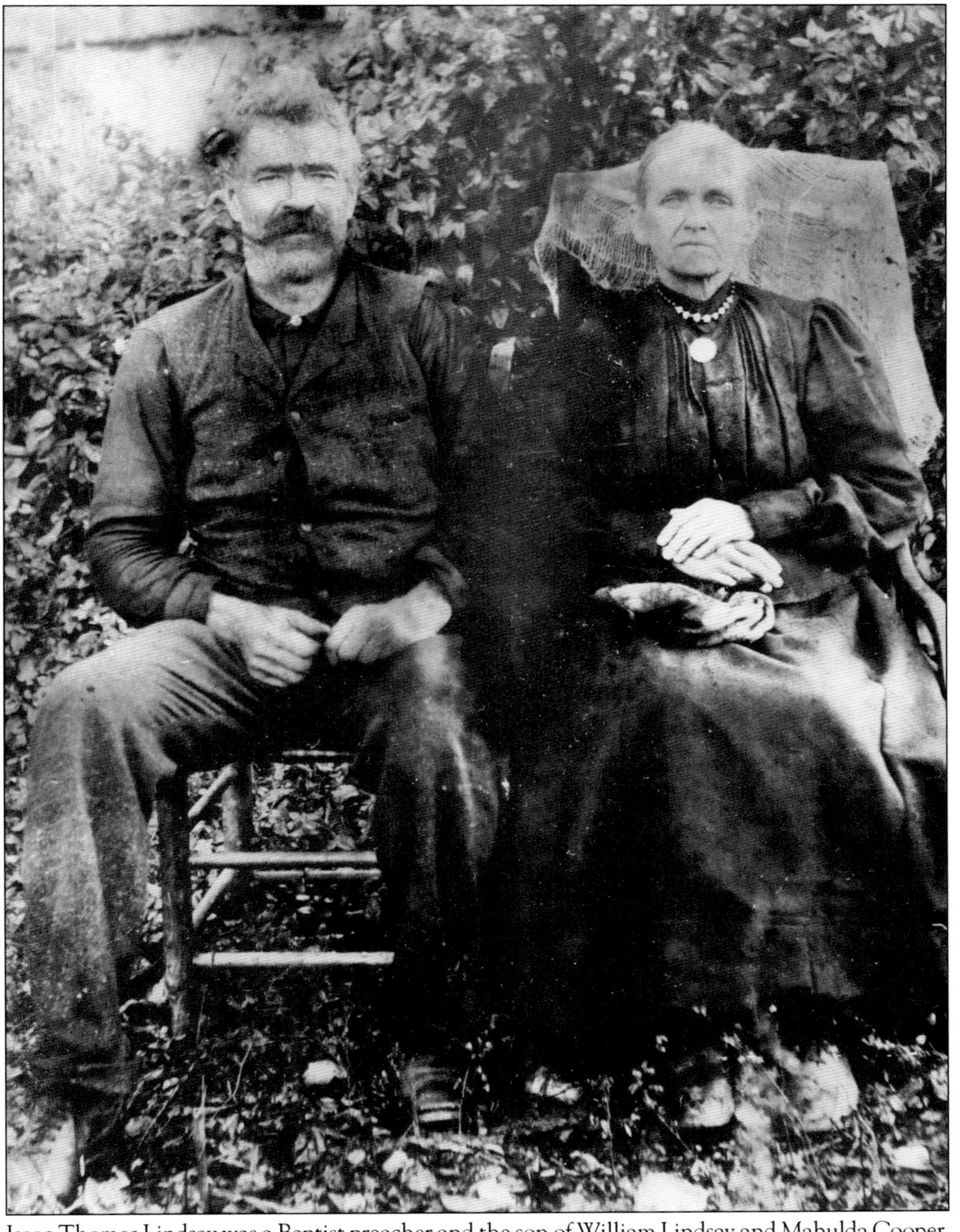

Isaac Thomas Lindsay was a Baptist preacher and the son of William Lindsay and Mahulda Cooper. He was born in 1857 and died in 1939. In 1877, he married Nancy Arminda Bullock, who was born in 1851 and died in 1929. She was the daughter of Francis Bullock and Milly Beach. Thomas and Nancy Lindsay were the parents of Martha Tennessee Lindsay, who married Hubert Arthur Foust, and of Mahulda Lindsay, who married Charlie Hatmaker. Isaac Thomas Lindsay and Nancy Arminda Bullock Lindsay are buried in the Longfield Baptist Church Cemetery, located on the Norris Freeway outside Lake City. (Courtesy of Charles Hugh Abner.)

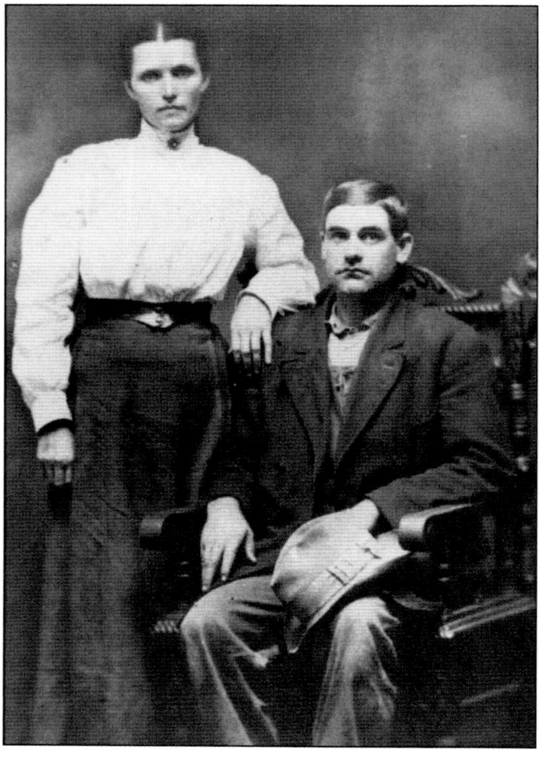

Jesse King Worthington was born in 1878 and died in 1923. In 1896, he married Martha Ellen Braden, who was born in 1879 and died in 1960, the daughter of Robert and Rachel Lawson Braden. Jesse and Martha were the parents of John Worthington and are buried in Sunset Cemetery in Clinton. (Courtesy of Judy Duncan Blakely.)

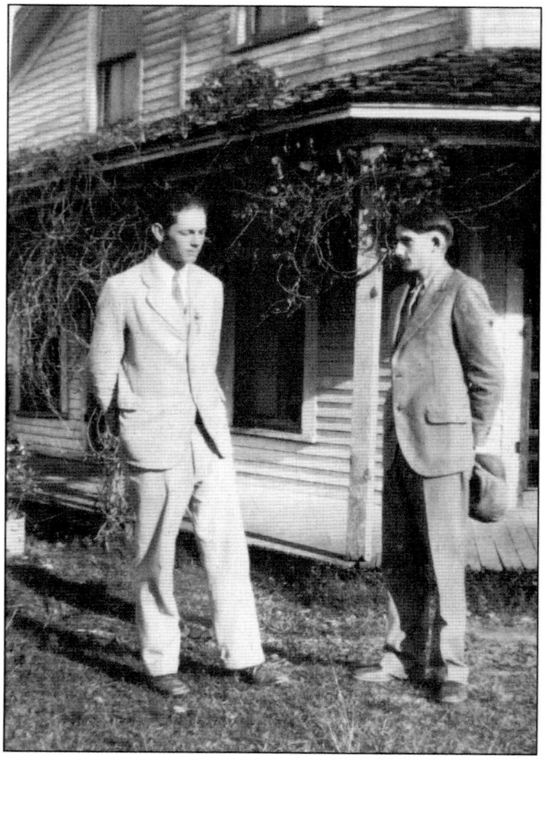

Herman Miller and Ralph Pyatt were from the Claxton-Edgemoor area of Anderson County. Ralph Pyatt was the son of John W. and Mary Anne Pyatt, who bought the old Laura McAdoo home on Carlock Street in Clinton. He married Ruth Keith, and they had three daughters: Betty Lynn, Sharon Ann, and Barbara. (Courtesy of Mary Elkins Barker.)

Samuel T. Pyatt, the son of John W. and Mary Anne Pyatt, was born and raised in the Claxton and Edgemoor communities of Anderson County but moved to Clinton after his parents bought the old McAdoo home. He was born in 1908 and died in 1987. He is pictured in this photograph with Murrell Ellis. (Courtesy of Mary Elkins Barker.)

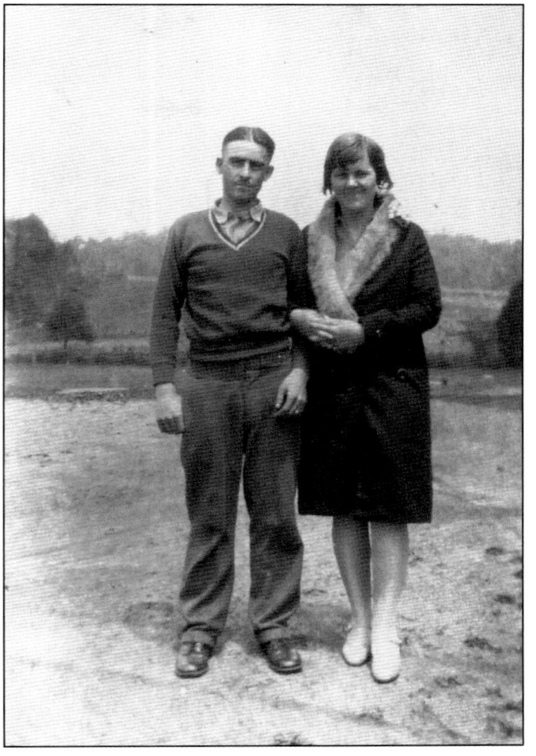

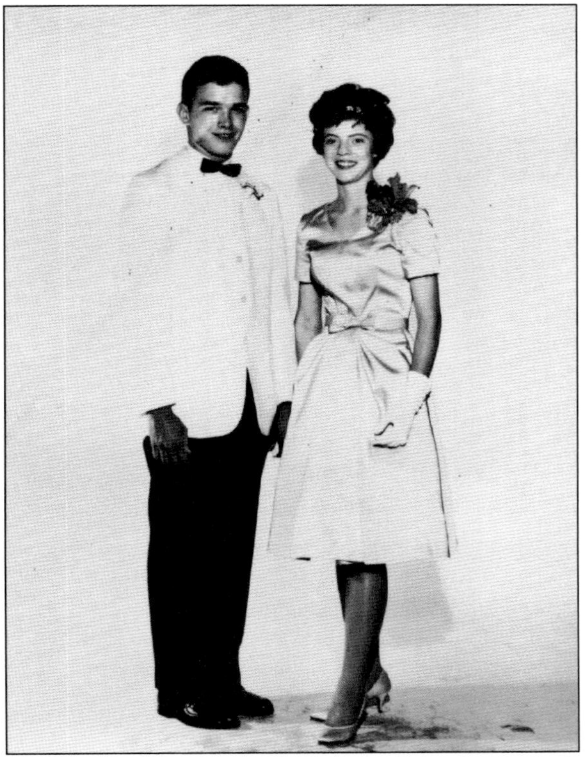

Art Barker and Mary Elkins, the daughter of Joe and Allie Ruth Moore Elkins, attended the 1962 Clinton High School senior prom as high school sweethearts and later married. They now live in Luttrell. Mary Elkins attended Claxton Elementary School through the eighth grade. (Courtesy of Mary Elkins Barker.)

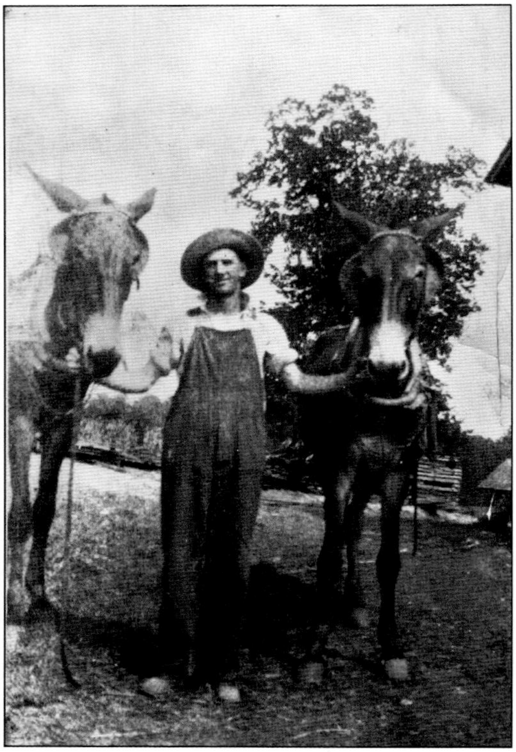

Frank Alonzo Rutherford (left) was born in 1906 and died in 1976. He married Ruby Weaver, who was born in 1909 and died in 1943, the daughter of Rufus and Mary Johnson Weaver. Rufus Weaver's farm once included all the land on which Anderson County High School now sits. The family of his wife, Mary Johnson, owned the land that is now the Alex Haley farm, across State Highway 61 from the Museum of Appalachia in the Bethel community near Norris. Frank's farm in the 1950s backed up against the land that became the Haley farm. In 1950, he and his son Bobby Frank Rutherford built the Norsonian Restaurant in Norris. Frank and Ruby Rutherford (below) are buried in Norris Memorial Gardens; Rufus and Mary Johnson Weaver are buried in Bethel Baptist Church Cemetery. (Both, courtesy of Doug Rutherford.)

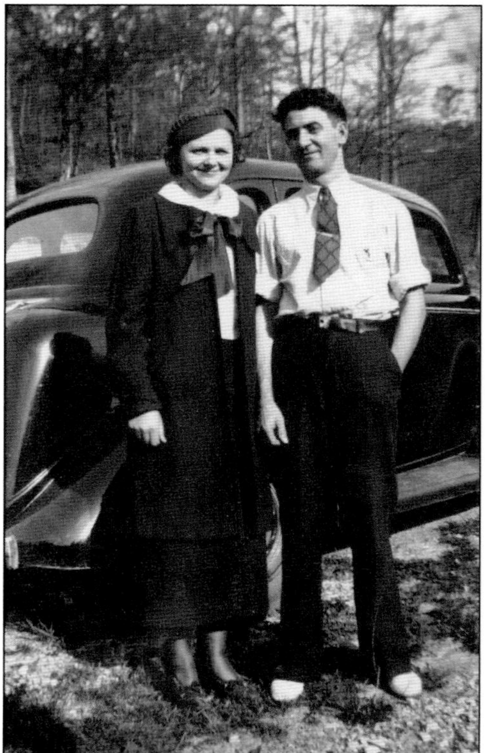

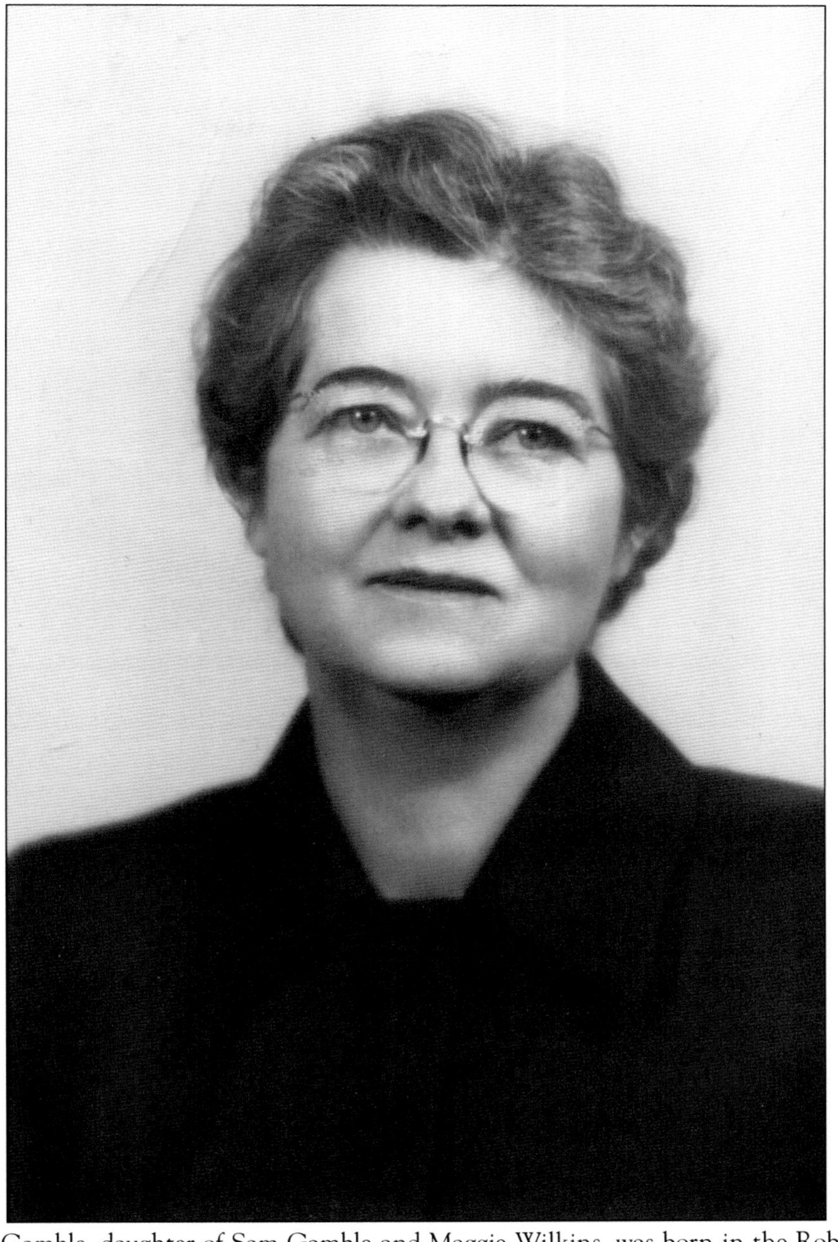

Ida Inez Gamble, daughter of Sam Gamble and Maggie Wilkins, was born in the Robertsville community in 1897 and died at her home in Clinton in 1993. Her family was among those displaced when the federal government took land in 1943 to build Oak Ridge as part of the Manhattan Project. She graduated from Clinton High School and the University of Tennessee. She taught Latin and English at Etowah, Decatur, Coal Creek (now Lake City), and Powell for 43 years. She was a member of Memorial United Methodist Church of Clinton and the Delta Kappa Gamma sorority, a charter member of the Retired Teachers Association, and a 50-year member of the Order of the Eastern Star. She had one sister, Frances Freels, and four brothers, Eugene, Oscar, John, and Young Gamble. She is buried in the Gamble Cemetery at Kern United Methodist Church in Oak Ridge. (Courtesy of Mary Elkins Barker.)

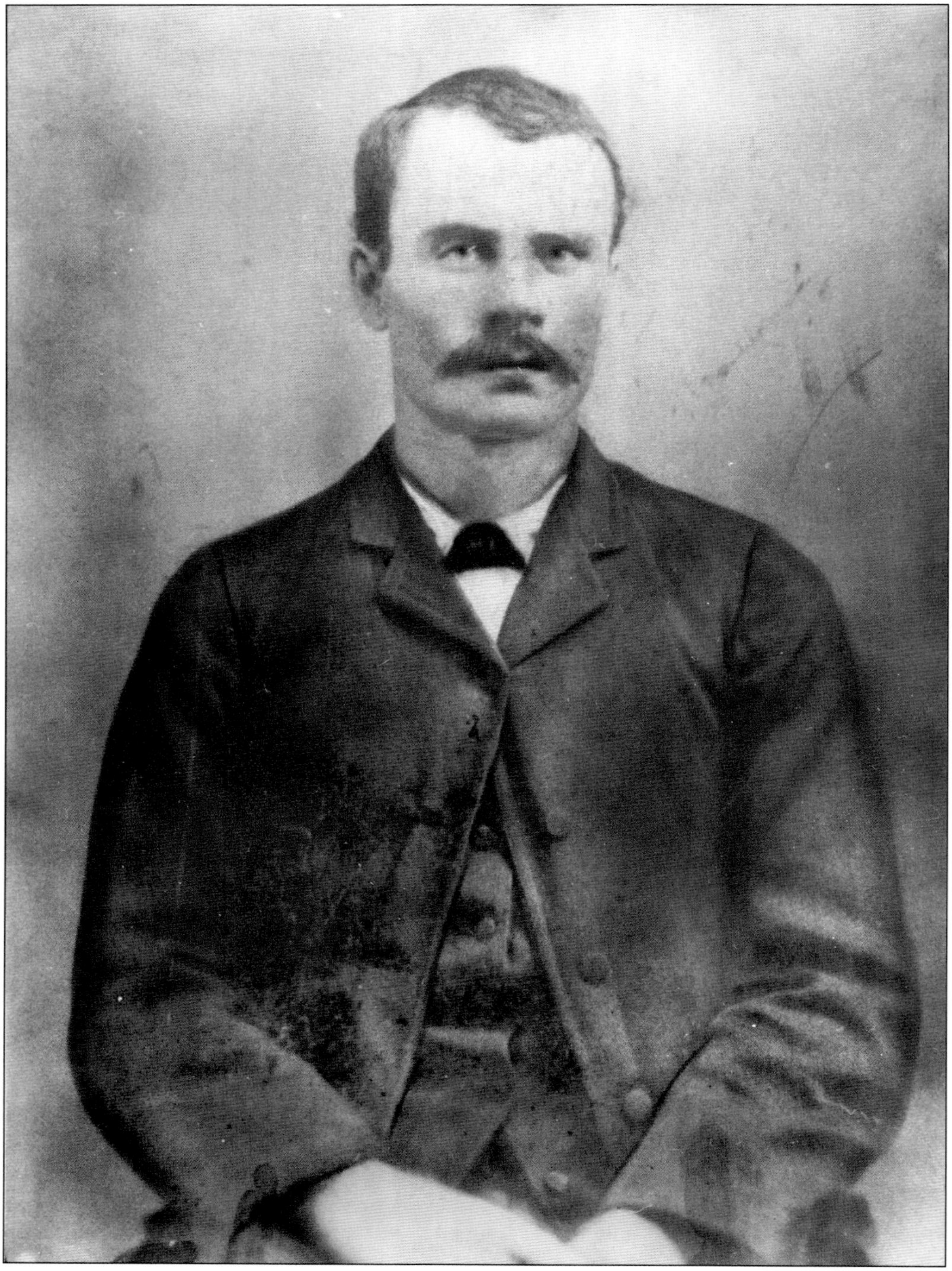

Elihu Abner was born in Kentucky in 1862 and died in 1906 in a coal mining accident. He married Martha Jane Willoughby, who was born in 1873 and died in 1941, the daughter of James B. and Rachel Willoughby. Elihu and Martha were the parents of Buel Abner and are both buried in unmarked graves in Ross Cemetery, located in the Medford section of Anderson County. (Courtesy of Charles Hugh Abner.)

Charles Hugh Abner was born in the Clear Branch community of Anderson County and graduated from Lake City High School and the University of Tennessee with a bachelor's degree in engineering. He is a mechanical engineer who worked at Oak Ridge National Laboratory for more than 40 years and is a member of the Pellissippi Genealogical and Historical Society. He is married to the former Wanda Lou Shetterly, and they have two children, Delores and Byron. (Courtesy of Charles Hugh Abner.)

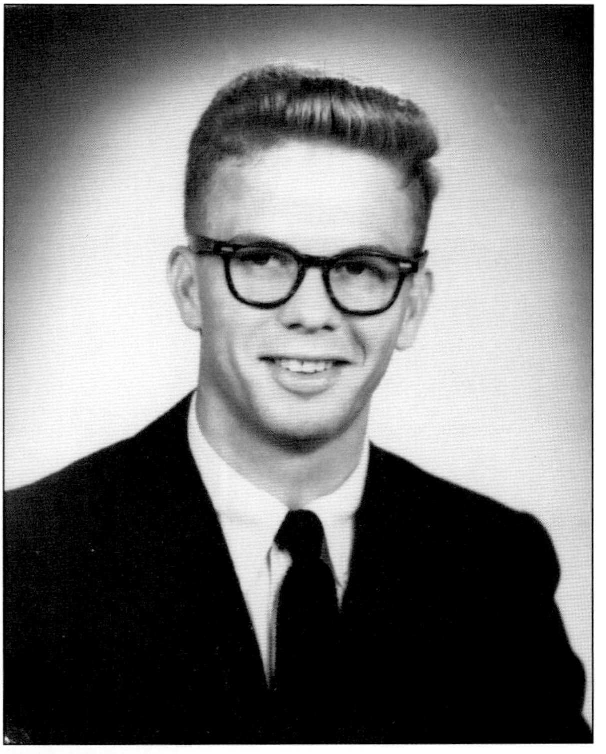

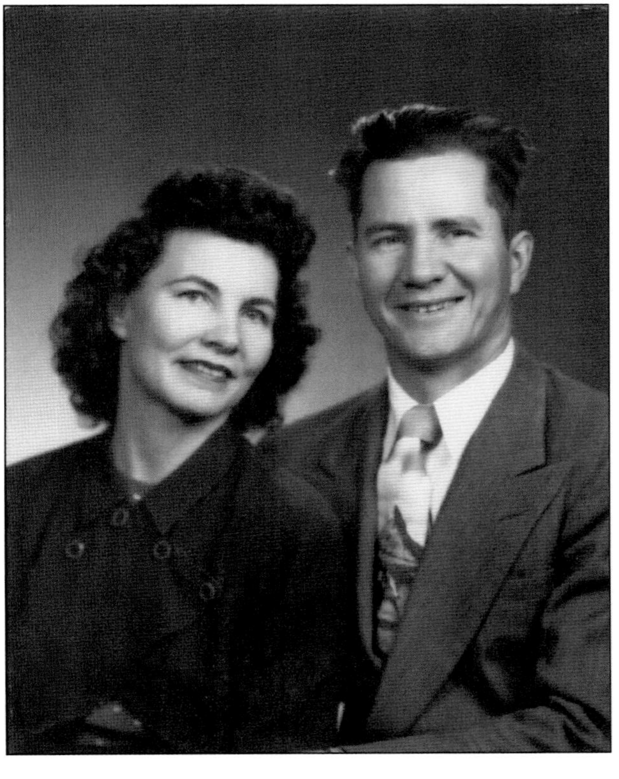

Franklin Roosevelt Shetterly married Lula Bernice Brown, who was born in 1913 and died in 2003, daughter of Eli Lowe and Mary Jane Seiber Brown. Franklin and Lula were the parents of Wanda Lou Shetterly, who is the wife of Charles Hugh Abner. They lived in the Black Oak community of Clinton. (Courtesy of Charles Hugh Abner.)

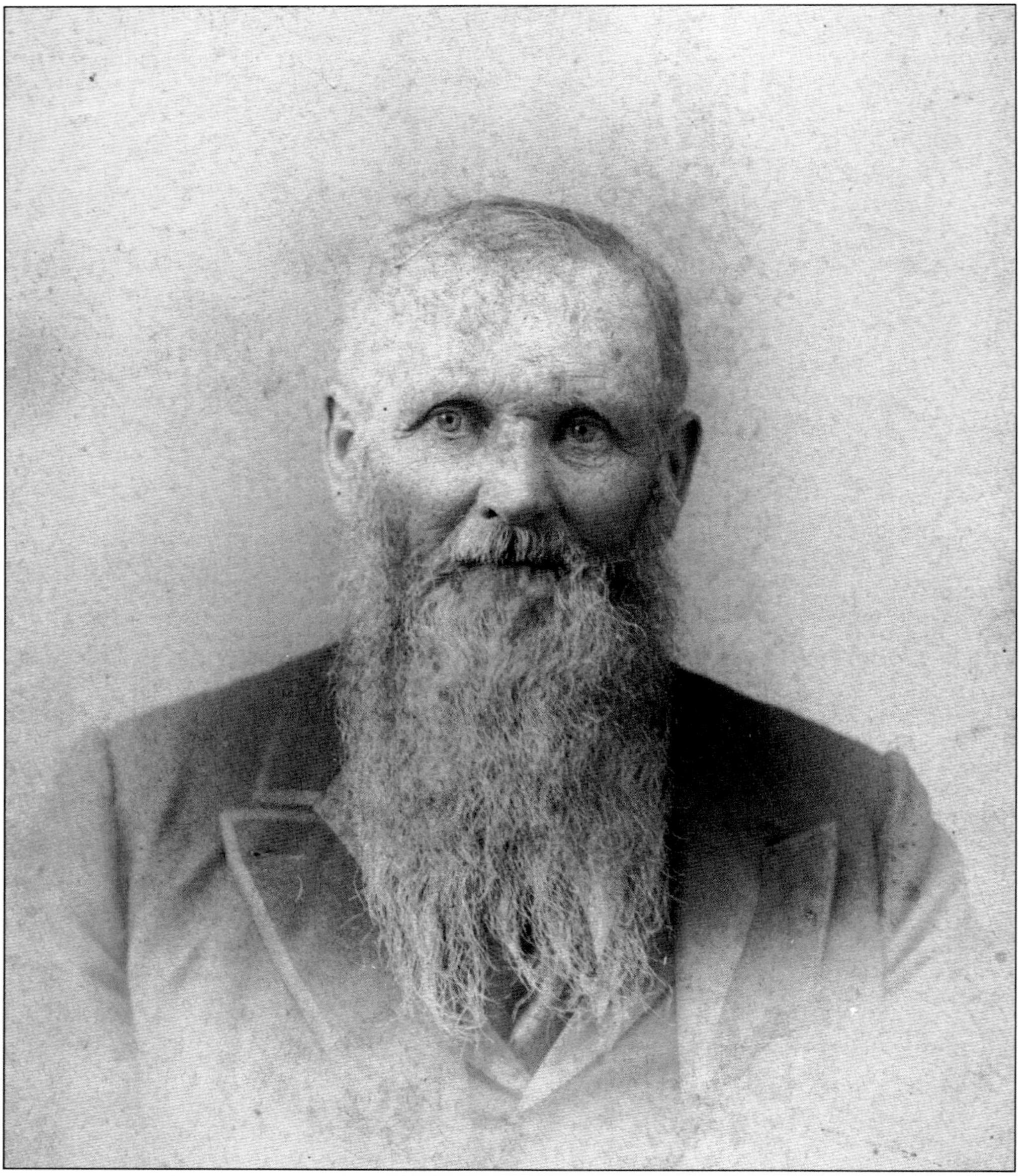

Frank P. Rutherford was the oldest son of Mark and Paulina Gibbs Rutherford, two of the organizing members of the Andersonville Baptist Church. Mark Rutherford was born in 1835 and died in 1916. Paulina Gibbs Rutherford was the daughter of Howard and Nancy Taylor Gibbs. She was born in 1836 and died in 1919. Frank P. Rutherford was a deacon in the Andersonville Baptist Church and president of the Board of Trustees for Andersonville Institute from 1897 through 1902. He owned and operated a store in Andersonville in partnership with his brother Charles N. Rutherford. The building is still standing and was also the site of the old Andersonville Post Office. His youngest brother, William Howard Rutherford, was the first ordained minister of Andersonville Baptist Church. Frank Rutherford married Martha "Mattie" Wallace, a daughter of John Wallace and Rosannah Mills Lamar, of Andersonville. He moved with his family to Oklahoma in later years. This picture is dated October 1892. (Courtesy of Kay Crowell Davis.)

Ida Marie Davidson Shetterly was a native of Morgan County, the daughter of Morgan Taylor and Martha Howard Davidson. She was born in 1871 and died in 1953. She married John Henry Shetterly, son of George Washington and Katherine Frances Marshall Shetterly. Ida and John were the parents of Franklin Roosevelt Shetterly. She is buried in Sunset Cemetery in Clinton. (Courtesy of Charles Hugh Abner.)

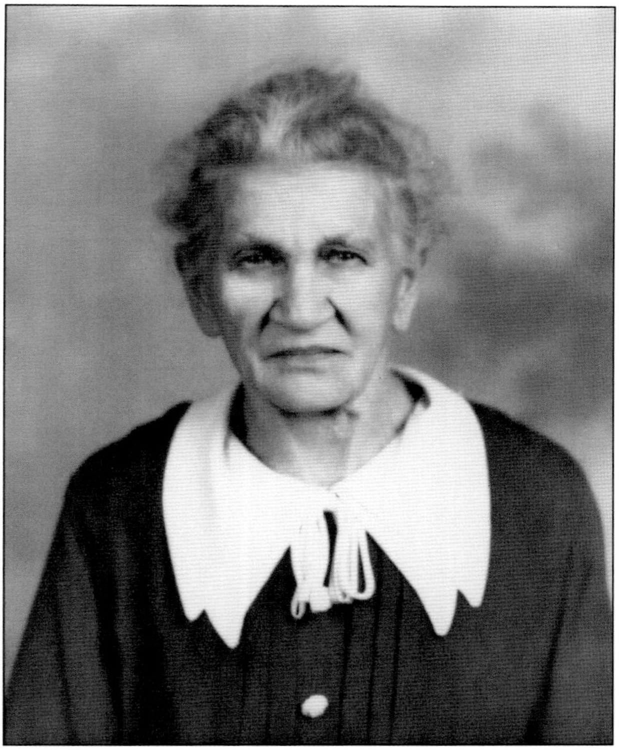

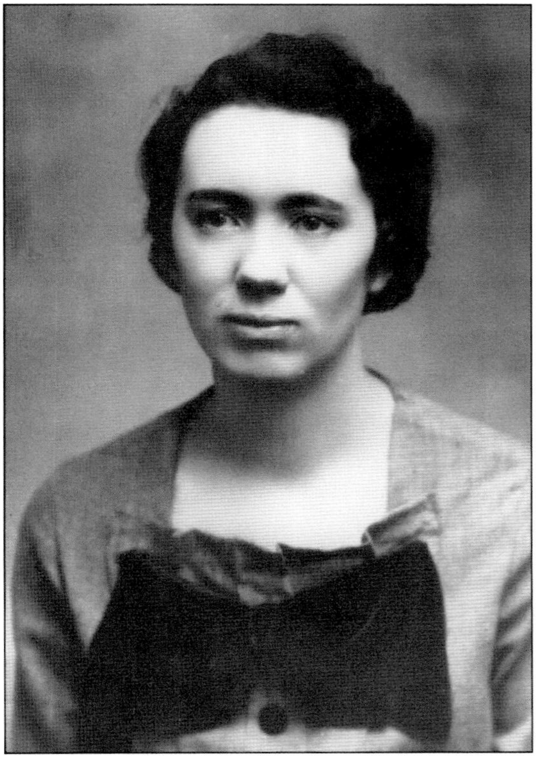

Josephine Wallace Crowell was born in 1911 and died in 1996. She was the daughter of J. Shields and Nora Murray Wallace. She married Robert Crowell, the son of Esker and Mary Blair Crowell, who was born in 1906 and died in 1992. Josephine and Robert Crowell are buried in Andersonville Cemetery. (Courtesy of Kay Crowell Davis.)

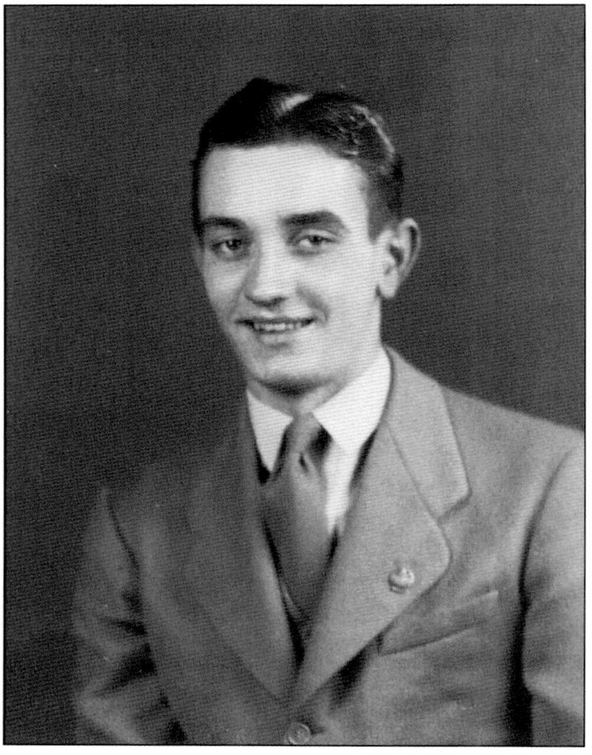

Hugh M. Wallace was the son of J. Shields Wallace and Nora Murray Wallace. He married Louise Nerren and lived in Oak Ridge, where he worked at the post office. He grew prize roses and was a judge for the rose society. They had no children and left their estate to the University of Tennessee. They are both buried in Andersonville Cemetery. (Courtesy of Kay Crowell Davis.)

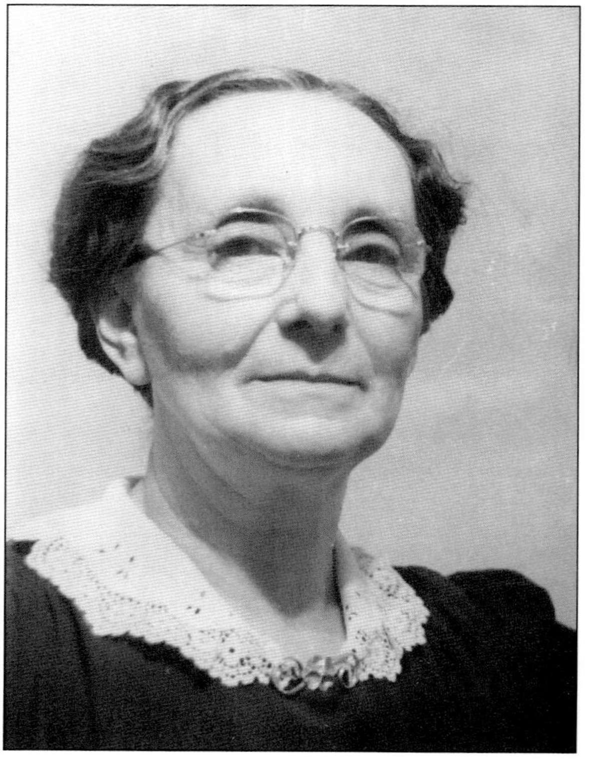

Nora Murray Wallace was the wife of J. Shields Wallace. She started a free lunch program in the Andersonville schools and was active with Andersonville's Tomato Club, which taught young women modern methods of canning and food preservation. Tomato Clubs evolved into the Home Demonstration and 4-H Clubs of the University of Tennessee Extension Service. (Courtesy of Kay Crowell Davis.)

Pleasant Eblis Slover, left, was the son of Sam and Amanda Carver Slover. Charlie Hatmaker, right, the son of Lindsay Joseph and Mary Ann Hatmaker, was born in 1874 and died in 1939. He was married to Minnie Mahulda Lindsay, and they were the parents of Bertha Alice Hatmaker. (Courtesy of Charles Hugh Abner.)

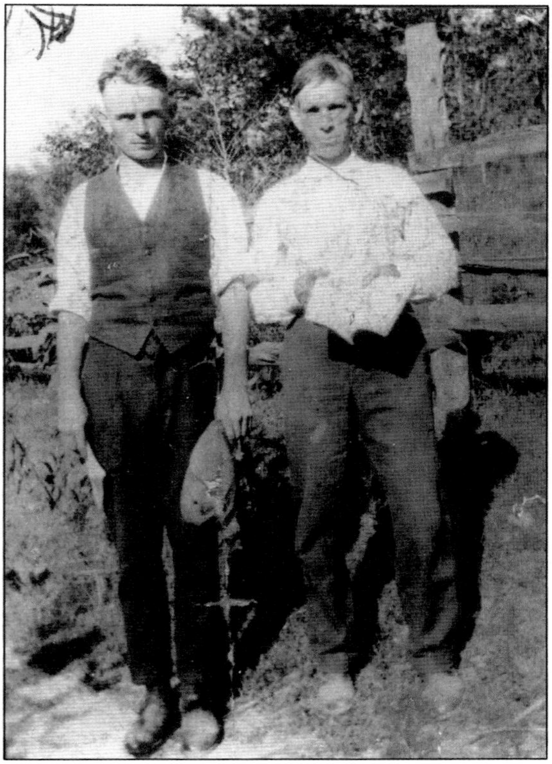

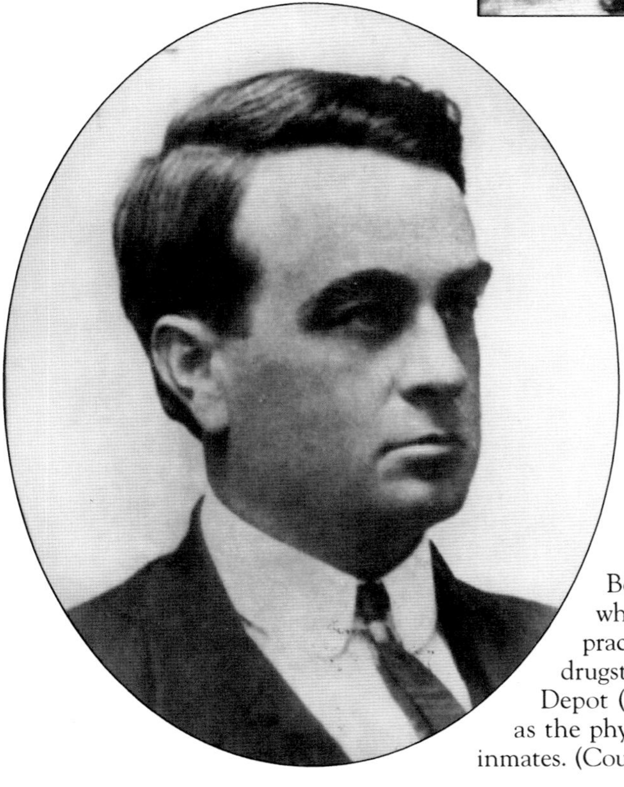

Beginning in 1884, Dr. Samuel B. Hall, who was born in 1864 and died in 1933, practiced medicine in Clinton and ran a drugstore next to his office, located at 358 Depot (now Market) Street. He also served as the physician for both county and city jail inmates. (Courtesy of the *Clinton Courier-News*.)

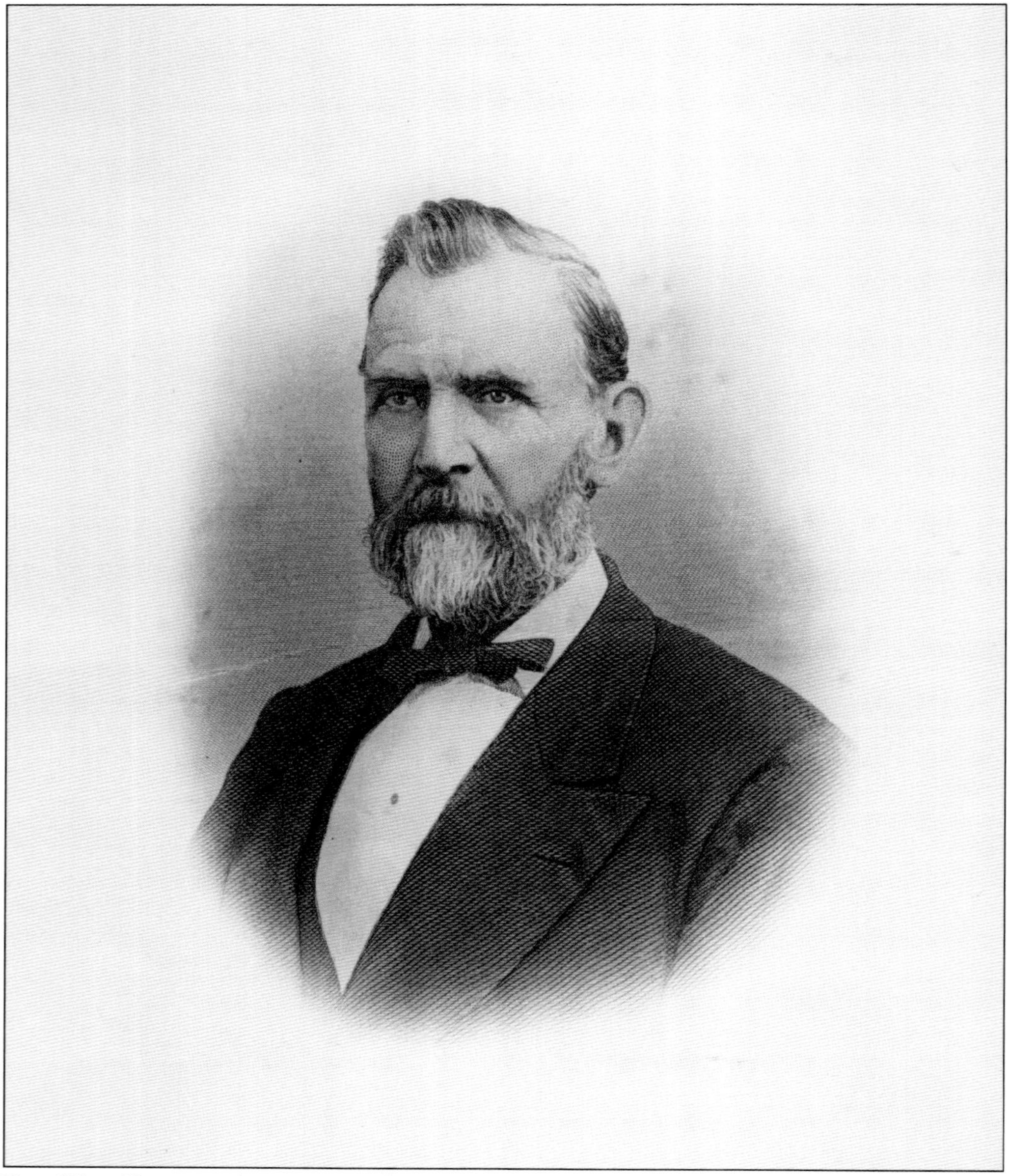

David King Young was born in 1826, the son of Samuel Clarkston and Charlotte Brazel Hall Young. He was the grandson of David Hall, a Revolutionary War soldier who was living in Anderson County when it was created. He attended Holston College and read law under Judge Thomas A.R. Nelson in Knoxville. After being admitted to the bar, he practiced law in Clinton until the Civil War, at which time he joined the Union army. He married Elizabeth Woodson, and they had 10 children: Josephine, John, Horace Woodson, Charlotte Alice, William Baxter, Minnie, Samuel, James Walter, Etta Iola, and David King Jr. The family lived on a large farm in the Eagle Bend of the Clinch River. After retiring as judge of the 16th Judicial Circuit, he served as president of Union Bank of Clinton and as a director of Clinton High School. He was a member of the Methodist Episcopal Church, South, of Clinton, and helped raise the money for a new church building in 1887. (Courtesy of the *Clinton Courier-News.*)

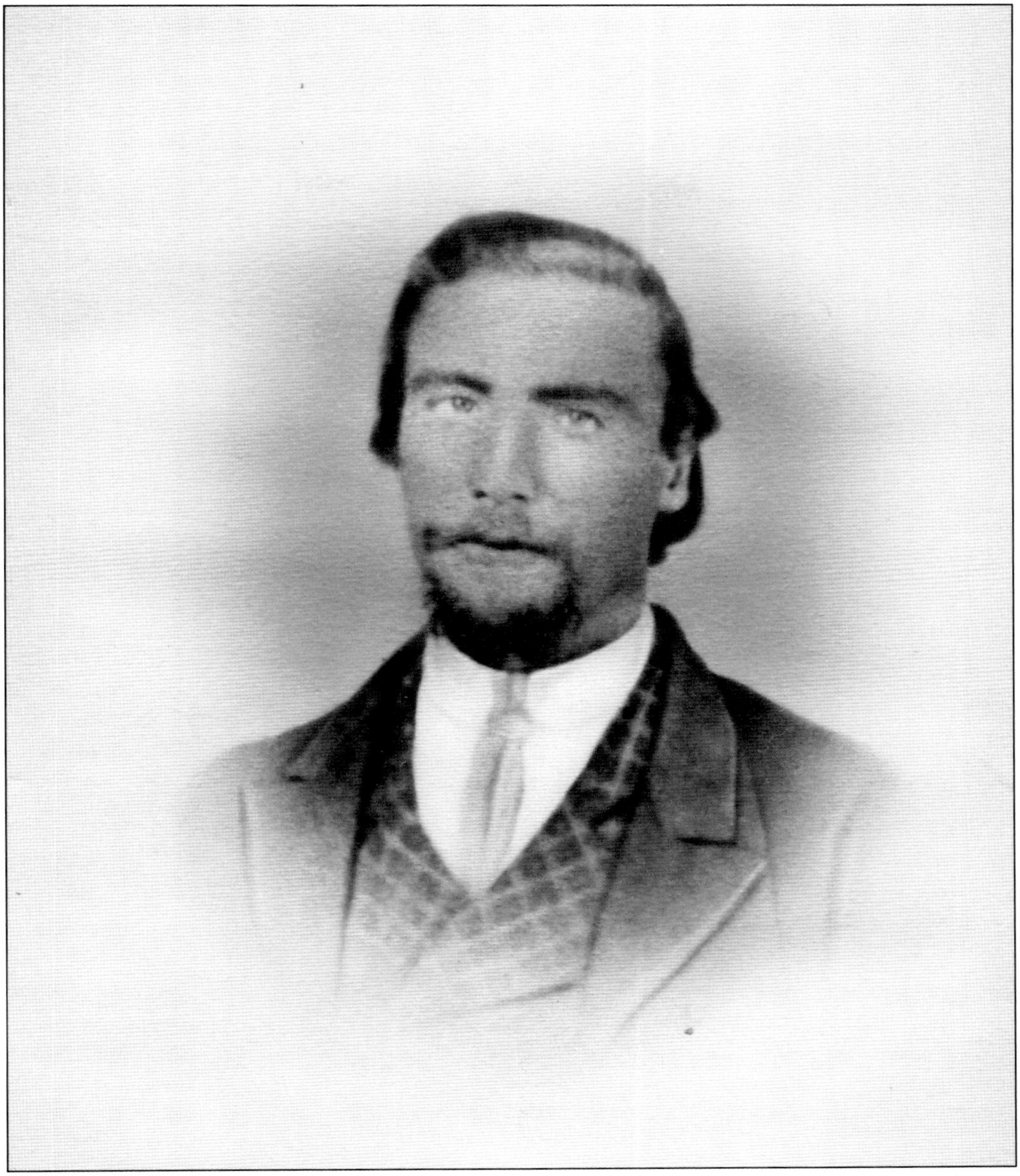

Born in 1842 in Dutch Valley, Robert Newton Baker was the son of George William and Ann McAdoo Baker. During the Civil War, he served in the Union army, having walked across the mountains to enlist in Kentucky. Returning home after the Civil War, he taught for several years, farmed, ran a general store, and served as county school superintendent. He also served in the 40th and 41st sessions of the Tennessee General Assembly and was elected county court clerk, justice of the peace, chairman of the court, and circuit court clerk. He married Susan Delilah Rains in 1879, and they had nine children: Annie, Julia, Horace, Howard, John, William, Lucy, Martha, and Nelle. Susan Baker served as postmistress for the Low's Sulphur Springs post office from 1879 until 1892. Robert Newton Baker died in 1911. (Courtesy of the *Clinton Courier-News*.)

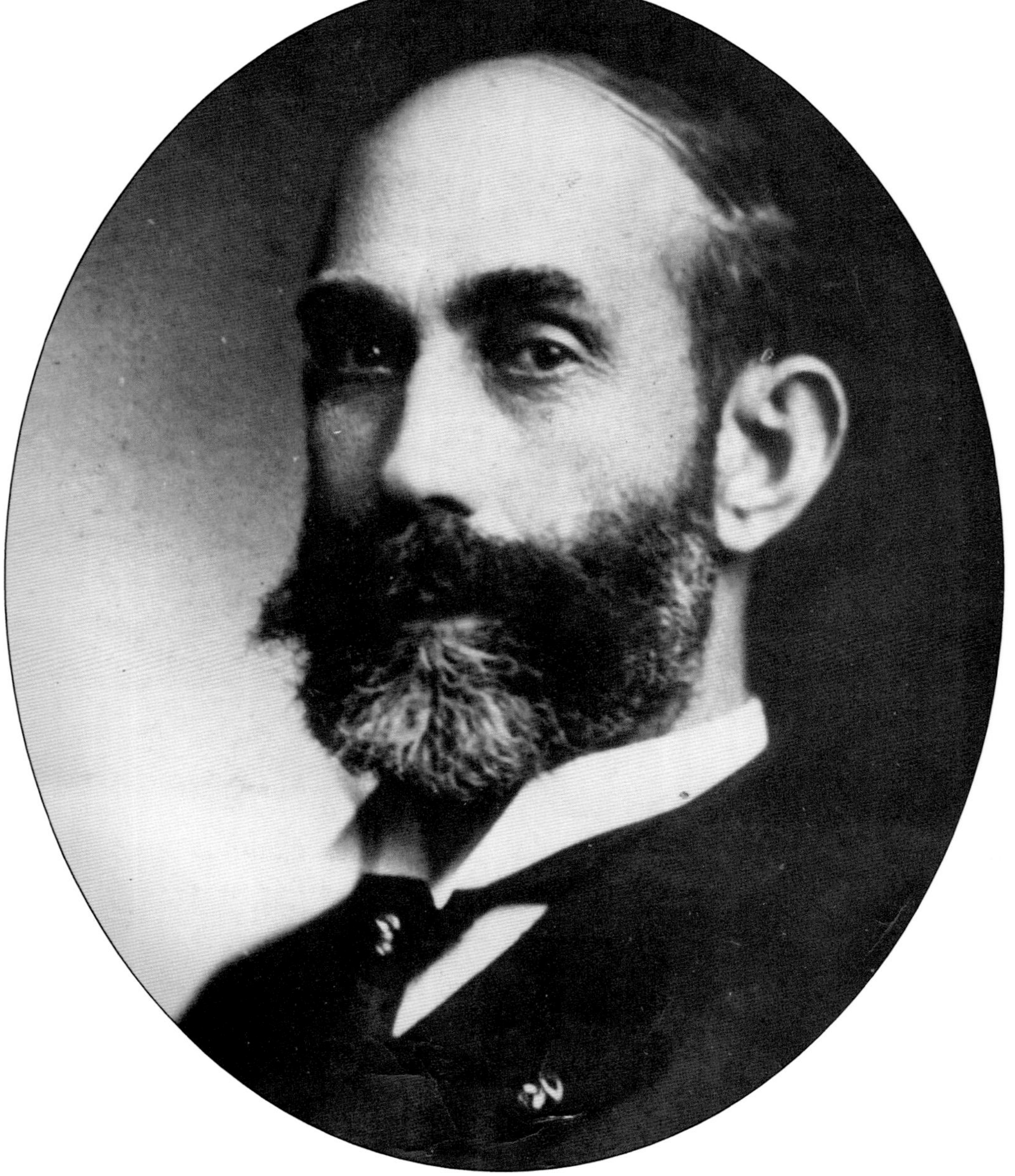

Sam Leath served as clerk and master of Chancery Court from 1882 until 1886, when he was elected county court clerk. He held the clerk's position until 1890. In 1894, he helped to incorporate the First Bank of Clinton. In 1905, Magnet Knitting Mill was incorporated with Sam Leath as its first president. He served two terms as a state representative, from 1911 to 1913 and from 1918 to 1921, and was chairman of the Clinton Board of Education in 1911, when the city and county high schools were consolidated. He purchased the Southern Hotel, and after it burned during Clinton's 1908 fire, he built the Leath Inn, which he sold in 1920 to pursue other business interests. He married Mary Trevathan, who had moved to Clinton from Knoxville. She ran a private school for girls and then taught at Clinton High School before becoming assistant principal. Sam and Mary Leath lived in Clinton until 1925, when they moved to Knoxville. (Courtesy of the *Clinton Courier-News*.)

Horace V. Wells began publication of the *Clinton Courier* on August 31, 1933. In 1939, he bought the *Anderson County News*, and the combined papers became the *Clinton Courier-News*. Friday, August 26, 1983, was declared H.V. Wells Jr. Day in Clinton in celebration of the paper's 50th anniversary. (Courtesy of the *Clinton Courier-News*.)

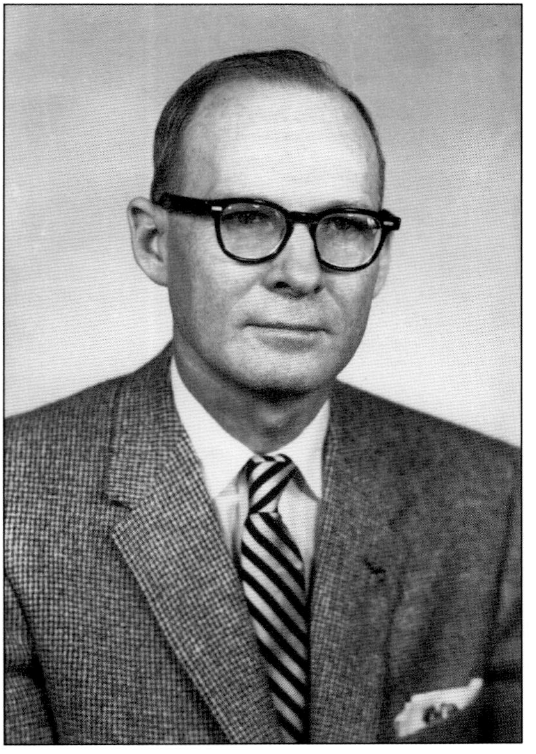

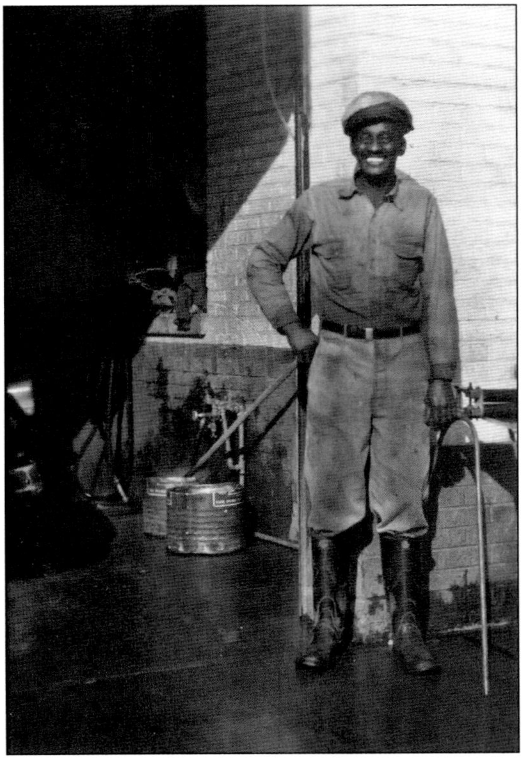

Sam Adams worked at the Clinton Service Station, which was owned and operated by John Rose, who bought the business in 1932. The station was located across Main Street from the First Baptist Church and is now a parking lot for the church. The old Pure Gas pumps were still in place as late as 1992, although the service station building had been demolished. (Courtesy of Jo Ann Allen Boyce.)

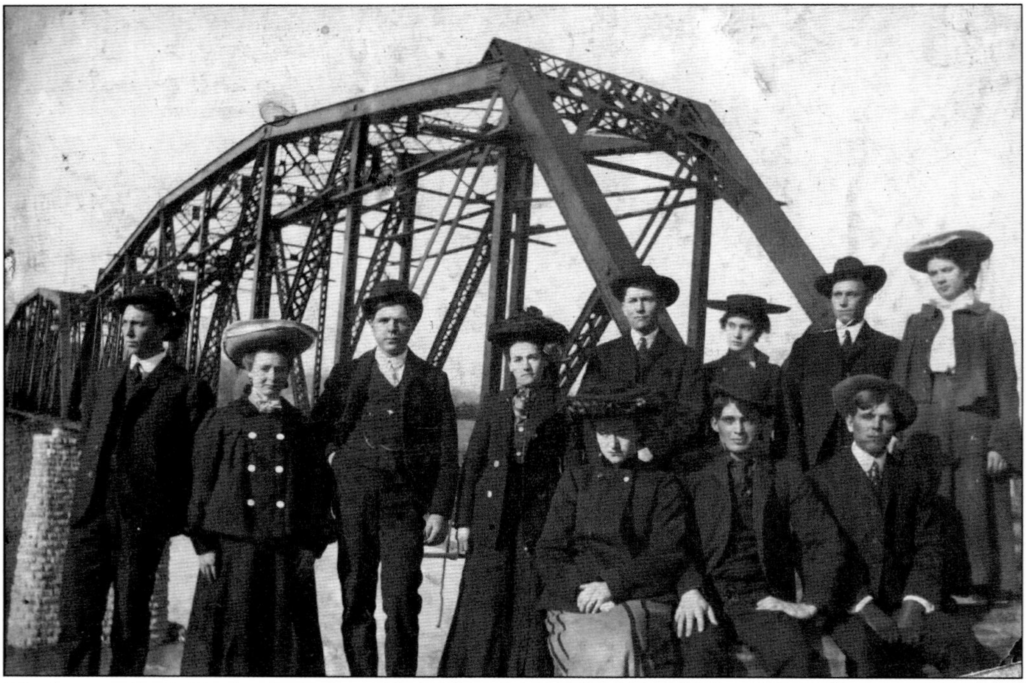

The Louisville & Nashville Railroad (L&N) trestle at Elza was a favorite place for young people to take photographs at the turn of the century. Birdie Worthington, who was born in 1881 and died in 1957, posed for this photograph with friends. Birdie (fourth from left) married Henry Duncan, who was born in 1876 and died in 1955, a veteran of the Spanish-American War. (Courtesy of Judy Duncan Blakely.)

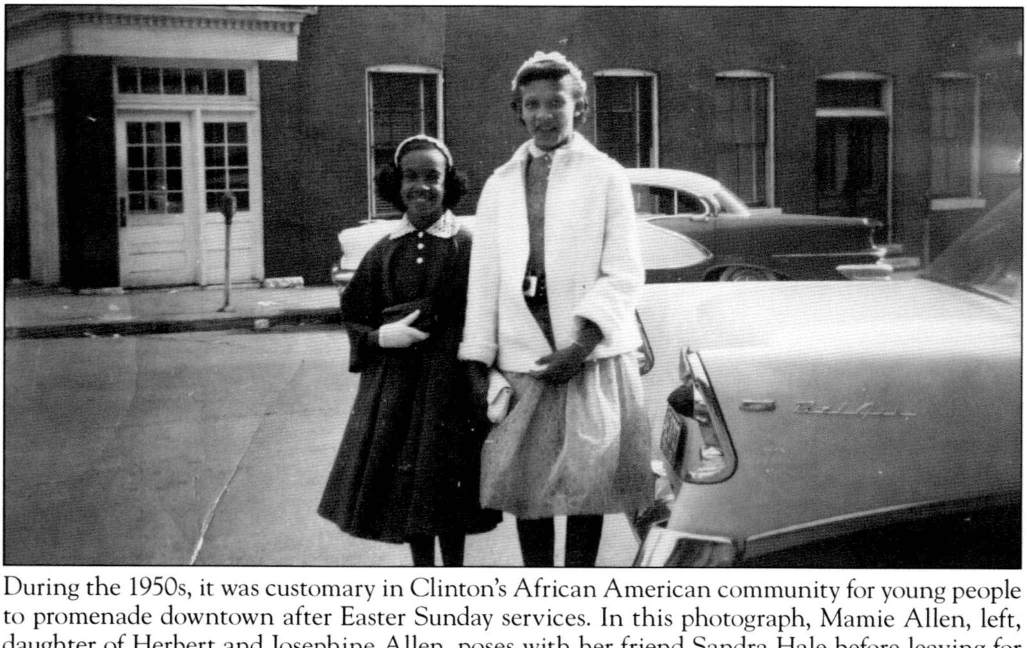

During the 1950s, it was customary in Clinton's African American community for young people to promenade downtown after Easter Sunday services. In this photograph, Mamie Allen, left, daughter of Herbert and Josephine Allen, poses with her friend Sandra Hale before leaving for the Easter Parade. (Courtesy of Jo Ann Allen Boyce.)

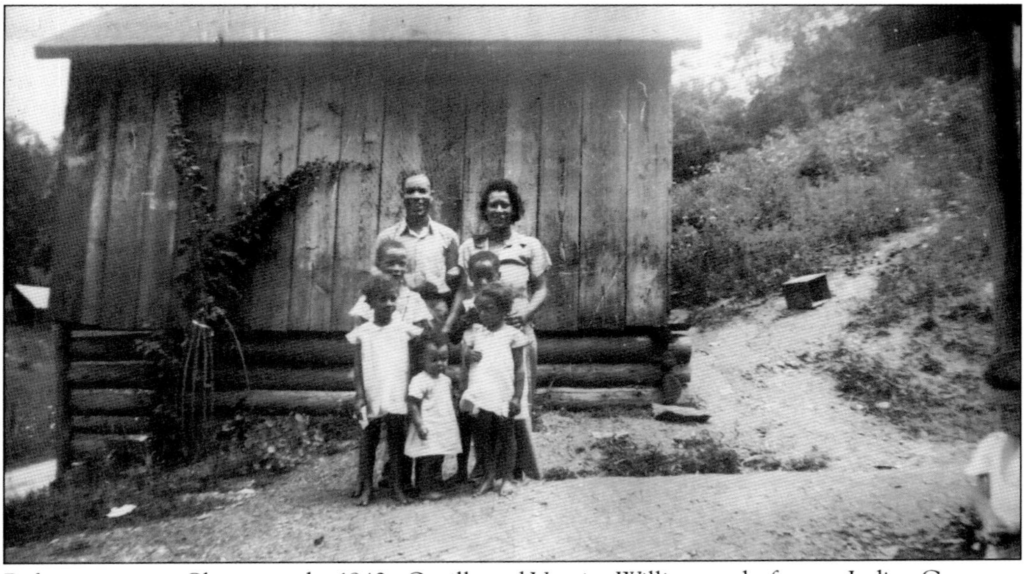

Before moving to Clinton in the 1940s, Orville and Vernice Willis rented a farm at Indian Gap, near Andersonville, where five of their 10 children were born. Reverend Willis was the head pastor of Mount Sinai Baptist Church in Clinton until his death. (Courtesy of Emily Wallace Haverkemp.)

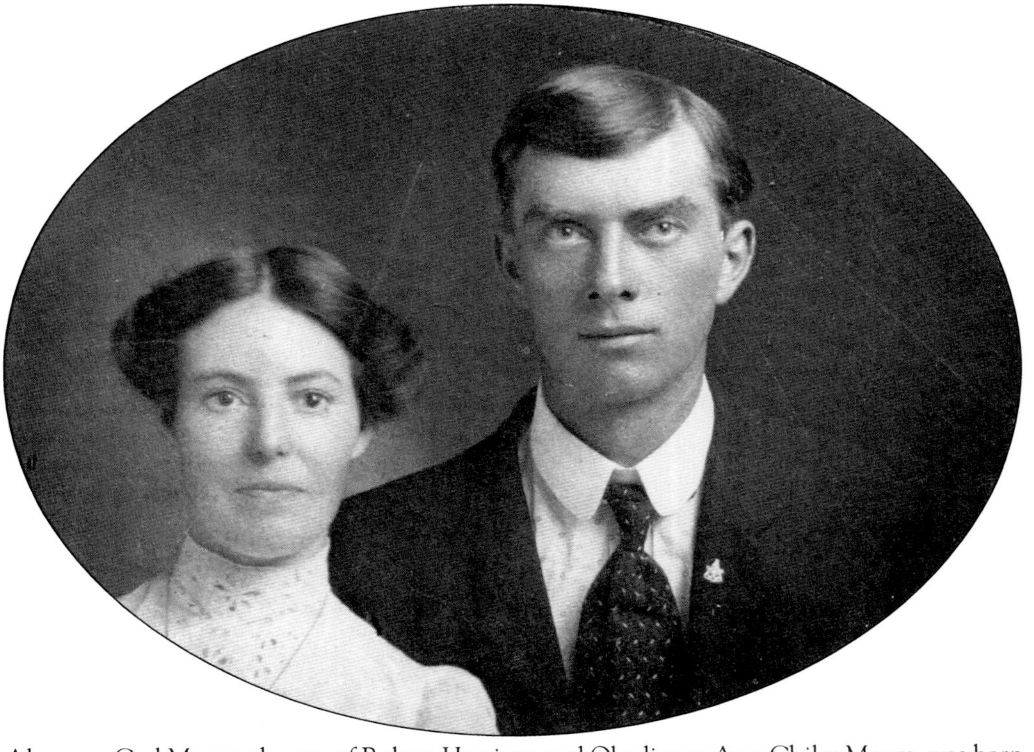

Algernon Carl Moore, the son of Robert Harrison and Obedience Ann Chiles Moore, was born in 1878 and died in 1944. He married Ida Florence Gammon, who was born in 1879 and died in 1944. A.C. Moore was a farmer and miller whose farm was located below the old Solway Bridge in Anderson County. (Courtesy of Mary Elkins Barker.)

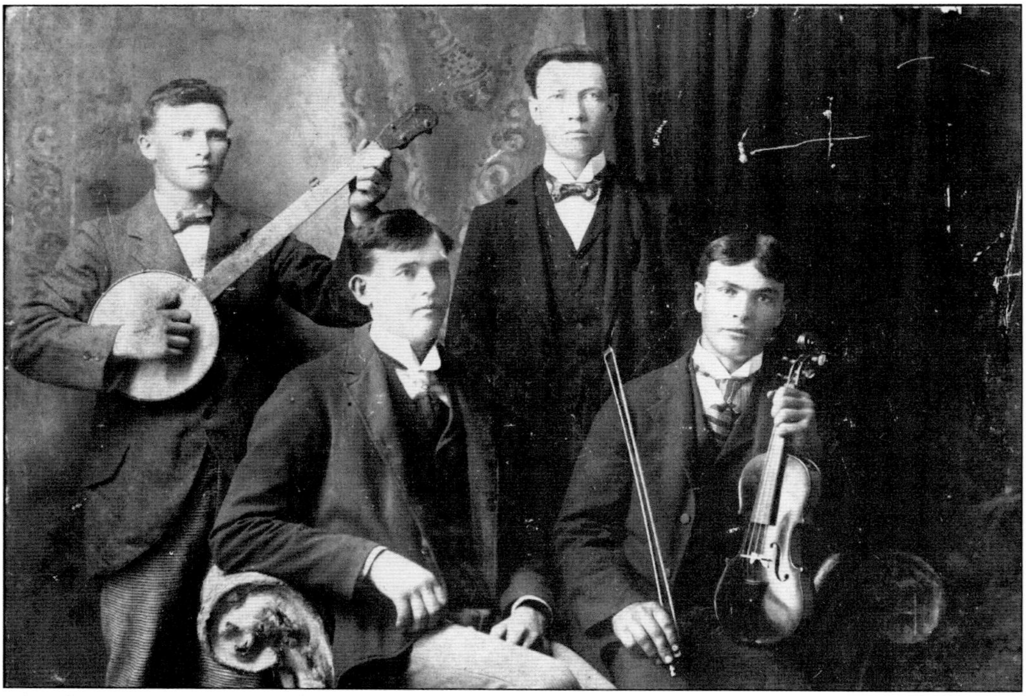

The above quartet featured David Nelson on the fiddle. Dave, who was born in 1879 and died in 1928, was the son of Jave and Ellen Evans Nelson. He traveled the area teaching singing schools in churches, and he was the local school bus contractor. He married Nancy Eleanor Johnson, who was born in 1877 and died in 1949. (Courtesy of Carolyn Johnson.)

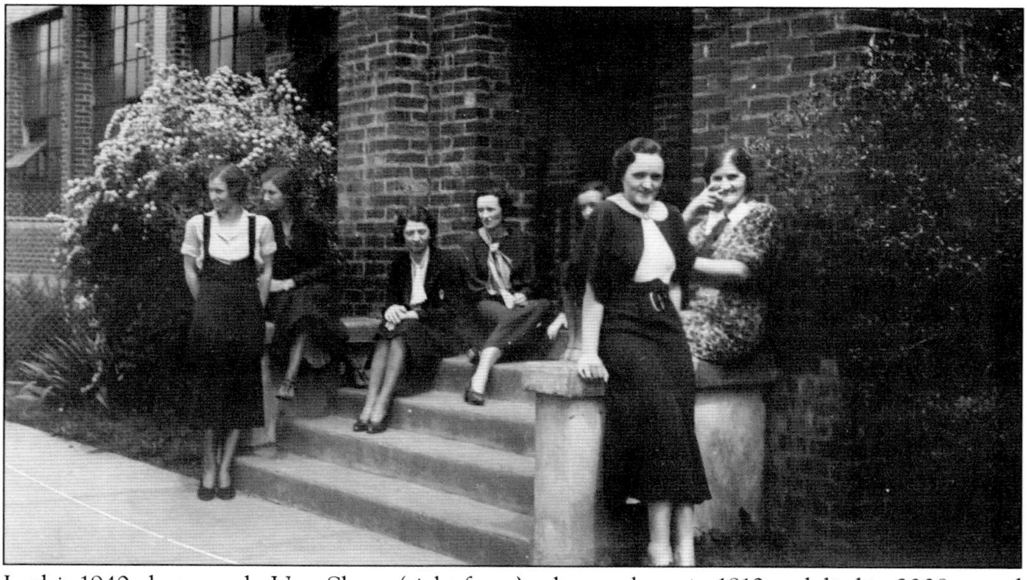

In this 1940 photograph, Ursa Sharp (right front), who was born in 1910 and died in 2008, posed with six fellow mill employees at the entrance to Magnet Mills, Inc. She was a native of Clinton, the daughter of William Russell and Effie Florence Rogers Sharp. She is buried in Woodhaven Memorial Gardens in the Claxton community. (Courtesy of Jerry Patterson.)

Members of the J. Shields Wallace family posed for a family portrait at the Wallace home during the summer of 1938. From left to right are (first row) John B. Wallace, Laura Wallace Anderson, and J. Shields Wallace; (second row) Frank W. Wallace and R. Lawrence Wallace. (Courtesy of Kay Crowell Davis.)

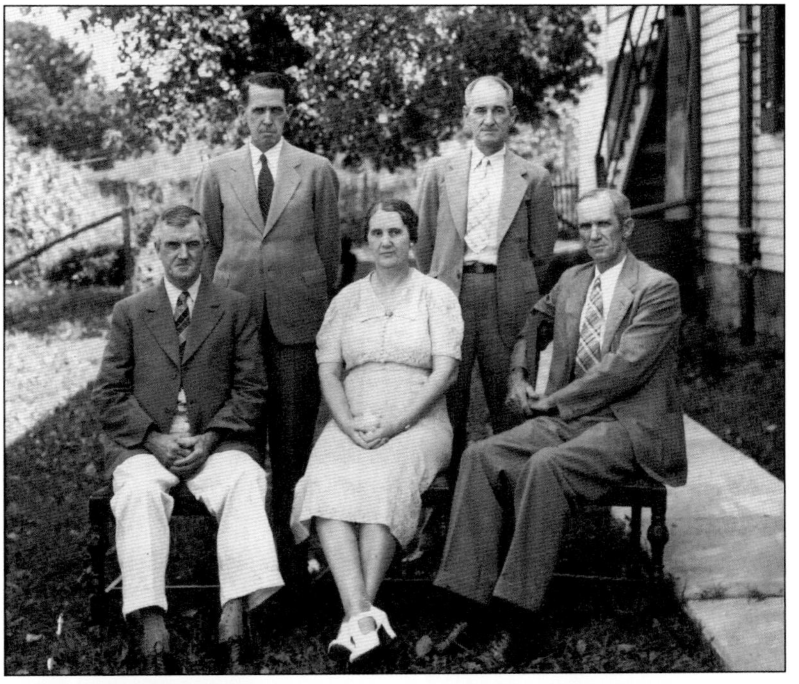

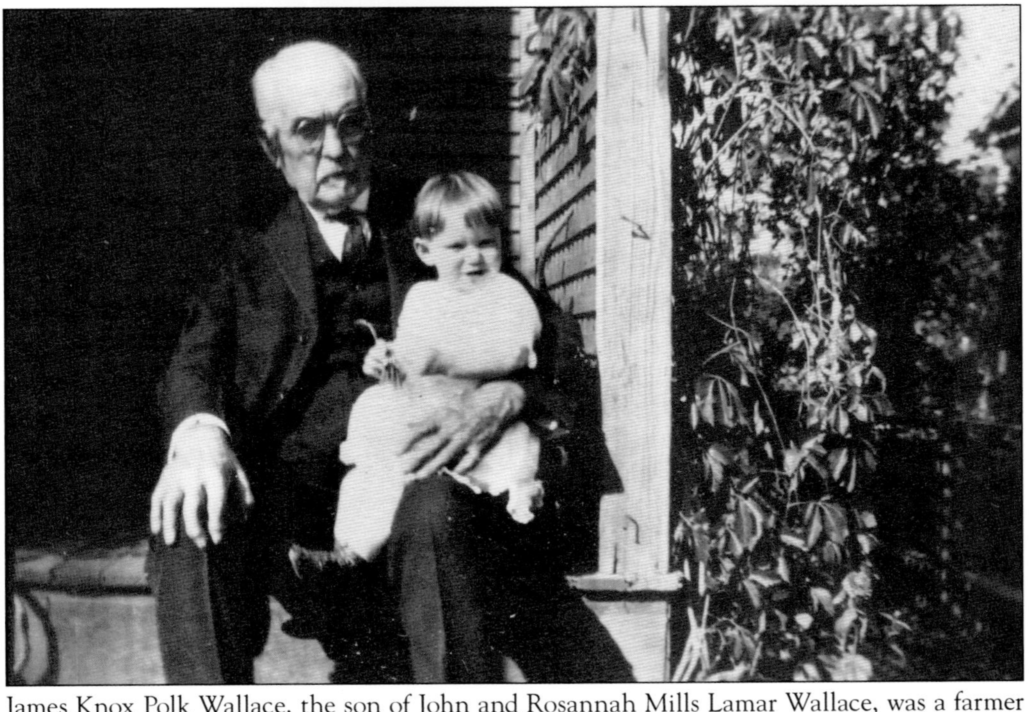

James Knox Polk Wallace, the son of John and Rosannah Mills Lamar Wallace, was a farmer and businessman in the Andersonville area. His first wife was Laura Caledonia McKinney; his second wife was Emma Rutherford. J.K.P. Wallace attended Mossy College (now Carson-Newman) and was the author of a series of travel articles that appeared in the Clinton newspaper in 1924. (Courtesy of Kay Crowell Davis.)

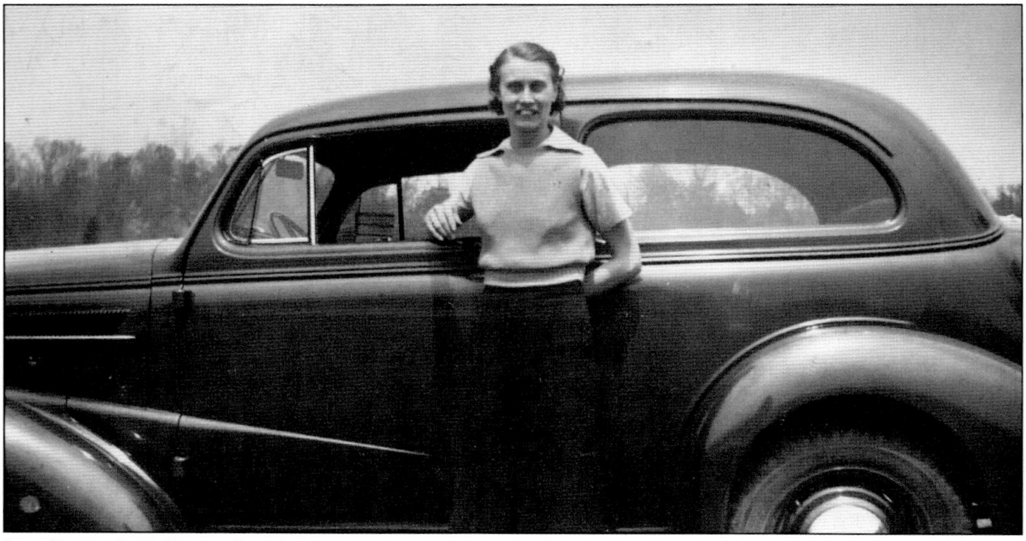

Lucille Peck Hill was the elementary supervisor for the Anderson County schools from 1940 until 1973. She was the daughter of Ernest A. and Sephie Lou Crozier Peck and a native of the Scarboro area. Her husband was H.H. "County" Hill, a former sheriff of Anderson County. (Courtesy of Mary Elkins Barker.)

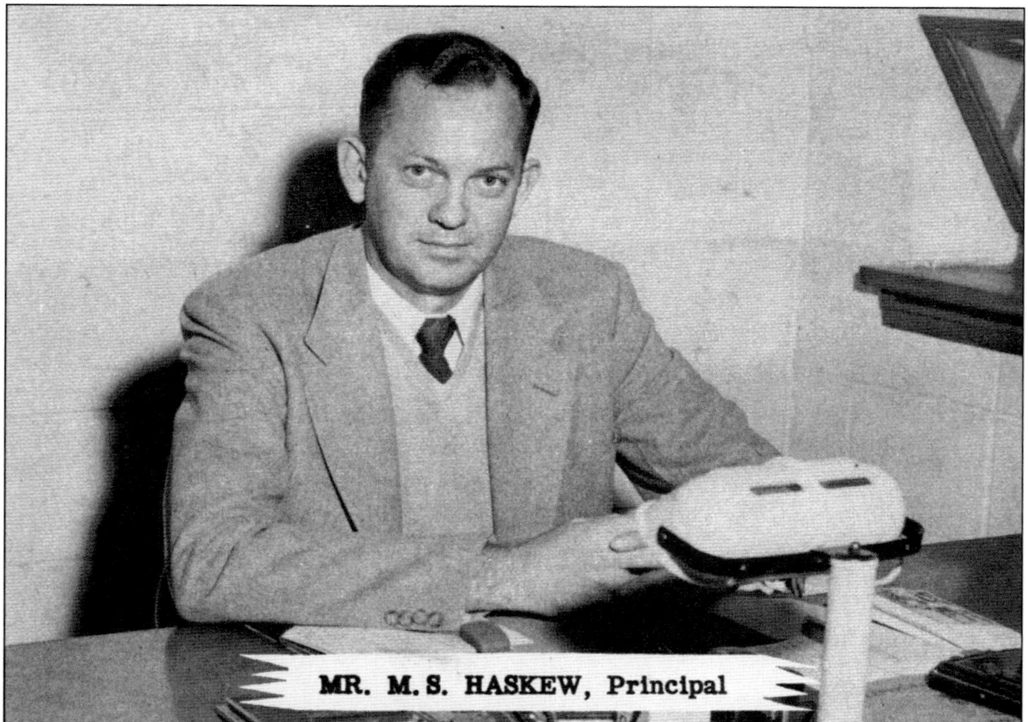

Monty S. Haskew was the principal of Claxton Elementary School for 14 years, and at the time of his death in 1969, he was employed as the director of special education in Anderson County schools. He lived in Powell and had two children, Sheila Ann and Mark Wayne. (Courtesy of Mary Elkins Barker.)

From left to right are Boyd Moore, Dennis Elkins, and Ralph Goodman. This photograph was taken in 1931 at Fort Oglethorpe, Georgia, where the three of them were in training. Boyd Moore was the son of Algernon Carl "A.C." and Ida Florence Gammon Moore. (Courtesy of Mary Elkins Barker.)

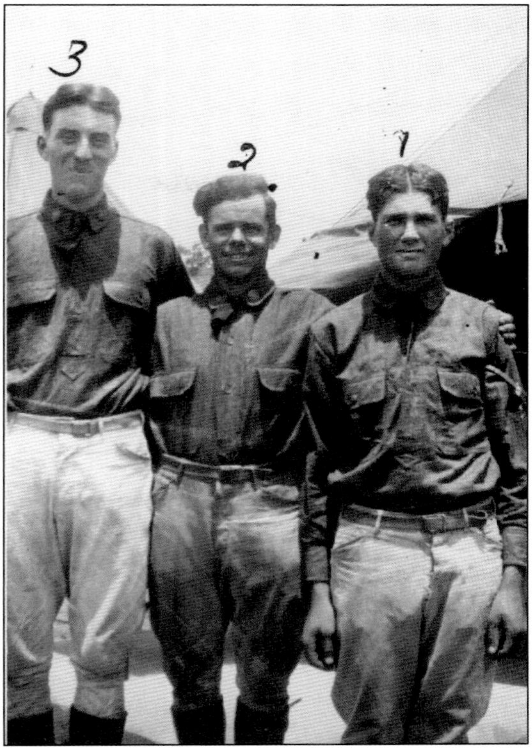

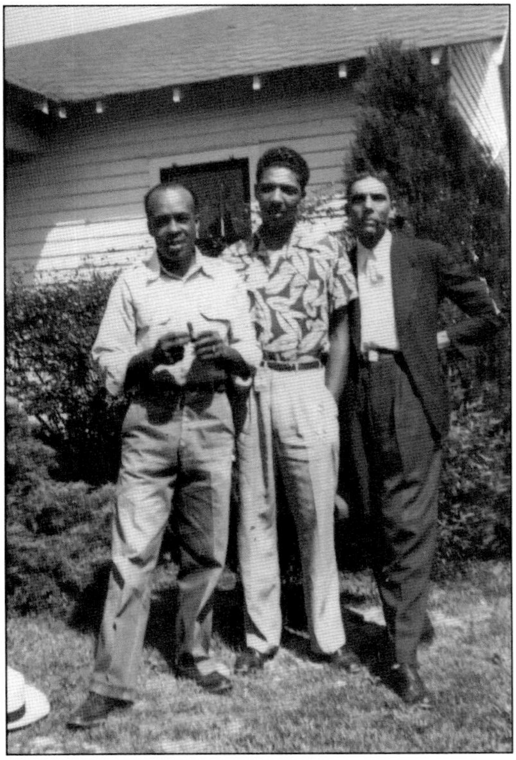

From left to right, Herbert Allen, Raymond "June" Willis Jr., and George Worthington posed in front of the Allen residence for this photograph. For five years, they made the weekly trip north on US Highway 25W to work in an automobile factory in Detroit, Michigan. Herbert Allen moved his family to Los Angeles in 1958, seeking better employment and education opportunities. (Courtesy of Jo Ann Allen Boyce.)

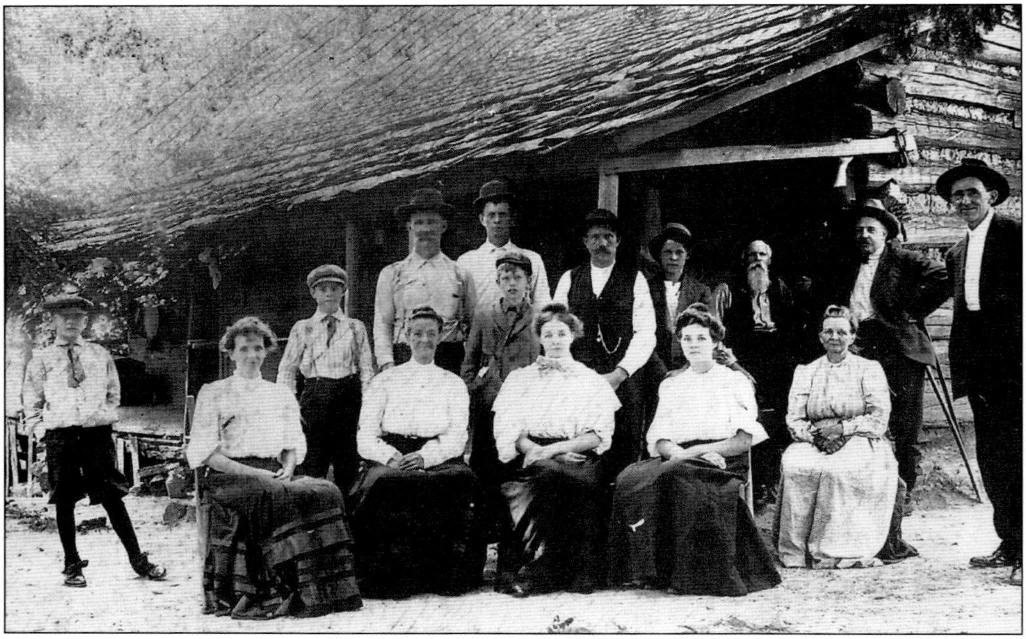

Harrison Riley Daugherty married Rosa Jane White in 1852, and they had nine children: Duncan, Elizabeth, Serelda, Julia, Barbara, Phoebe Eliza, Alice, Cordelia, and Naomi. For this photograph, the family posed in front of the family log home. Daughters Serelda and Barbara are not pictured. (Courtesy of Charles Hugh Abner.)

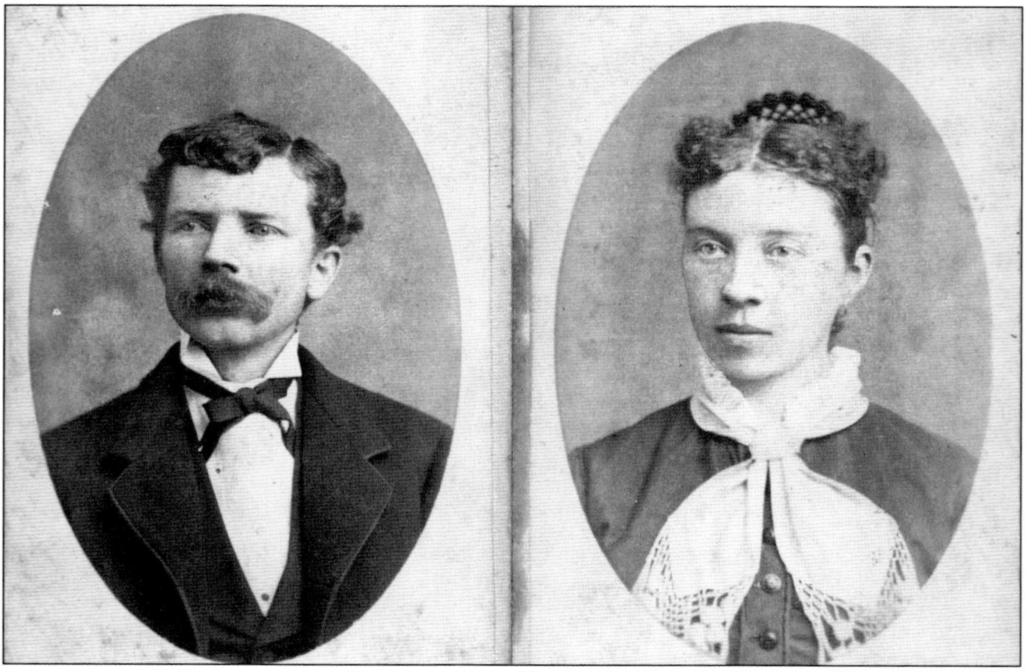

Robert Harrison Moore married Obedience Ann "Annie" Chiles, the daughter of Col. John Coffee Chiles. They settled in the Edgemoor community of Anderson County and were the parents of Algernon Carl "A.C." Moore, who married Ida Florence Gammon. (Courtesy of Mary Elkins Barker.)

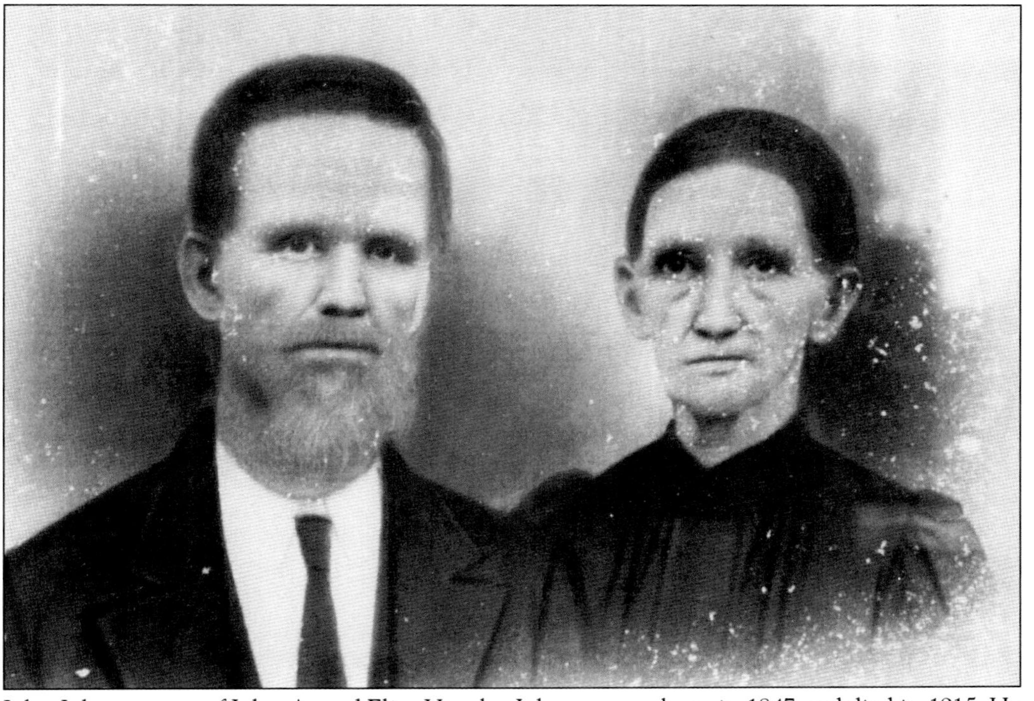

John Johnson, son of John A. and Eliza Hensley Johnson, was born in 1847 and died in 1915. He was pastor of Farmer's Grove Baptist Church, located in the Blockhouse Valley area of South Clinton. He married Mary Farmer, daughter of John and Betsy Henderson Farmer, who was born in 1848 and died in 1921. (Courtesy of Carolyn Johnson.)

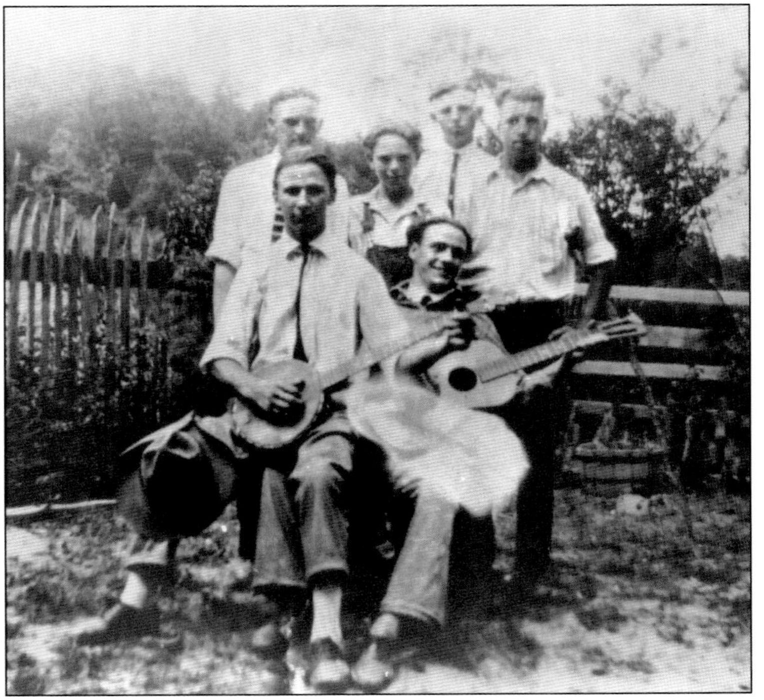

Pictured in front in this photograph are brothers Burley, left, and Lawrence Nelson, sons of David and Nancy Eleanor Johnson Nelson, who were popular local musicians. Standing in back, from left to right, are Joe May, John May, Jackie York, and Claude Lane. Burley Nelson was born in 1903 and died in 1988. He retired from the Bush Brothers Cannery in Clinton. (Courtesy of Carolyn Johnson.)

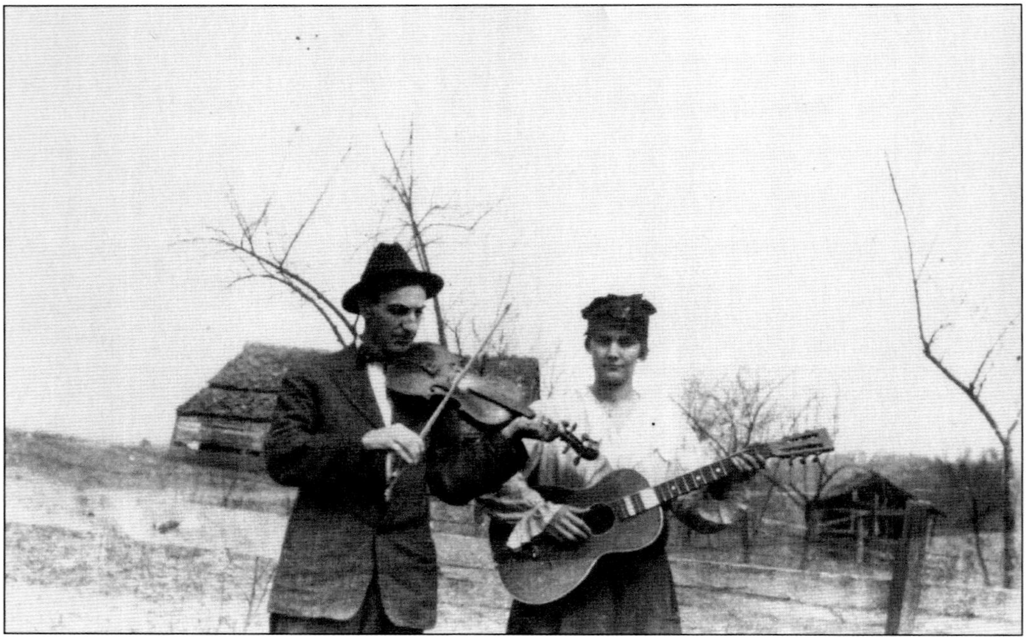

Benjamin Harrison Kelley was a fiddle maker, clock maker, and avid foxhunter. He is pictured with his wife, Susie Nelson, a native of Anderson County and the daughter of David and Nancy Eleanor Nelson. Harrison and Susie Kelley lived on Byington-Solway Road in Karns and are buried in Bethel Cemetery on Emory Road in Knox County. (Courtesy of Carolyn Johnson.)

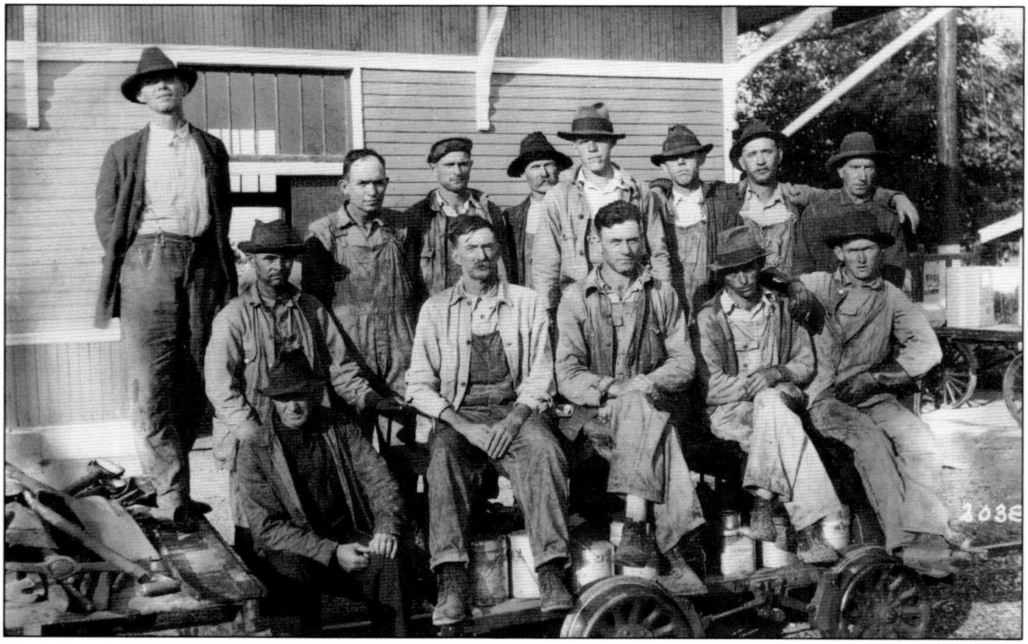

Both the Louisville & Nashville Railroad and the Southern Railway built lines through Anderson County. The L&N track ran across the Clinch River at Elza and on through Marlow and the Dossett tunnel. Will King, second from left in the front row, poses about 1900 with other members of his section gang at the L&N depot, where they were working. (Courtesy of Maxine Meade Holbrook.)

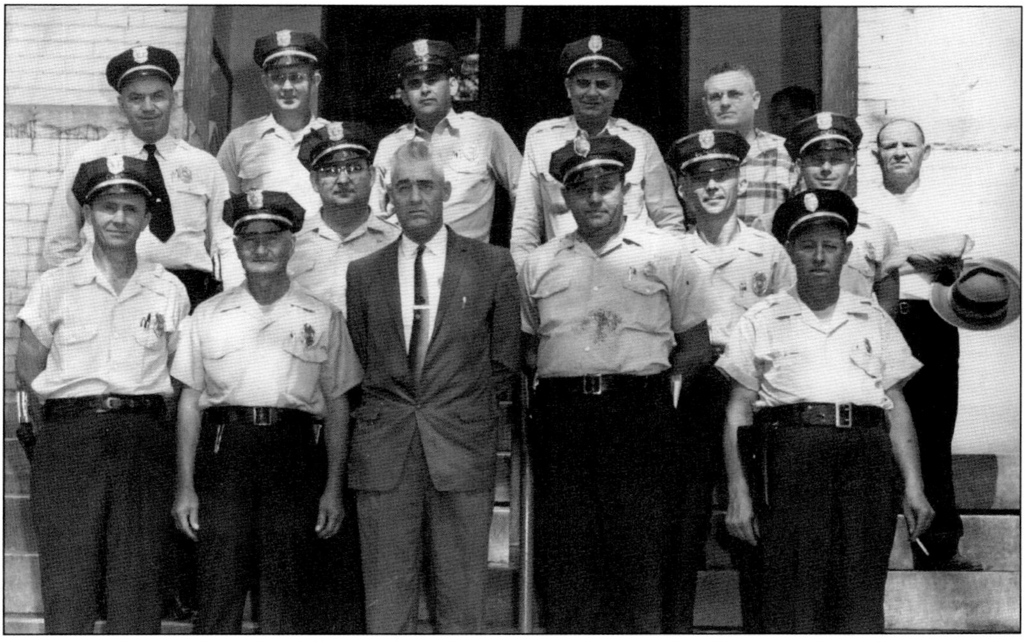

Anderson County sheriff and deputies in 1958 were, from left to right, (first row) Frank Pratt, Charley Brown, Sheriff Glad Woodward, J.W. Daniels, and J.C. Cantrell; (second row) W.C. Shorter, Sam Davis, and J.C. Daniels; (third row) Frank Butler, Clyde Shultz, Charles Rouse, H.H. "County" Hill, Shellie Jones, and Kelly Foust of Lake City. (Courtesy of the *Clinton Courier-News.*)

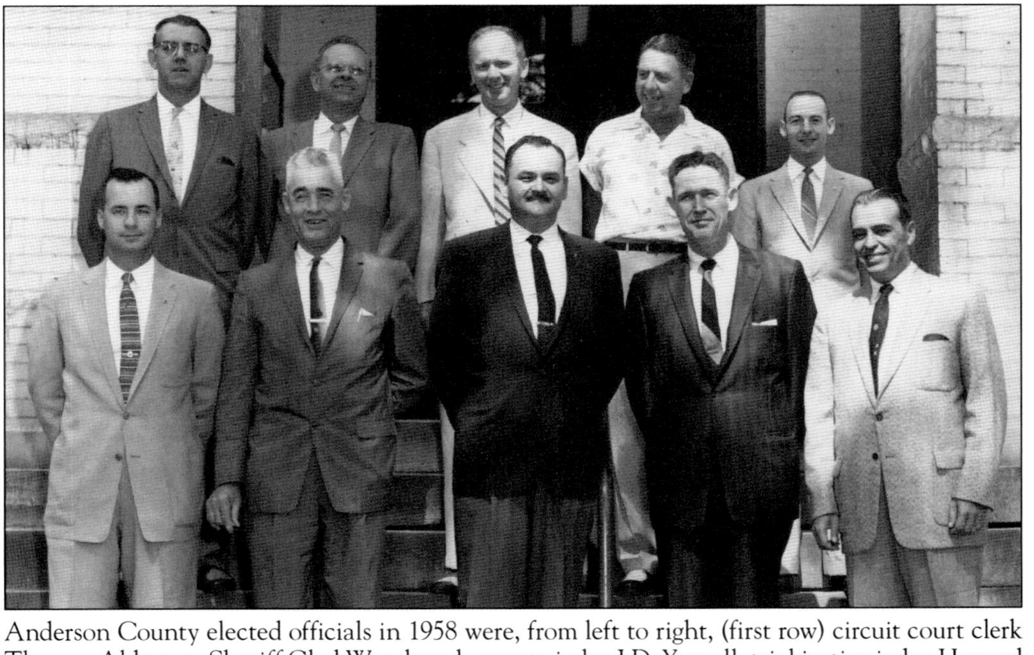

Anderson County elected officials in 1958 were, from left to right, (first row) circuit court clerk Thomas Alderson, Sheriff Glad Woodward, county judge J.D. Yarnell, trial justice judge Howard Woodside, and trustee George Ridenour; (second row) county court clerk John M. Purdy, tax assessor Carl J. Irwin, county attorney Gene Joyce, road superintendent Charles E. Shoopman, and register of deeds Joel Meredith. (Courtesy of the *Clinton Courier-News.*)

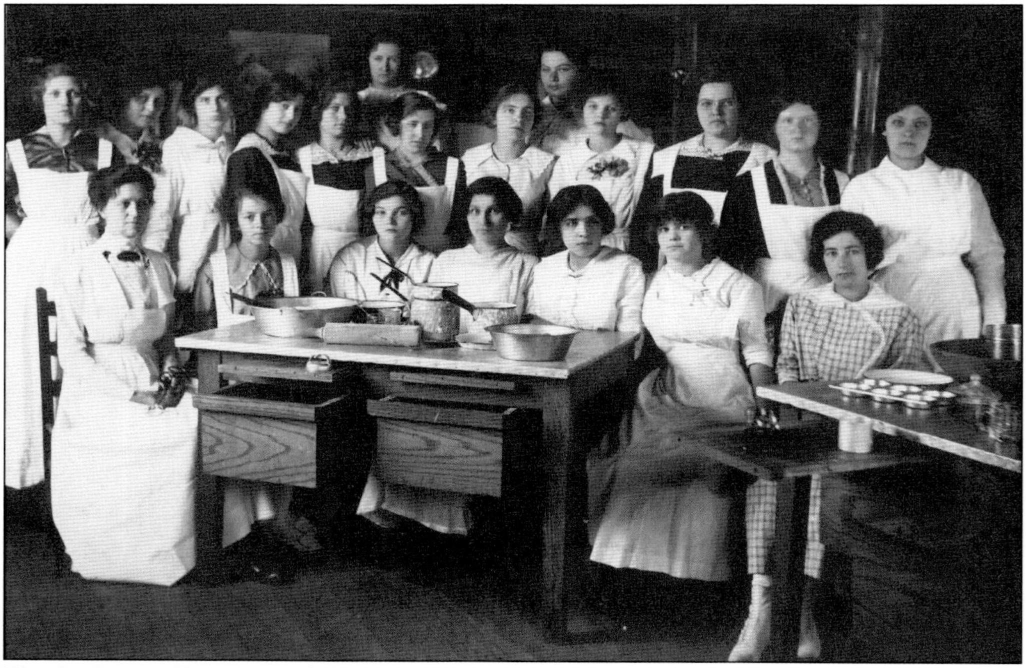

The Andersonville Tomato Club posed for this photograph, taken about 1918. Tomato Clubs taught young women modern methods of canning and food preservation. Young men were encouraged to join Corn Clubs to learn modern methods of farming and husbandry. Today's 4-H and Home Demonstration Clubs evolved from these Tomato and Corn Clubs. (Courtesy of Kay Crowell Davis.)

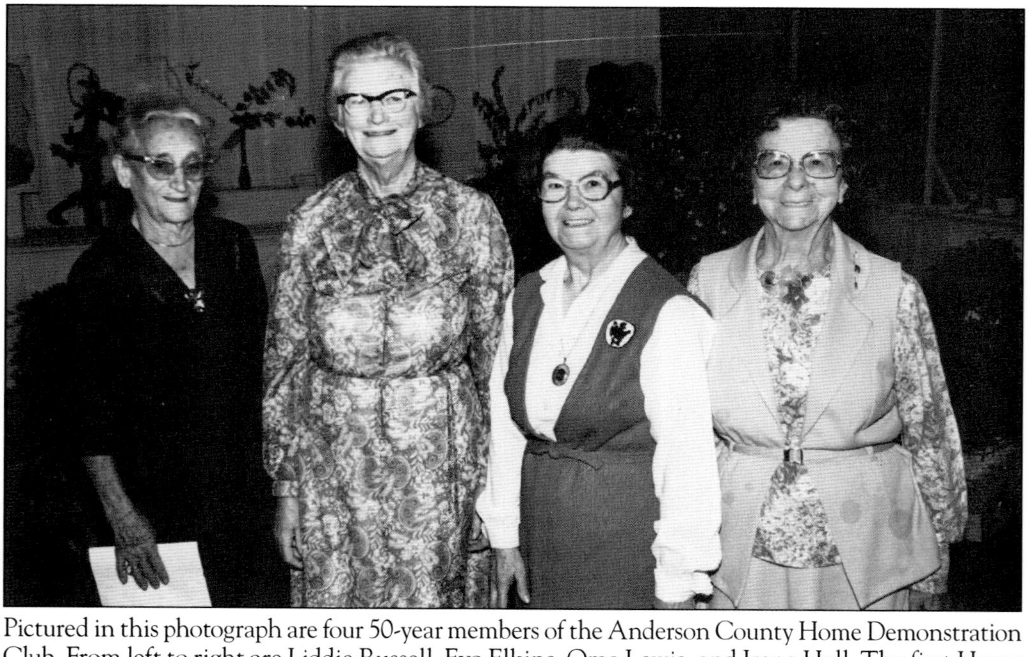

Pictured in this photograph are four 50-year members of the Anderson County Home Demonstration Club. From left to right are Liddie Russell, Eva Elkins, Oma Lewis, and Irene Hall. The first Home Demonstration Club in Anderson County was formed in the Glen Alpine community in 1923. The Clinton Hometttes group was formed in 1965. (Courtesy Mary Elkins Barker.)

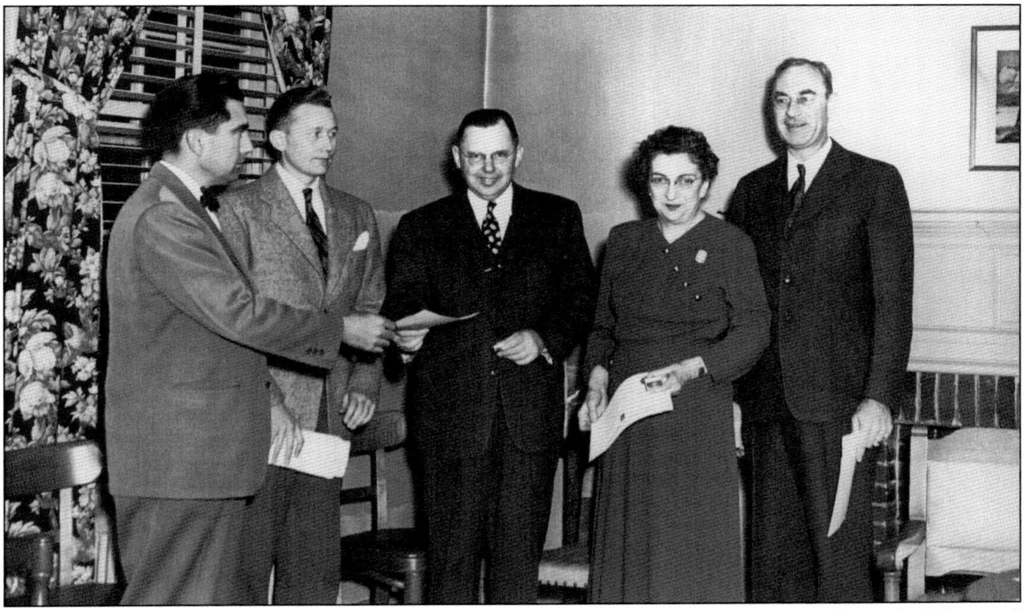

In December 1948, three area residents were awarded certificates of appreciation from the National Foundation of Infantile Paralysis for their 10 years of service to the March of Dimes. From left to right are Jared Maddux, honorary state chairman; Fred Wankan Jr., of the state foundation; A.D. Crenshaw and Eloise Wynne, of Clinton; and Harry Tour, of Norris. (Courtesy of the Pellissippi Genealogical and Historical Society.)

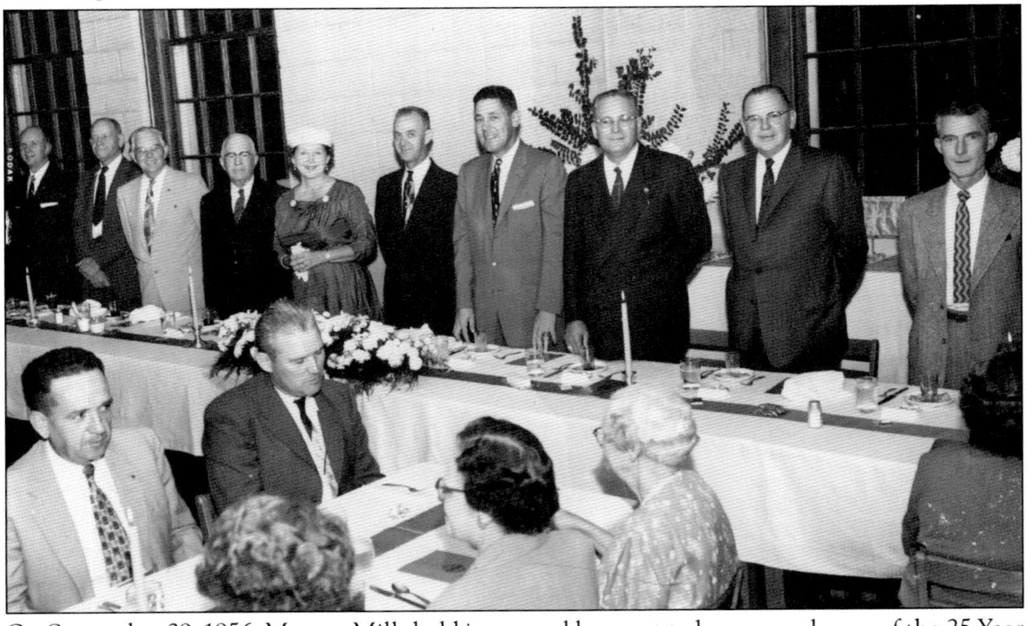

On September 29, 1956, Magnet Mills held its annual banquet to honor employees of the 25-Year Club. Seated at the head table were the following officials and guests, from left to right: C.F. Thompson, Ed Cureton, D.O. Wright, C.S. Kincaid, Mrs. Ramsey Pollard (Della), Othel Duncan, Lloyd N. Williams, guest speaker Dr. Ramsey Pollard, A.D. Crenshaw, and Wayne Pebley. (Courtesy of the *Clinton Courier-News*.)

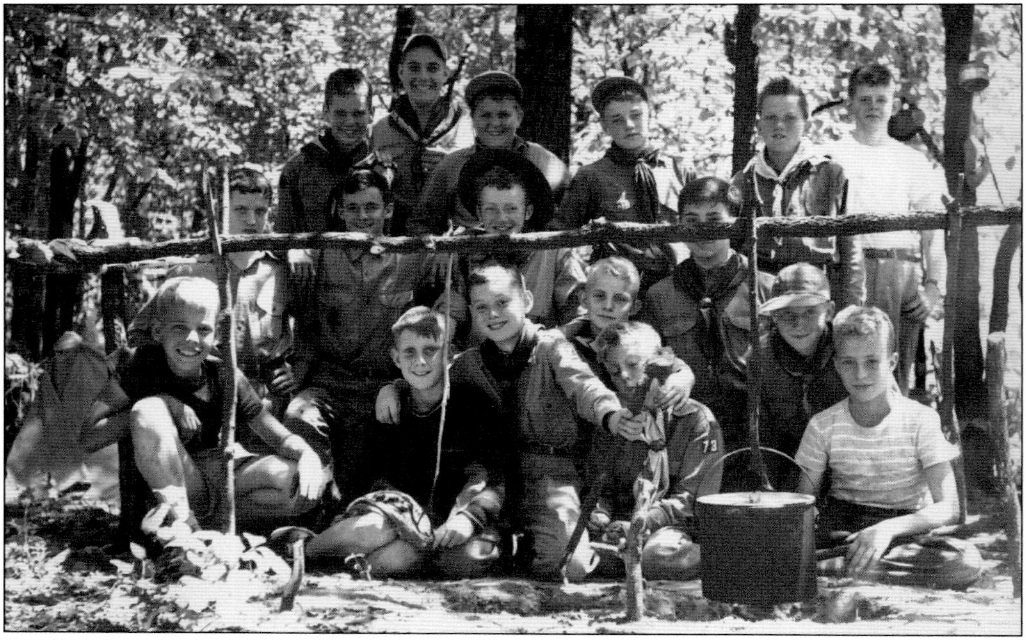

The Boy Scouts of America have always had active participation from Anderson County's young men, with troops from Clinton, Oak Ridge, and Norris. Pictured here is Boy Scout Troop 73 of Norris about 1943. A longtime Scoutmaster with the Norris troop was Joe Feemon. (Courtesy of the Norris Museum.)

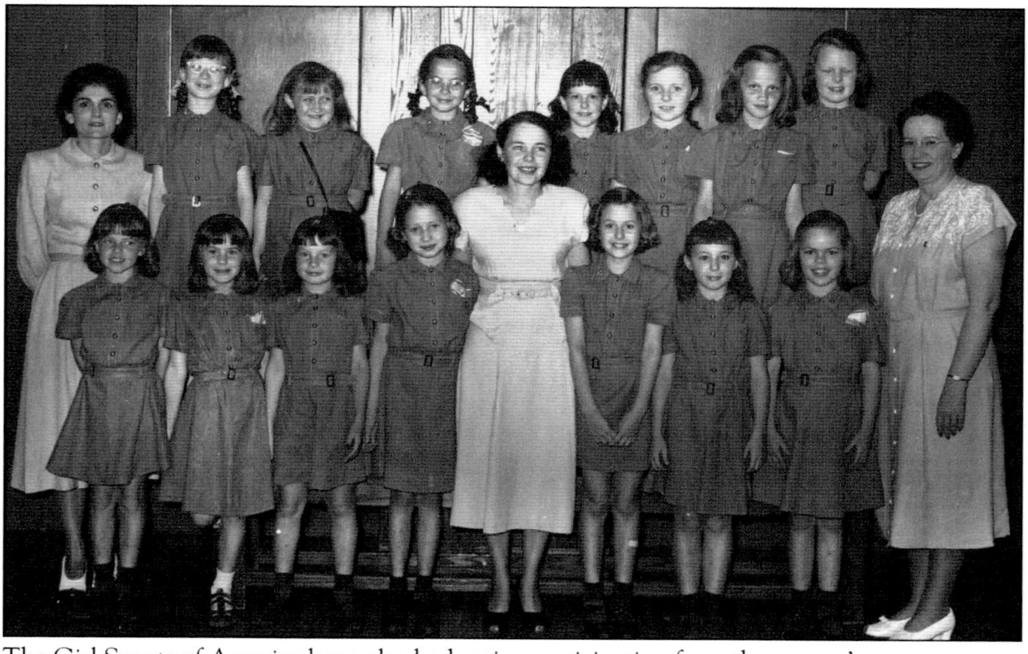

The Girl Scouts of America have also had active participation from the county's young women, with troops formed in Clinton, Norris, and Oak Ridge. Norris Brownie troop members posed for this 1950s photograph. Pictured in the middle of the front row is Ella Lynn Crossno. (Courtesy of the Norris Museum.)

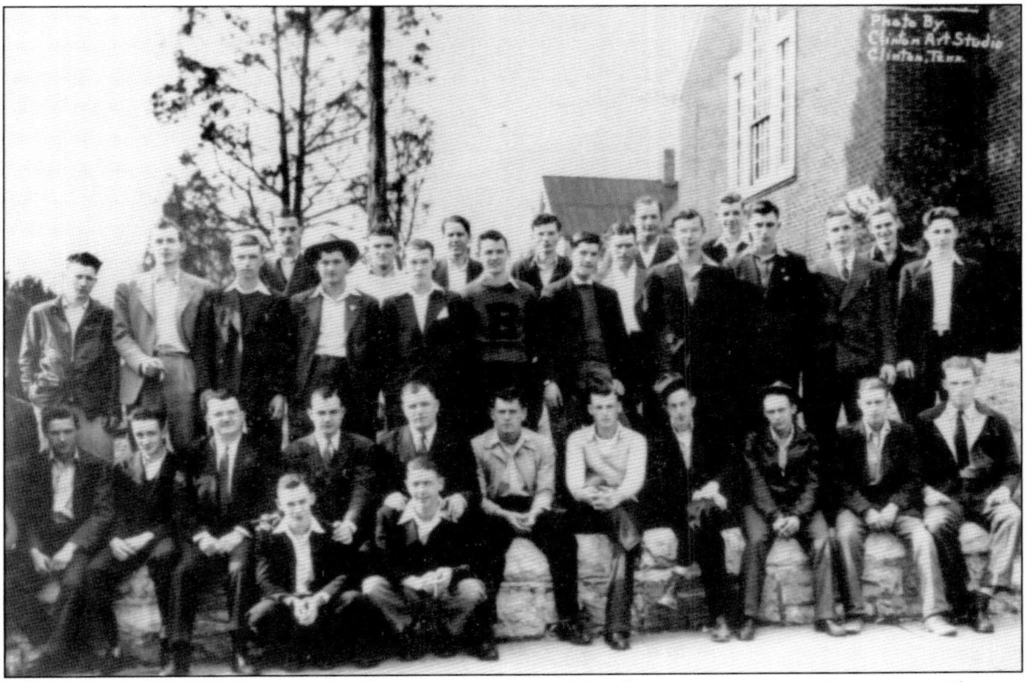

World War II US Army inductees from Clinton posed for this photograph in downtown Clinton before boarding the troop train for Knoxville in March 1943. Clinton-area military inductees routinely posed for a group photograph prior to entraining for Knoxville. After passenger train service from Clinton was stopped, inductees were bused to Knoxville. (Courtesy of Mary Harris.)

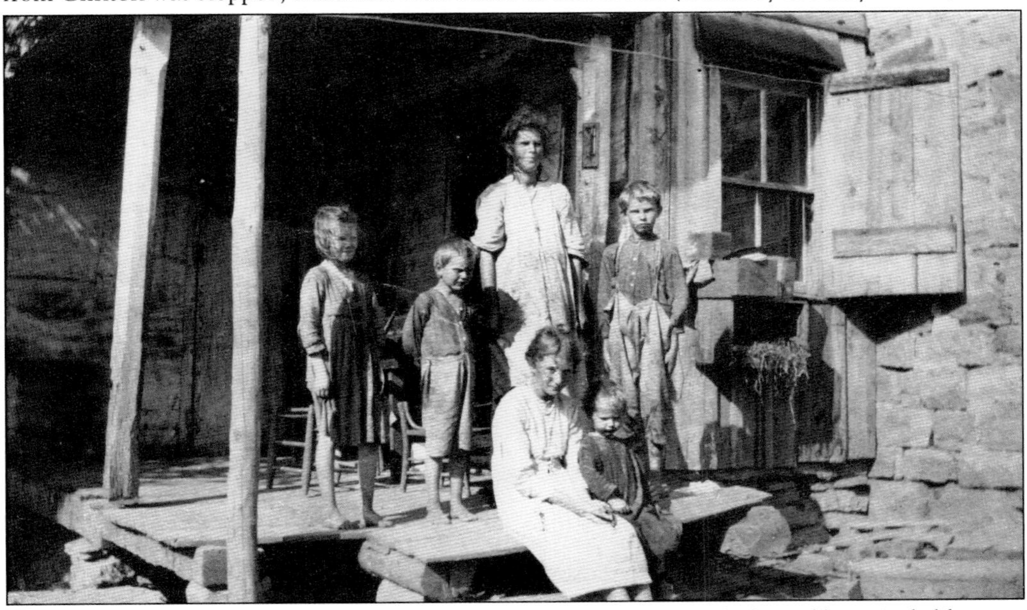

Nannie Thomason, wife of Walter Scott Thomason, is shown with five of her 10 children on the front porch of the David Hall cabin. From left to right are (first row) Marie holding Ransom; (second row) Rova, Roscoe, Nannie, and Columbus. A roosting box is attached below the window. (Courtesy of Elizabeth Thomason Bumgardner.)

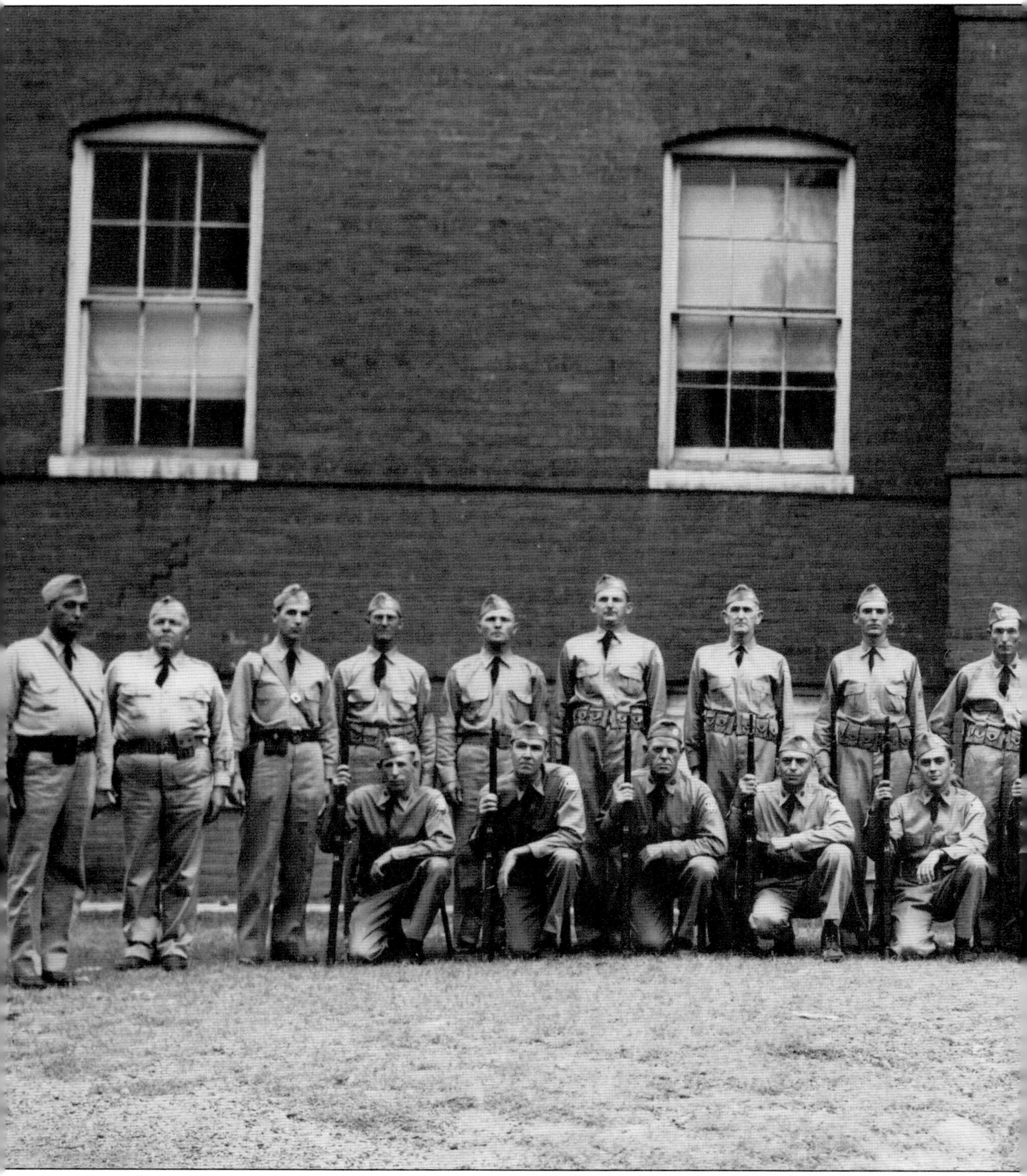

Capt. Edwin Wiley Wynne organized the first National Guard unit in Clinton since the General Assembly abolished the old-style militias. The unit mustered in on February 23, 1927, with the following members: Captain Wynne, 1st Lt. Edmund Cureton, 2nd Lt. Harold Lurvey, 1st Sgt. William Pemberton, S.Sgt. William Polk, S.Sgt. Edward Galyon, Sgt. Emile Duval, Pvt. Earl Bohanon, Pvt. Joe Brown, Pvt. Clarence Brummett, Pvt. Paul Burkett, Pvt. Edward Daniels,

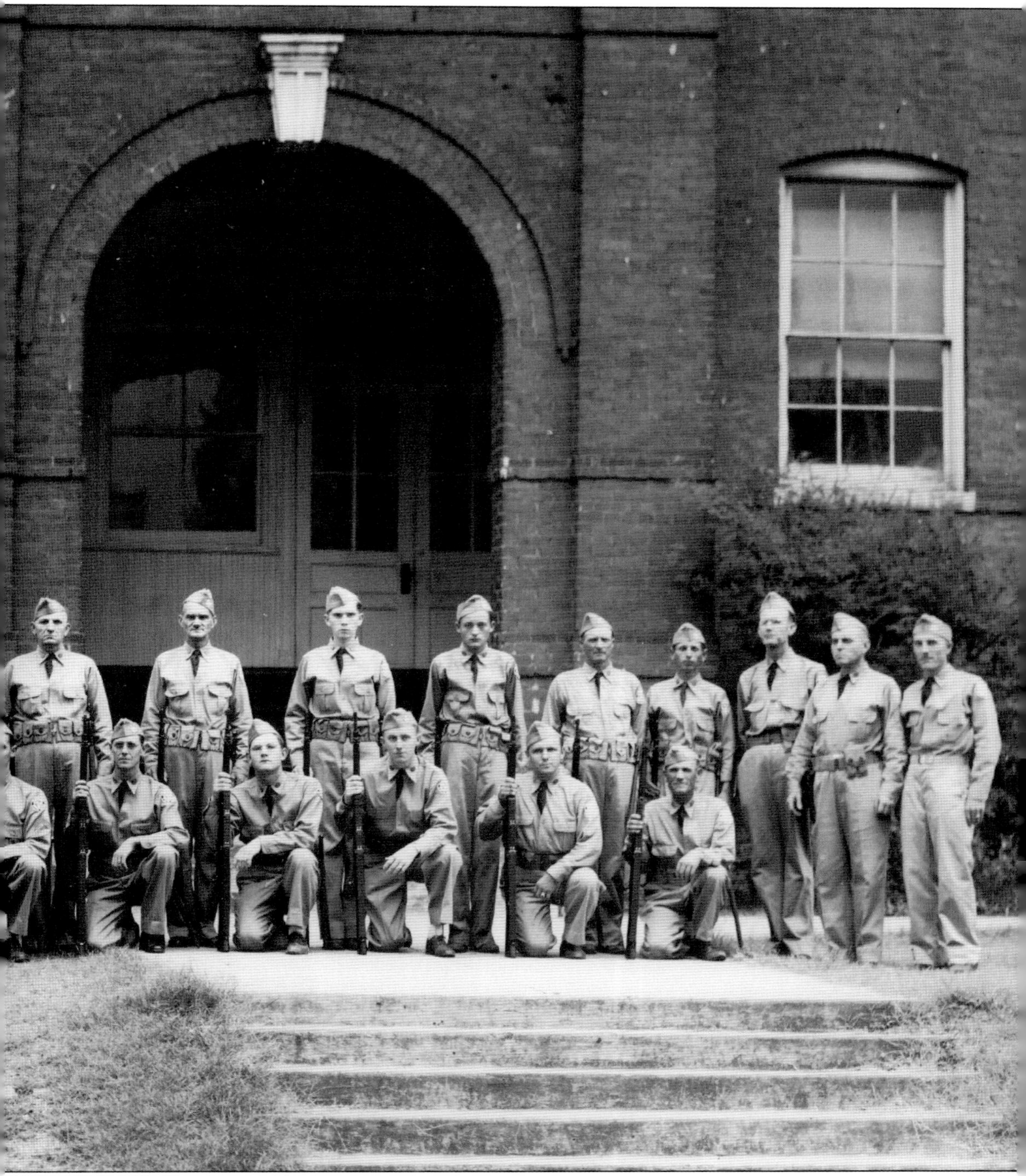

Pvt. John Daniels, Pvt. Edward Dail, Pvt. Vaughn Disney, Pvt. Earl Goans, Pvt. Everett Goans, Pvt. James Gowland, Pvt. Charles Haynes, Pvt. Richard Hensley, Pvt. Hugh Humphrey, Pvt. Don Lurvey, Pvt. Ernest Martin, Pvt. Harry Murray, Pvt. Kim Pierce, Pvt. Chandos Rhea, Pvt. Burleson Smith, Pvt. Earl Stokes, Pvt. Willie Viles, Pvt. Carl Weaver, Pvt. Glenn Wilson, and Pvt. John Wilson. (Courtesy of the Pellissippi Genealogical and Historical Society.)

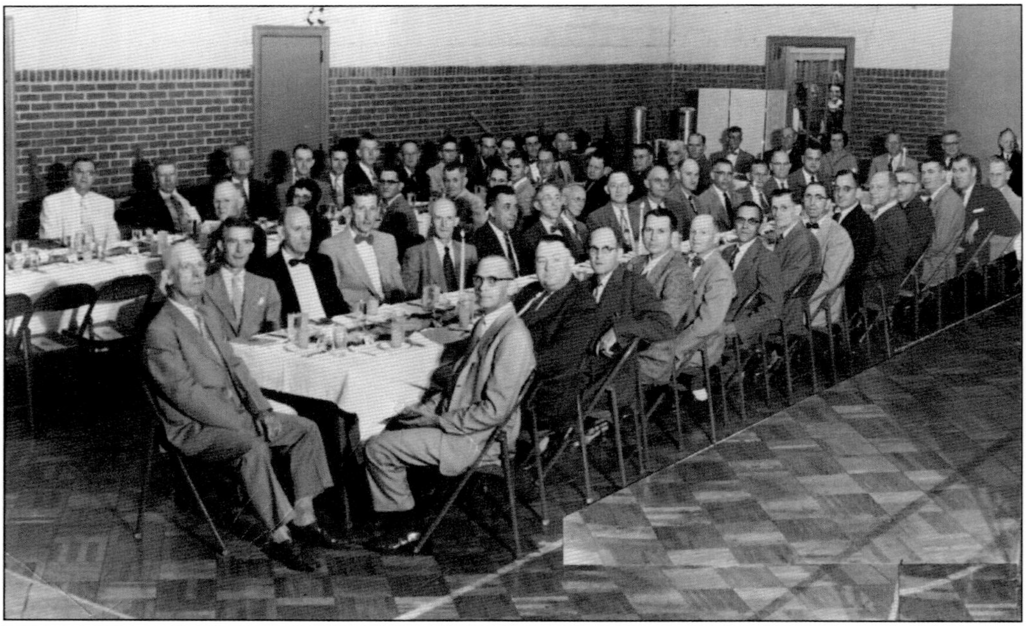

Magnet Mills, Inc., held annual banquets for its employees' 25-Year Club. Employees who reached 25 years of service with the mill were honored with a silver service pin. Employees who reached 30 years of service were honored with a gold watch. Certificates of appreciation were also awarded for 20 years of service. The banquets were held at various locations in Clinton, including the Park Hotel and Clinton High School's cafeteria and gym. The photographs above and below were taken at a banquet held in the gym of the city's Memorial Recreation Center, located on Broad Street. (Both, courtesy of Maxine Meade Holbrook.)

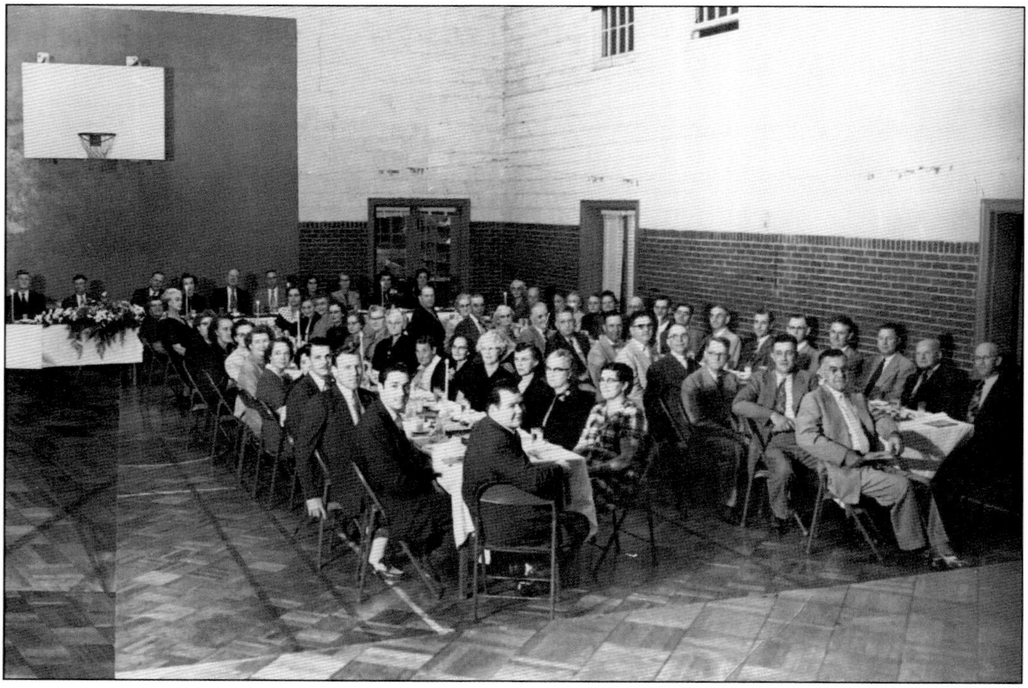

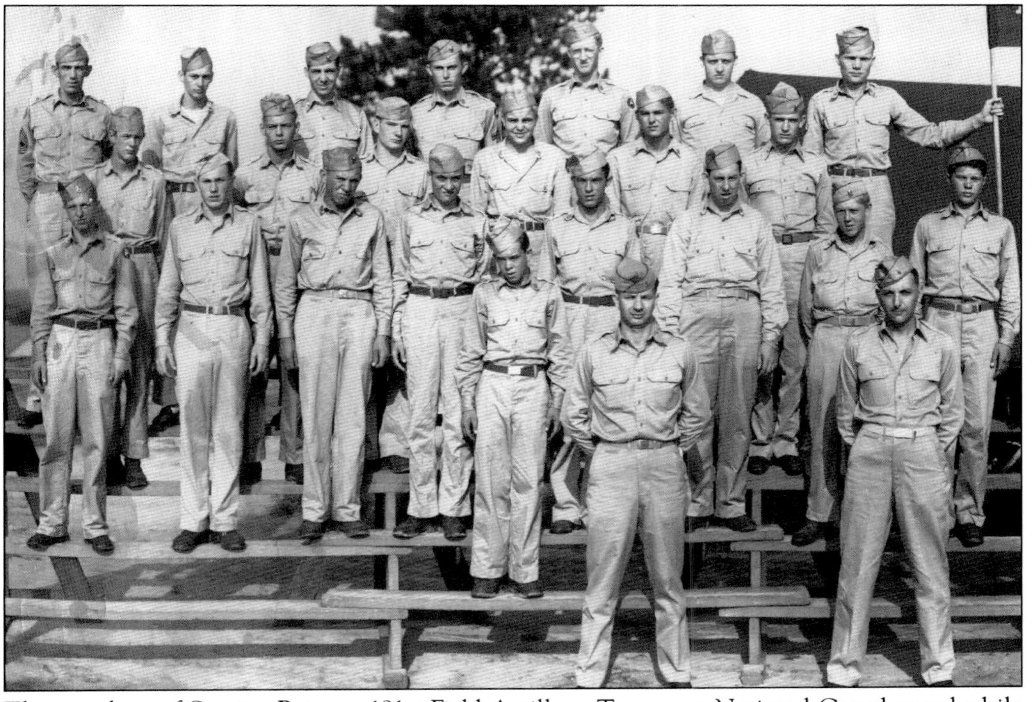

The members of Service Battery, 191st Field Artillery, Tennessee National Guard posed while at summer training at Fort Jackson, South Carolina, in 1949. The first National Guard unit based in Clinton in the 20th century was organized in 1927 by Capt. Edwin Wiley Wynne. He commanded the Clinton unit until he resigned in 1931. In 1938, the Clinton unit was designated Headquarters Battery CT (Combat Team) 2nd Battalion, 115th Field Artillery. Mobilization orders came in 1941, and the unit trained at Camp Forrest before deploying to Europe, where it saw action throughout World War II. It was deactivated in Germany in 1946. Some men from the Clinton unit again saw action during the Korean War and in September 1956, when a "law and order" operation existed in Clinton during the desegregation crisis that resulted in the bombing of Clinton High School. (Both, courtesy of Carolyn Spessard Braden.)

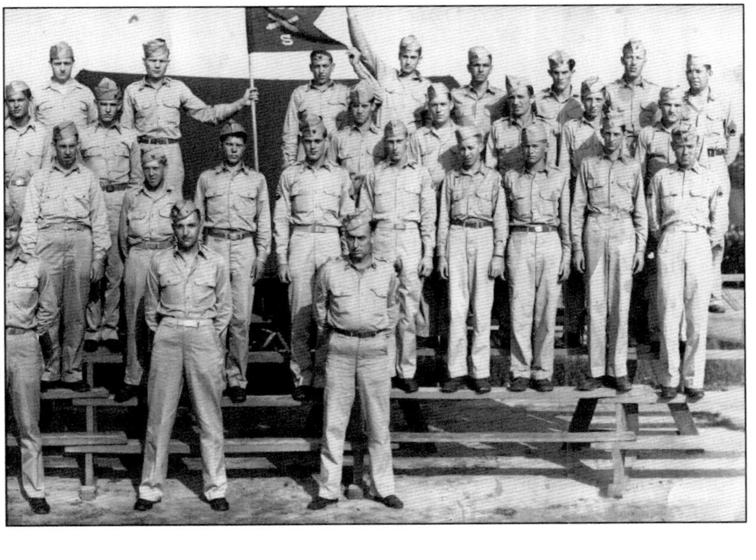

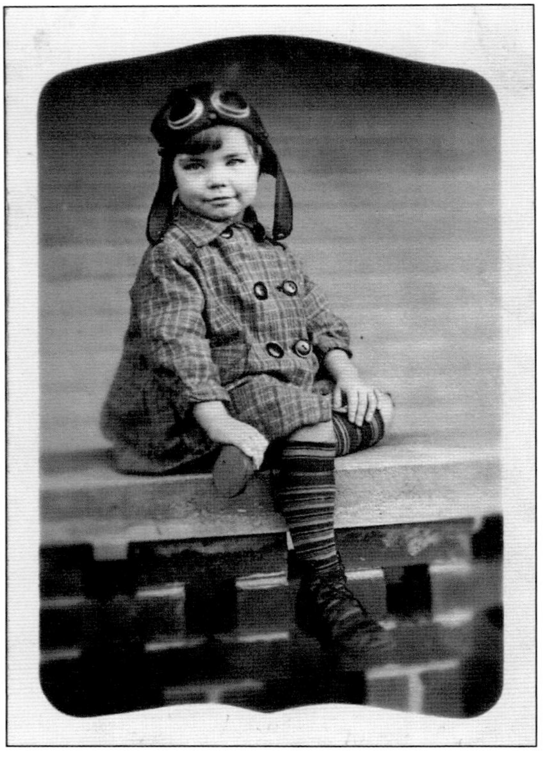

Wanda Lou Shetterly, wife of Charles Hugh Abner, is pictured in about 1937. She is the daughter of Franklin Roosevelt Shetterly and Lula Bernice Brown of the Black Oak community. She graduated from Clinton High School and Knoxville Business College and is retired from the personnel department of Y-12 in Oak Ridge. She has three children: Steven, Delores, and Byron. (Courtesy of Charles Hugh Abner.)

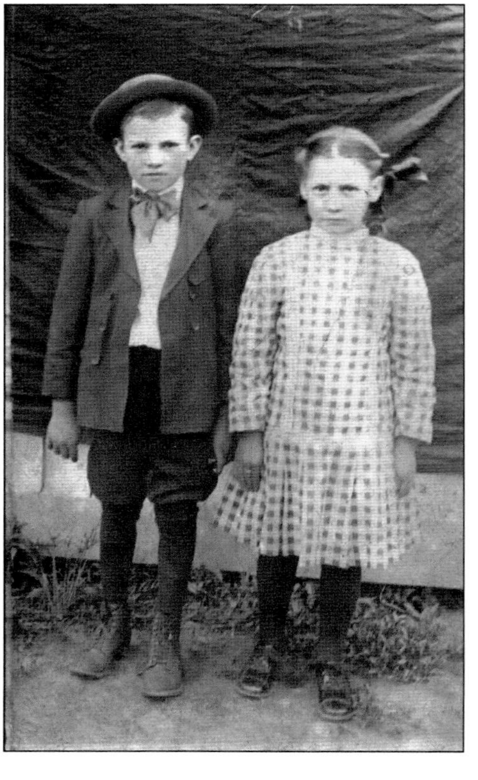

Acton and Ada Duncan were the two oldest children of Henry and Birdie Worthington Duncan. After their birth, Birdie and Henry divorced; Henry remarried and had children by his second wife. Henry and his second wife divorced; he remarried Birdie, and they had a second family. (Courtesy Judy Duncan Blakely.)

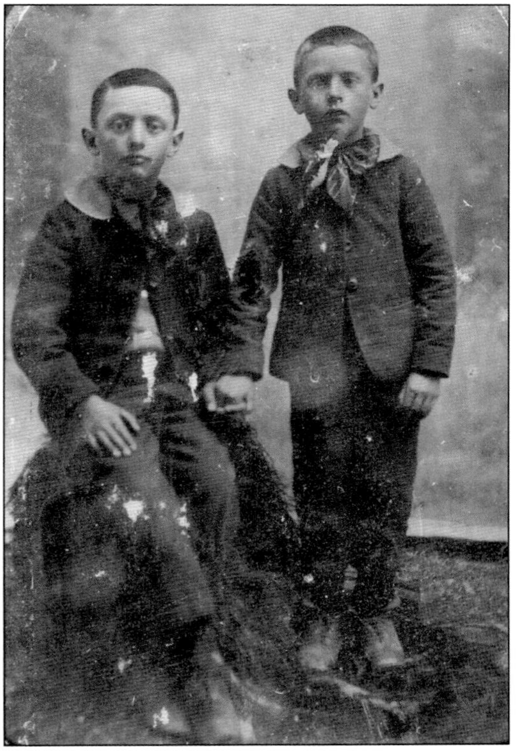

John Granville Arnold, who was born in 1811 and died in 1878, and his wife Sarah, who was born in 1812 and died in 1900, had William, Alfred, Katherine, Sarah, Emeline, Nancy, and Amanda. Emeline Arnold married Elijah Jennings and had two sons, Ernest and George, who posed for the photograph below in about 1880, when they were aged seven and 10, respectively. Alfred married and moved to Bristol to operate a lumber mill. William married Sarah Flannigan, and they continued to live in the Edgemoor community. William and Sarah had a son named Charles, who was age seven in 1880. The photograph at right, made in about 1880, is labeled simply, "the Arnold boys." These four boys are grandsons of Granville and Sarah Arnold, but it is unknown whether the Arnold boys are brothers or cousins. (Both, courtesy of Elizabeth Thomason Bumgardner.)

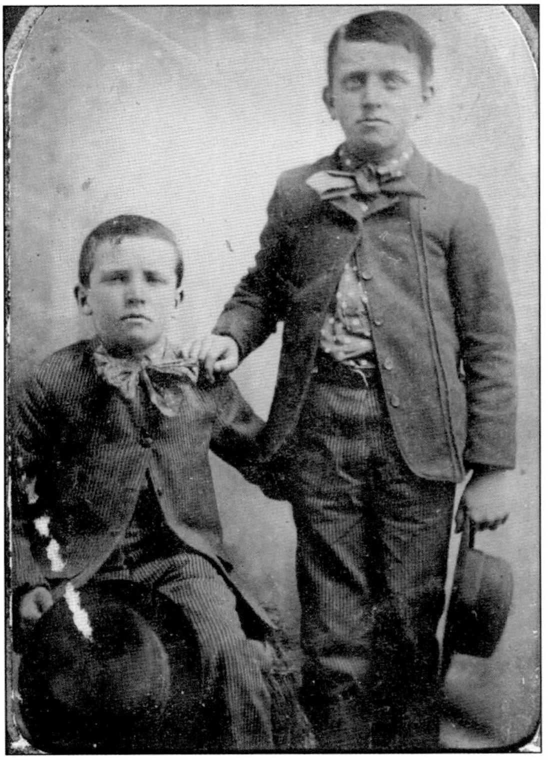

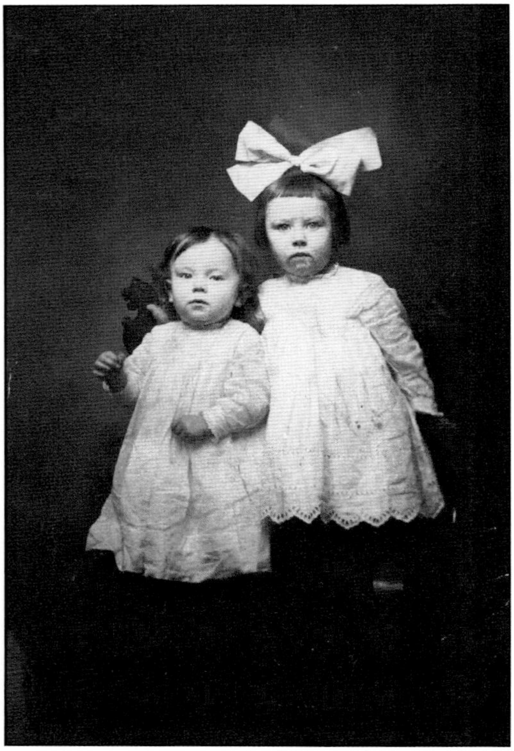

Robert, left, and Anna Ruth, right, were two of the nine children of J. Shields and Nora Murray Wallace. Anna Ruth Wallace was born in 1908 and married Hansford DeFoe. Robert Wallace was born in 1909 and married Ruby Hicks. They are both buried in the Andersonville Cemetery. (Courtesy of Kay Crowell Davis.)

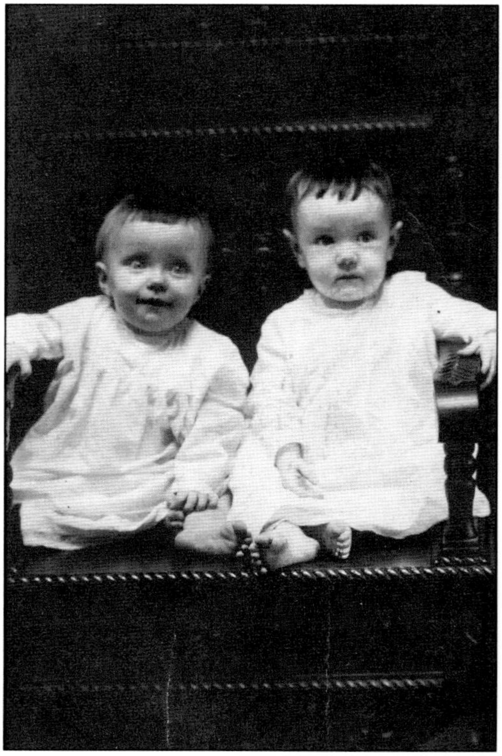

Hazel and Helen Wallace were the twin daughters of J. Shields and Nora Murray Wallace. Hazel and Helen were born in 1913. Helen Wallace married Claude Sharp. Hazel Wallace married Homer Lambert. (Courtesy of Kay Crowell Davis.)

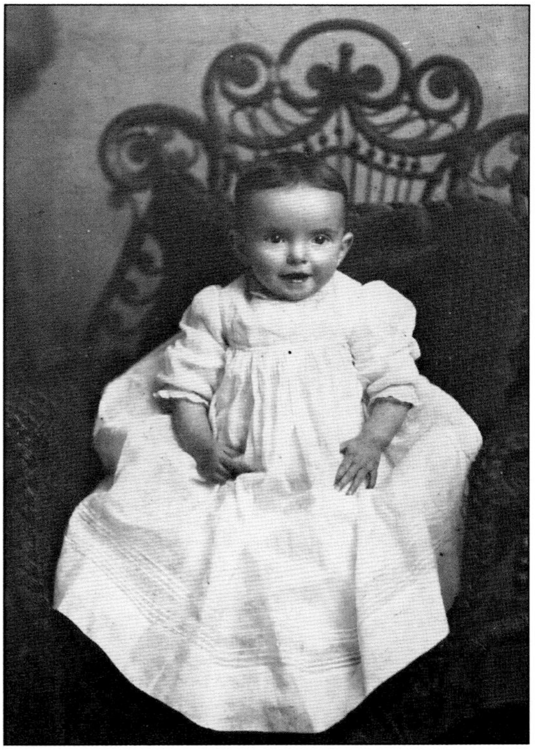

Emily Fowler (in the photograph at right) and Lyman and Alma Fowler (in the photograph below) were three of the children of Samuel Patton and Mary Lee Robertson Fowler. Emily was 10 months old when her photograph was taken. She died a month later, at the age of 11 months. Alma was age five and Lyman was age two in their photograph. Lyman and Alma Fowler grew up at The Hemlocks, the family home located in the Dutch Valley section of Anderson County. They attended school at the one-room schoolhouse Samuel Patton Fowler built and taught at. (Both, courtesy of Susan Fowler.)

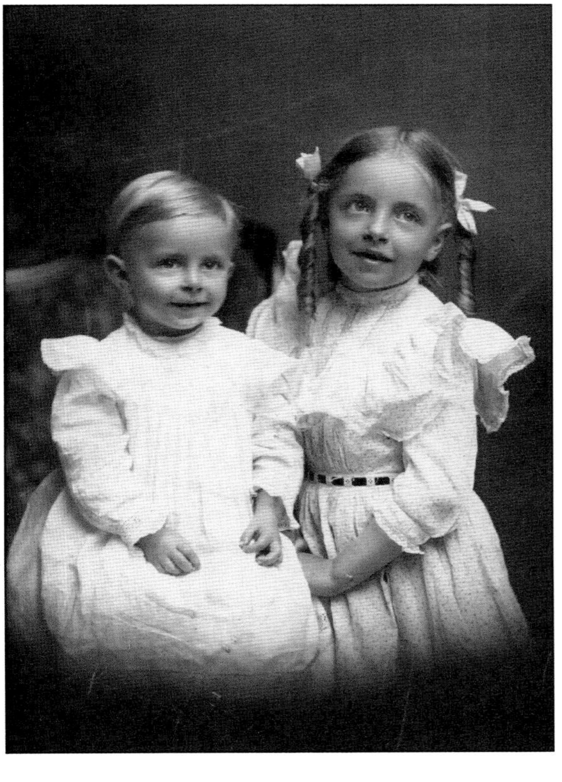

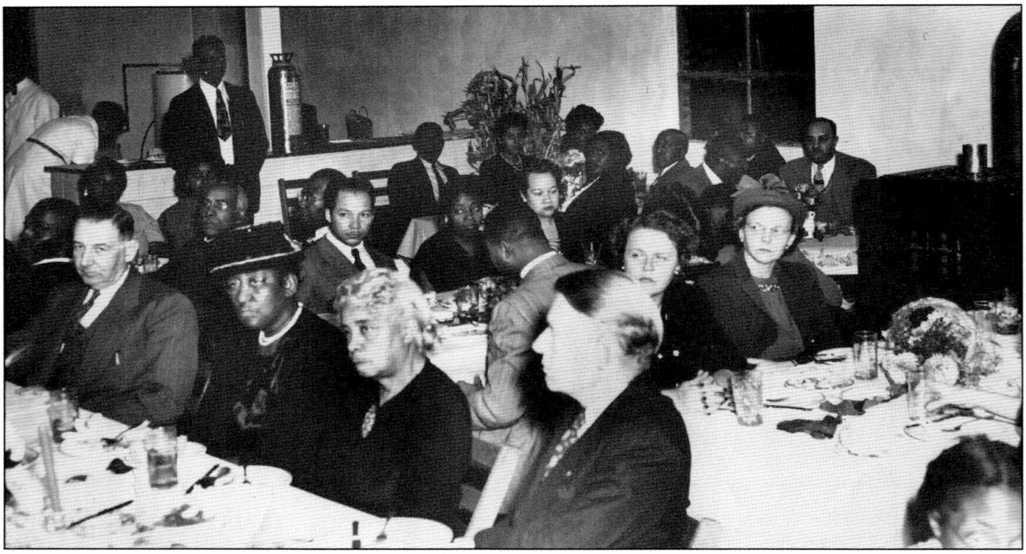

Before the integration of Clinton High School, African American children attending school past the eighth grade were bused to Knoxville. Because of the bus schedule, students from Clinton could not participate in extracurricular activities. Members of the African American and white communities came together in the 1950s to build the Green McAdoo Community Center to provide Clinton's African American children with recreational resources. (Courtesy of Jo Ann Allen Boyce.)

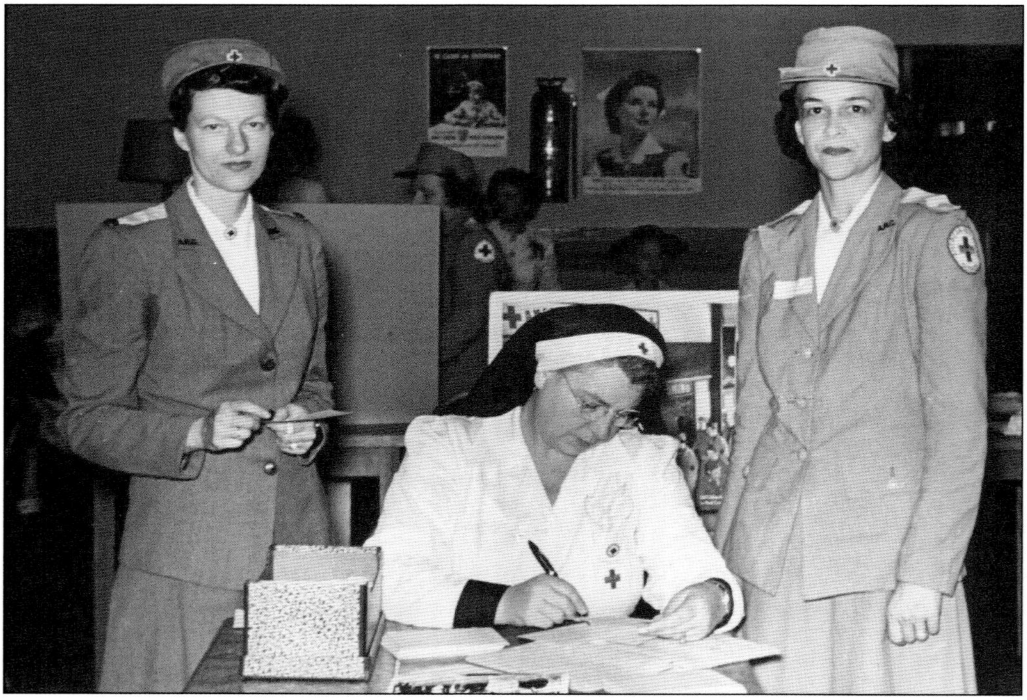

The Anderson County Chapter of the Red Cross was organized in Clinton in 1918. The Oak Ridge Chapter received its charter in 1947. In 1987, they combined to form the Appalachian Chapter of the Red Cross. Pictured in 1943 are, from left to right, Mrs. Weil, Mrs. Gatenby, and Mrs. Trayner. (Courtesy of the Appalachian Chapter of the Red Cross.)

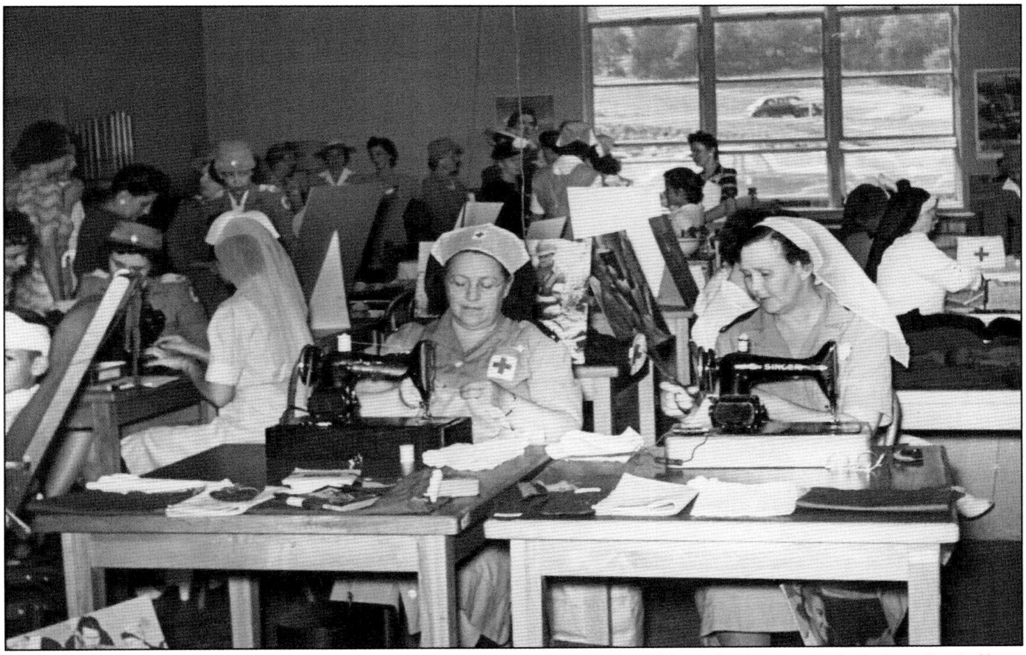

Members of the Red Cross are shown sewing and rolling surgical bandages in 1943. After the Jellico train wreck in 1944, hearses from Martin's Funeral Home in Lake City transported bodies and survivors of the wreck to the nearest hospital, which was located in Oak Ridge. Because Oak Ridge was a "secret city" not located on any civilian maps of the time, Oak Ridge officials were asked to send all notifications to the victims' next of kin from Clinton so that correspondence would have the Clinton postmark. (Both, courtesy of the Appalachian Chapter of the Red Cross.)

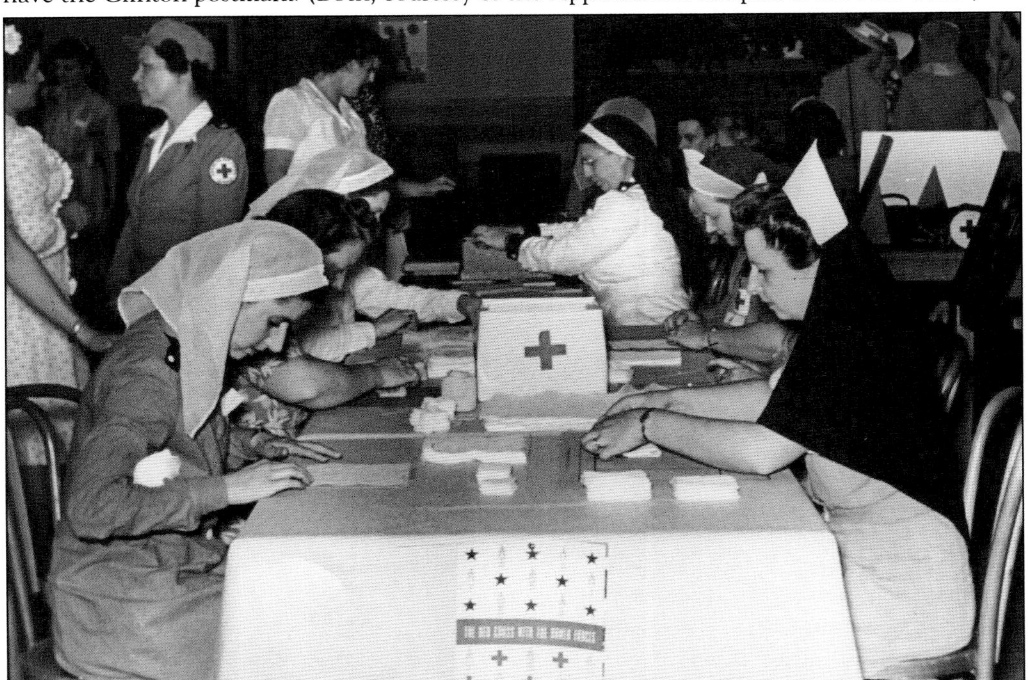

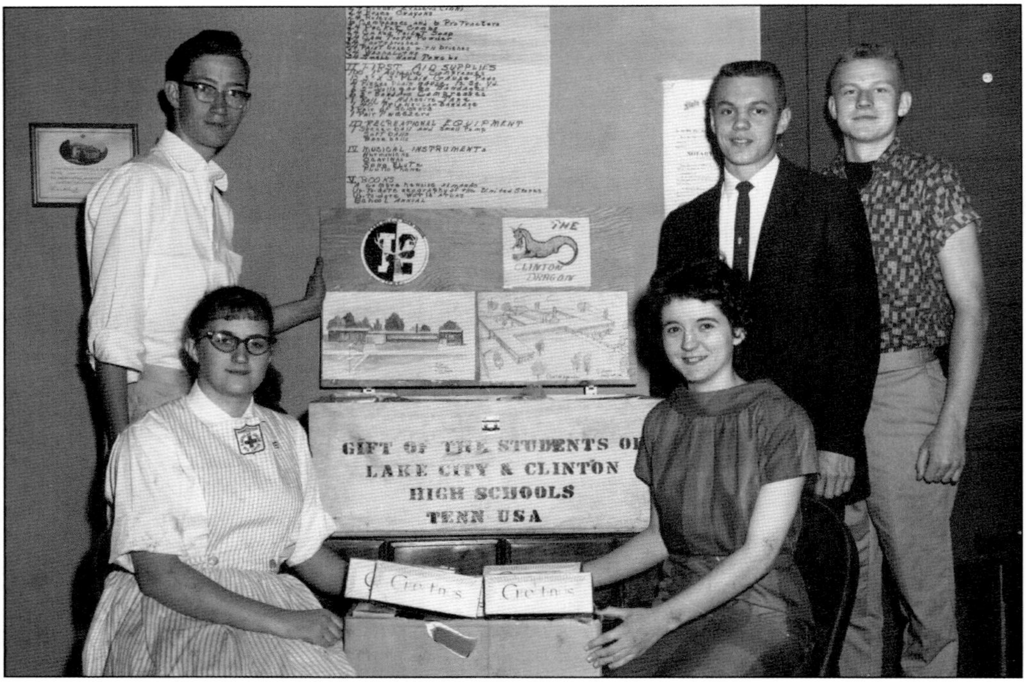

During the 1950s and 1960s, the Oak Ridge and Clinton Chapters of the Red Cross reached out to the young people of Anderson County through the Junior Red Cross program. In the photograph above, Junior Red Cross volunteers from Lake City and Clinton High Schools assemble a chest of goodies. On the wall above the chest is a list of the contents. It includes school and first-aid supplies, softballs and baseballs, US and world maps, and school annuals from both high schools. The photograph below shows Junior Red Cross volunteers from Norris Elementary School in the 1950s. (Both, courtesy of the Appalachian Chapter of the Red Cross.)

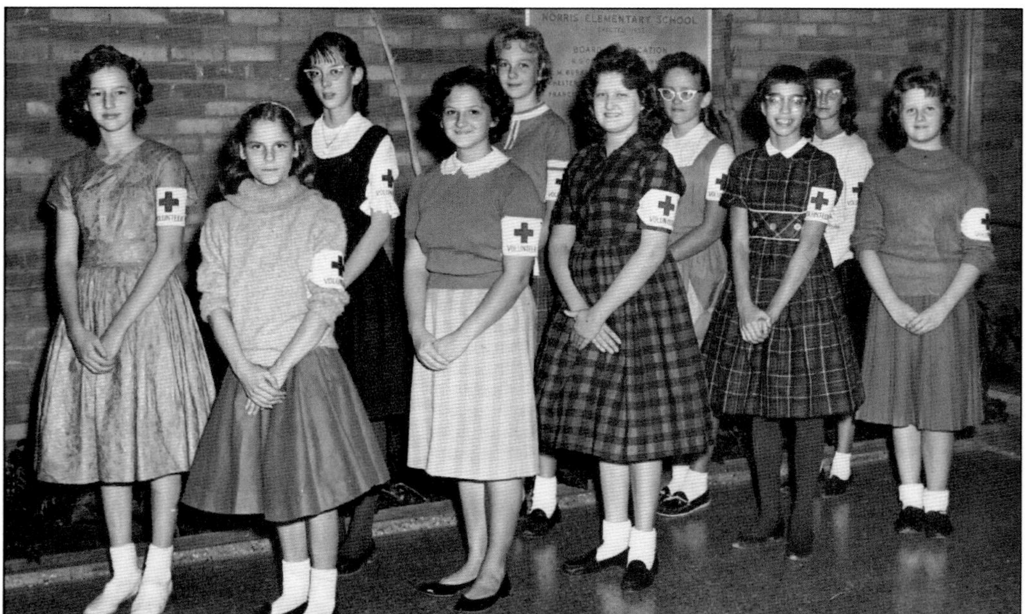

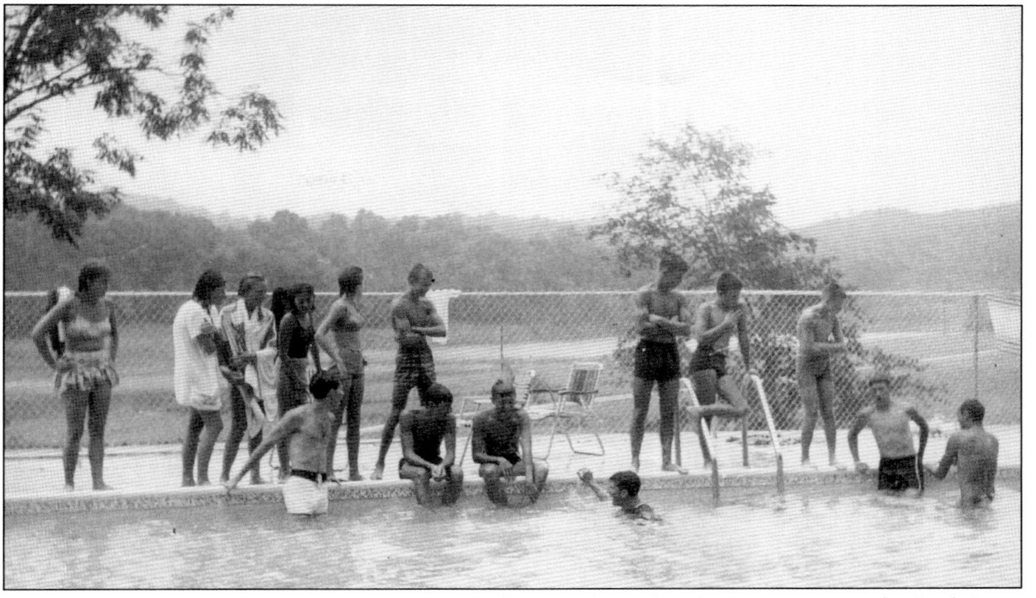

In addition to sewing and folding surgical bandages and supplies for use overseas, the Red Cross participates in disaster relief locally and abroad and offers life skills classes to members of the local communities. In this photograph from the 1960s, Clinton youth are shown receiving swimming and life-saving instruction at the community pool in Jaycee Park, which was dedicated in 1963. (Courtesy of the Appalachian Chapter of the Red Cross.)

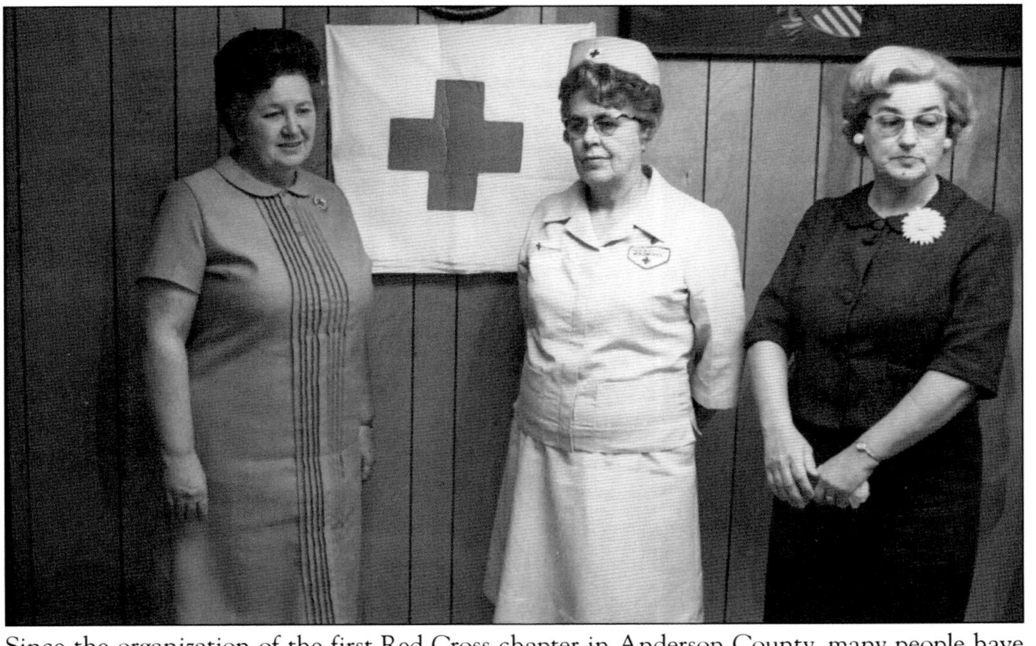

Since the organization of the first Red Cross chapter in Anderson County, many people have volunteered their time, energy, and money to further the cause. Many notable civic leaders have served on the Red Cross Council and in other positions of leadership. In this undated photograph, Mrs. Charles Stuckey is seen on the left at a meeting of the council. (Courtesy of the Appalachian Chapter of the Red Cross.)

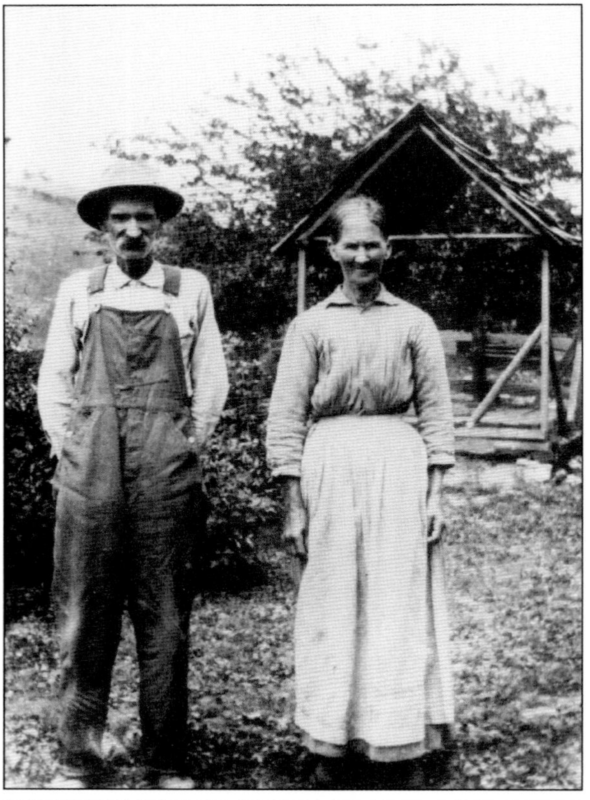

John L. Worthington was born in 1854 and died in 1923. He was the son John K. and Martha J. Worthington. He married Sarah Hutcherson on January 5, 1873. John L. and Sarah Worthington are buried in the Miller Cemetery at Island Home Baptist Church. (Courtesy of Charles Hugh Abner.)

The photograph below shows the Jesse Brown and Sarah Catherine Rhoda Jane Peak Worthington home about 1910. Pictured on the ground are, from left to right, Mae Pyatt, Jesse Brown Worthington, Sarah Worthington holding an unidentified baby, Martha Worthington, and three unidentified young ladies. Pictured on the roof are, from left to right, Samuel Worthington, Robert Worthington, an unidentified young boy, Pat Cook, Jesse Worthington, and Sallie Worthington. (Courtesy of Judy Duncan Blakely.)

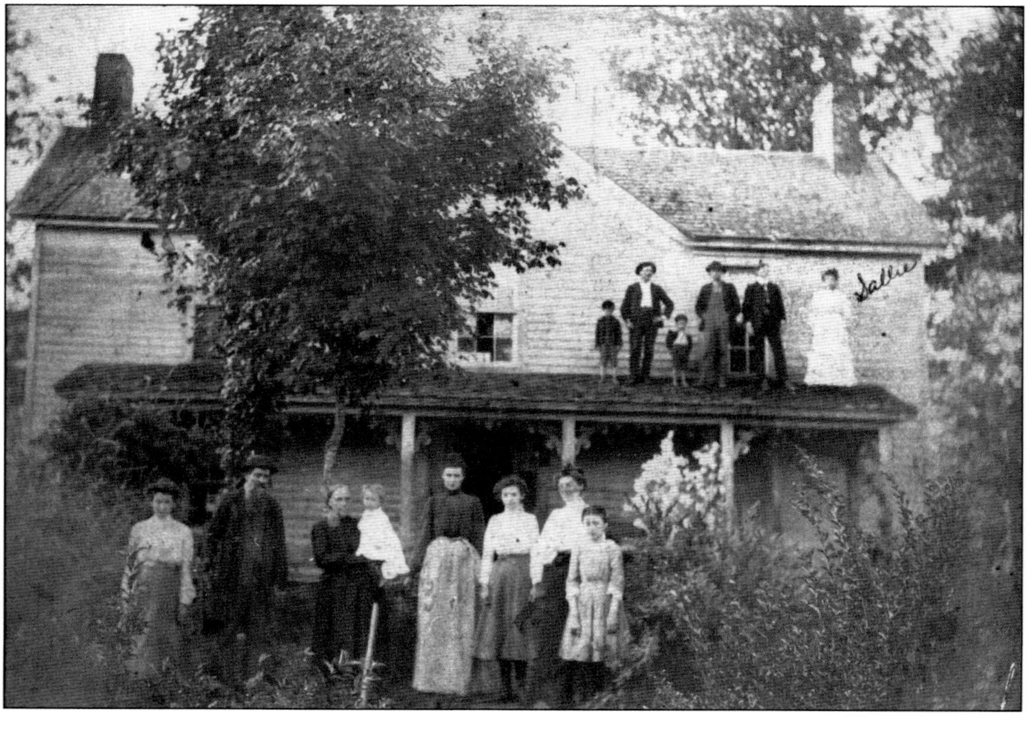

Two

CHURCHES

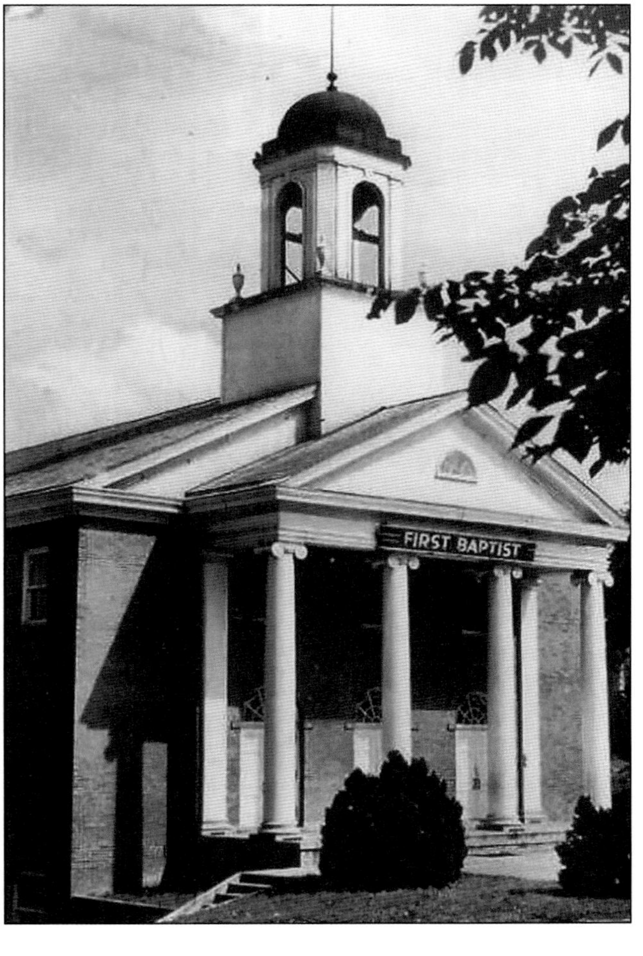

The First Baptist Church of Clinton was originally a frame building located near Edgewood and Delta Avenues. The church moved to Jacksboro (now Main) Street, where it stands today. The present building has seen much remodeling and many additions through the years, but its columned facade is still the same, although the neon sign above the entrance has been removed. (Courtesy of the *Clinton Courier-News*.)

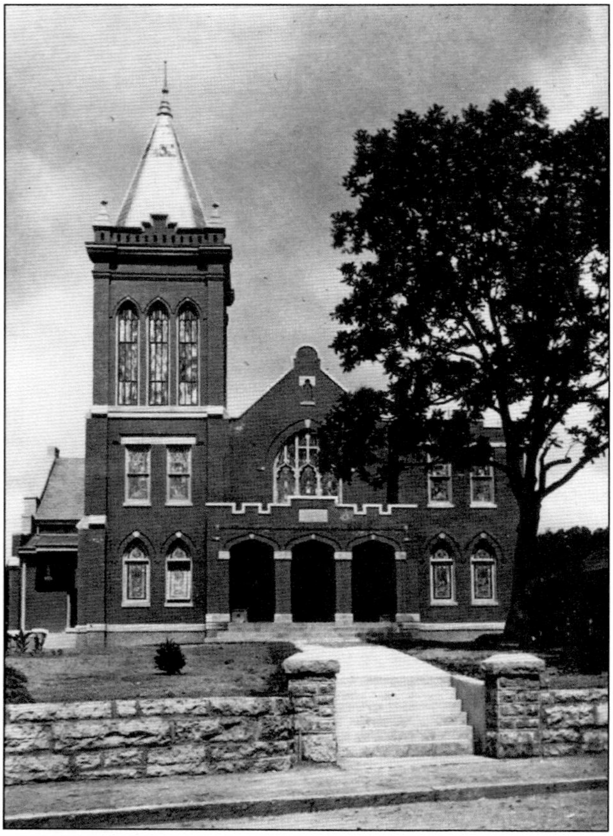

The Young Memorial Church was located on the lot where the Memorial United Methodist Church stands today in Clinton. Judge David K. Young Sr. was a member of the Methodist Episcopal Church, South, of Clinton, and in 1887, he was instrumental in raising the funds to build this new church building. (Courtesy of the *Clinton Courier-News*.)

Pictured below are members of the Lupton Church, once located off of Emory Valley Road in Oak Ridge. From left to right are (first row) Laura Steele Strader, Louise Bardill Howard, Edith B. Stair, Pearl Steele Henderson, Frances Gray Long, and Eva Butler Wilkins; (second row) Bob Worthington, John Bardill, John Gamble, Frank Hightower, and Homer Hackworth. (Courtesy of Mary Elkins Barker.)

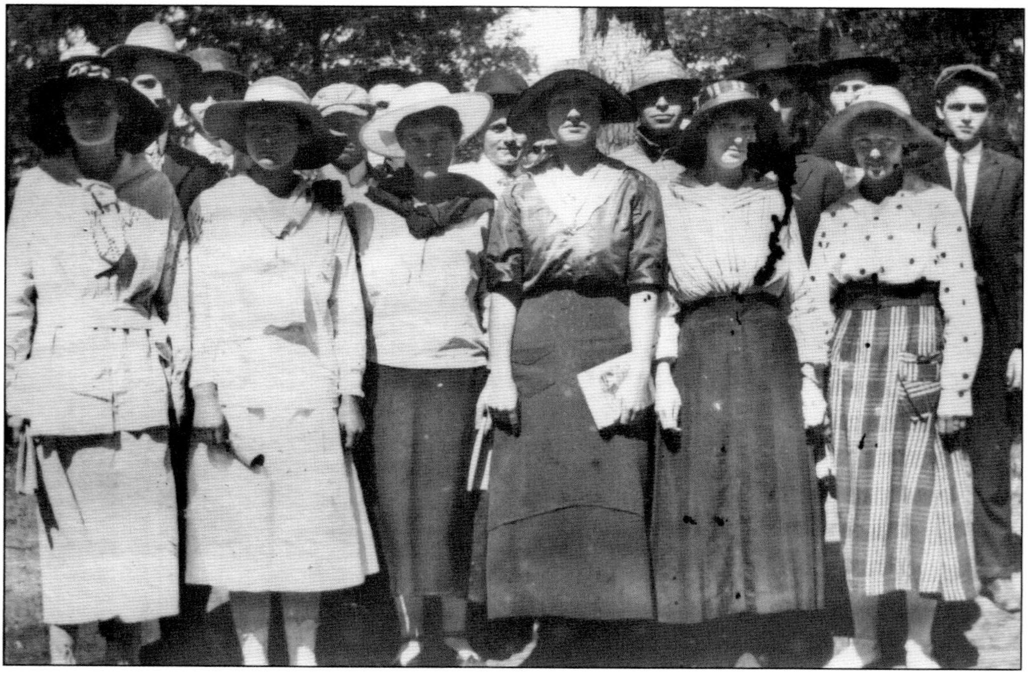

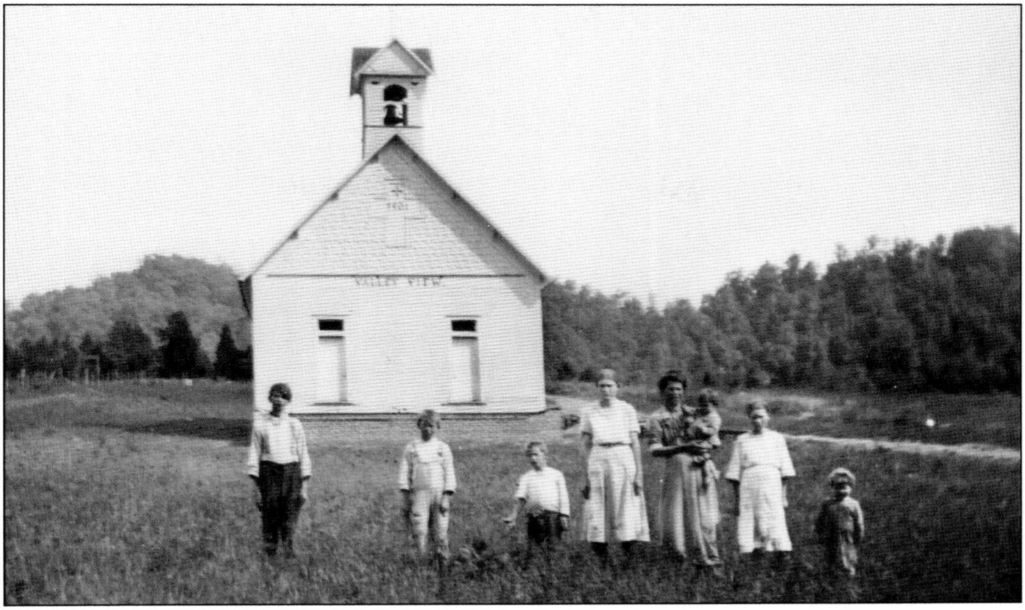

Established in 1901, Valley View United Methodist Church is located on Old Edgemoor Road, across from the David Hall cabin. Old Edgemoor Road was part of the Emory Trace, which crossed the Clinch River close to where the marina and rowing center are today on Melton Hill Drive. Pictured in 1921 in front of the church are Nannie Thomason and seven of her children. (Courtesy of Elizabeth Thomason Bumgardner.)

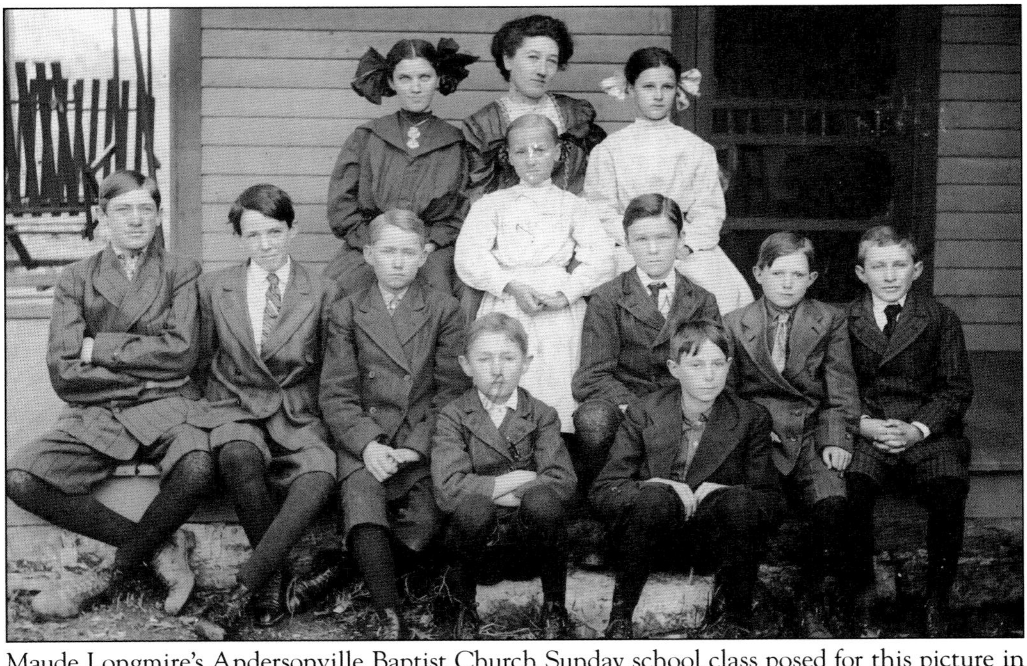

Maude Longmire's Andersonville Baptist Church Sunday school class posed for this picture in 1909. On the second row are Lon Williams (left) and Frank W. Wallace (second from left). Middle of the back row is Maude Longmire. Other class members are unidentified. Lon Williams is the well-known author of pulp fiction Westerns. (Courtesy of Kay Crowell Davis.)

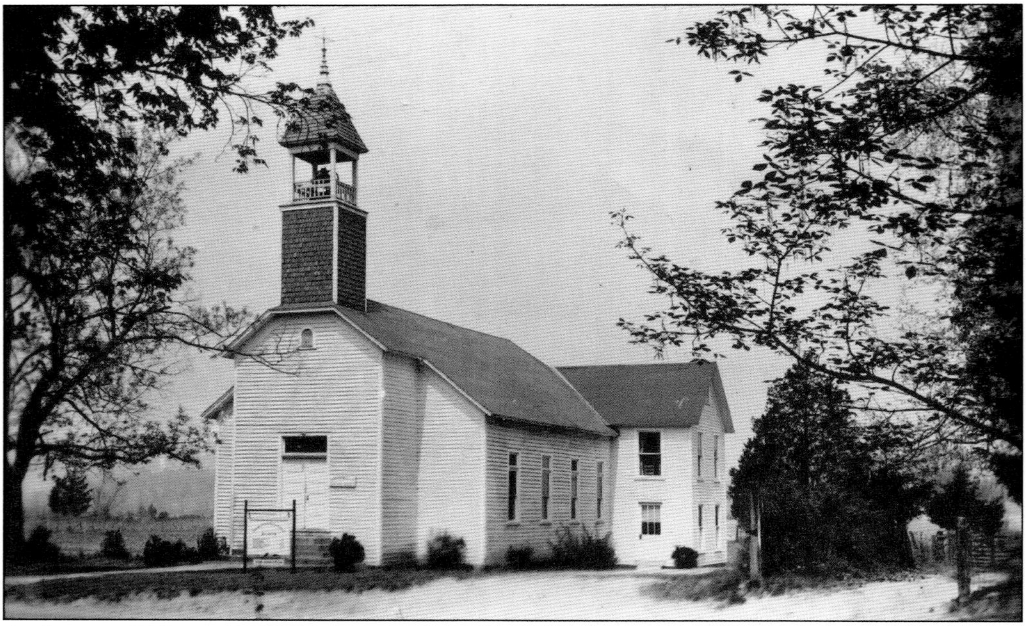

Andersonville Baptist Church was organized as the Baptist Church of Christ of Andersonville on May 26, 1883. The 13 organizing members were F.F. and Elizabeth Dawn, Rosannah Mills Lamar Wallace, J.K.P. Wallace, J.M. Jones, S.J. Jones, Mary E. Longmire, and William Howard Rutherford, of Bethel Baptist Church; Mark and Paulina Rutherford, Mary E. Foster, and Laura Caledonia McKinney Wallace (wife of J.K.P.), of Oak Grove Baptist Church; and Fannie Whitaker, of Red Hill Baptist Church. W.H. Rutherford, the first deacon of the church, was ordained a minister by the church and became its first pastor. The photograph above shows the original 1883 building (front) with the 1938 Sunday school room addition (rear). Below is a photograph of the interior of the church. (Both, courtesy of Emily Wallace Haverkamp.)

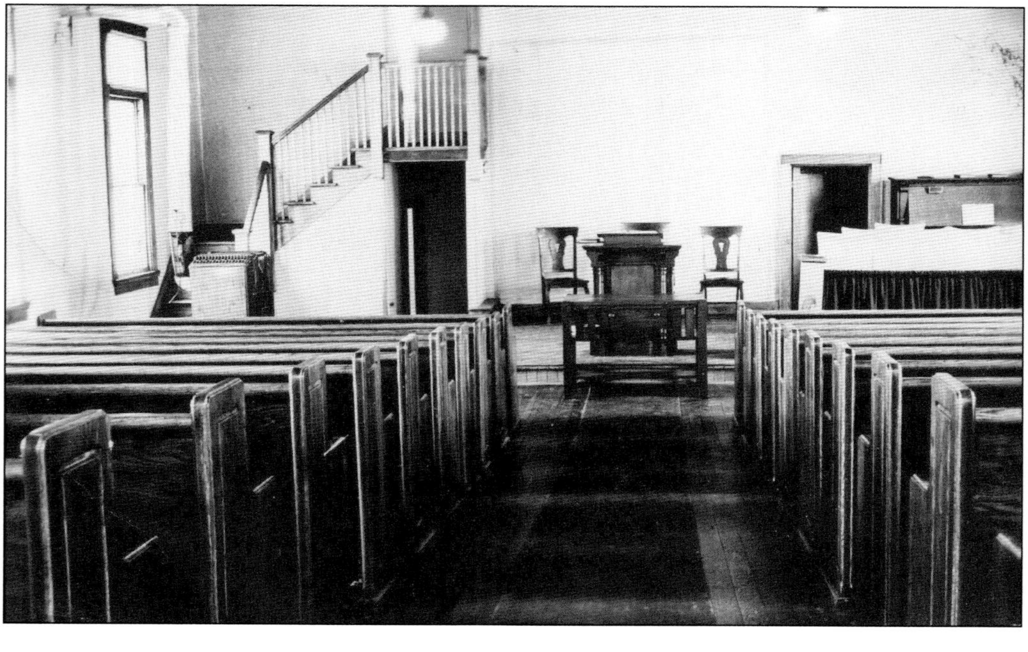

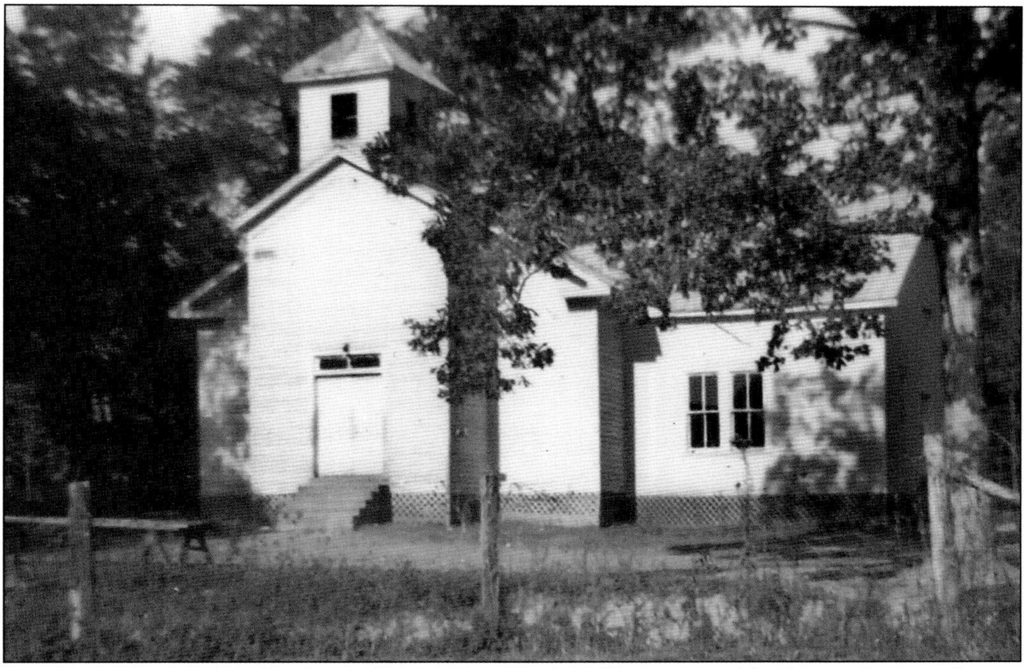

New Hope Baptist Church is located in the Bear Creek Valley section of Anderson County, close to the Y-12 complex in Oak Ridge. The homes located in Bear Creek Valley were taken by the federal government when the city of Oak Ridge was built during World War II as part of the Manhattan Project; most of the families relocated to other areas of the county. (Courtesy of Robert Copeland.)

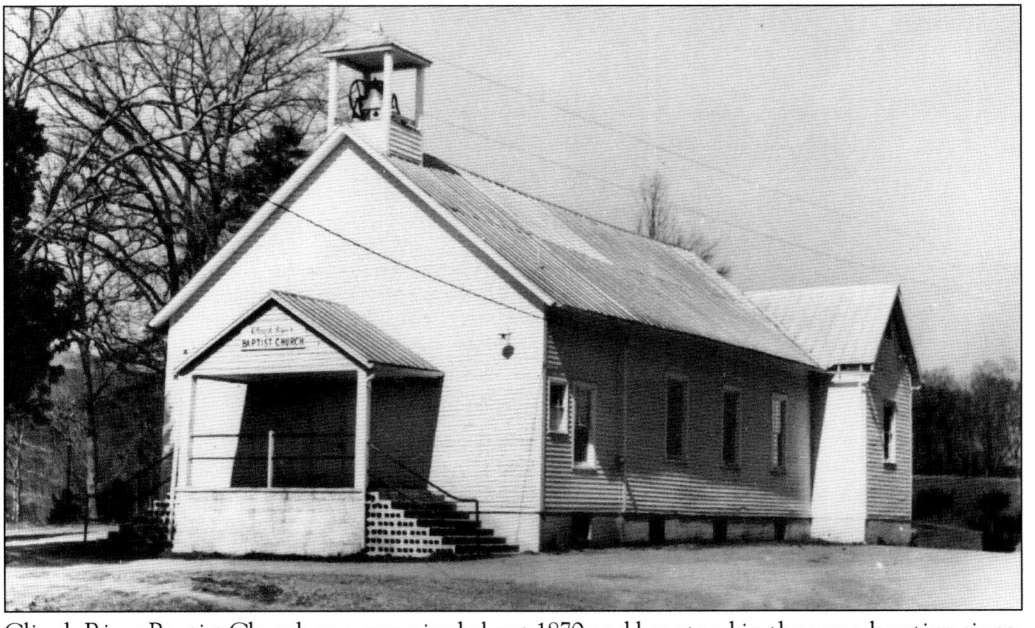

Clinch River Baptist Church was organized about 1870 and has stood in the same location since. The original white frame building was remodeled by adding windows and then by adding brick side steps outside the front entrance. The frame church was replaced by a new brick church in 1969. (Courtesy of Charles Hugh Abner.)

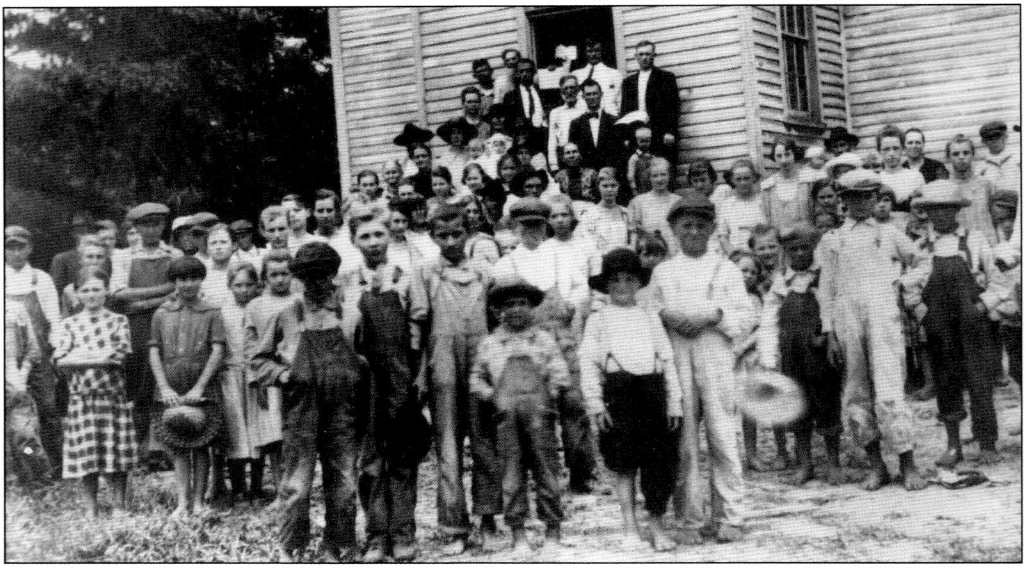

The photograph above shows one of Clinch River Baptist Church's early congregations. The photograph below shows members of its congregation during the 1950s. The Clinch River Baptist Church serves residents in the Lake City, Clear Branch, Medford, and Dutch Valley areas of Anderson County. It is a member of the Clinton Baptist Association, organized in 1853 and headquartered in Clinton, as well as the Tennessee Baptist Convention and the Southern Baptist Convention. As the church congregation has grown, services have been added, and today, it is known for its strong youth and children's programs. (Both, courtesy of Charles Hugh Abner.)

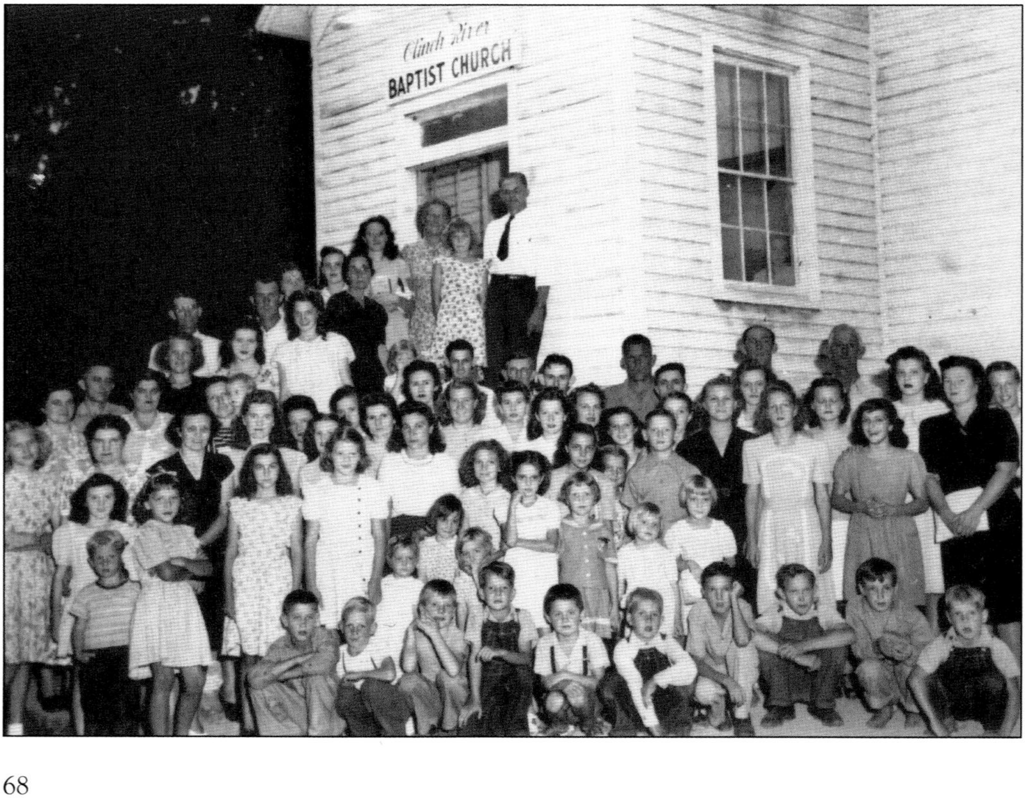

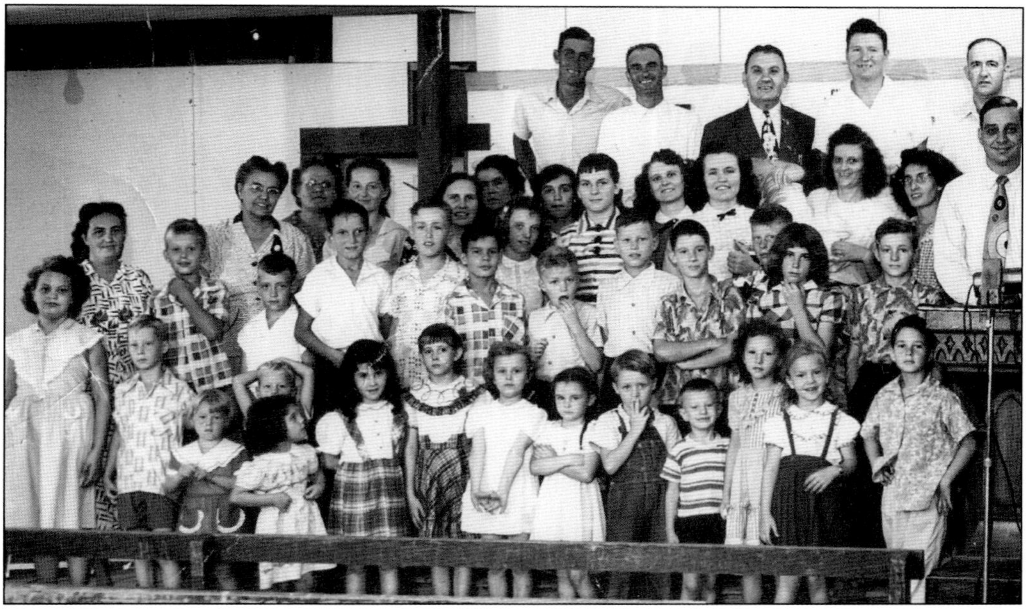

The Clinton Tabernacle Church of God was located at the corner of Scruggs Avenue and Sharp Street in Clinton. The church later moved to a location on State Highway 61 between Clinton and Oak Ridge. Identified members of the 1951–1952 congregation are Dewey Copeland, Murt Garner, Walter Webb, Norman Roberts, Roy Farmer, Reverend Kelly, Dan Richards, Edward Webb, Joe Brown, Eula Copeland, Jerry Copeland, Lela Mae Roberts (who is holding Thomas Garner), Jeanette Webb, John Copeland, Virgie Copeland, Kay Duncan, Camella Snellings, Bill Farmer, John Garrett, Gladys Dotson, Minnie Rayfield, Gene Corder, John Roach, Burt Giles, Ralph Garner, Archie Corder, Lorene Morgan, Louella Farmer, Homer Copeland, June Roberts, Kim Snellings, Violet Vandergriff, Leon Roberts, Bob Copeland, Glen Garner, Marilyn Webb, Bill Copeland, Linda Garner, Caroline Garrett, James Charles Farmer, Ruth Martin, Kitty Roberts, James Roberts, Mary French, and Silvey Roach. (Both, courtesy of Robert Copeland.)

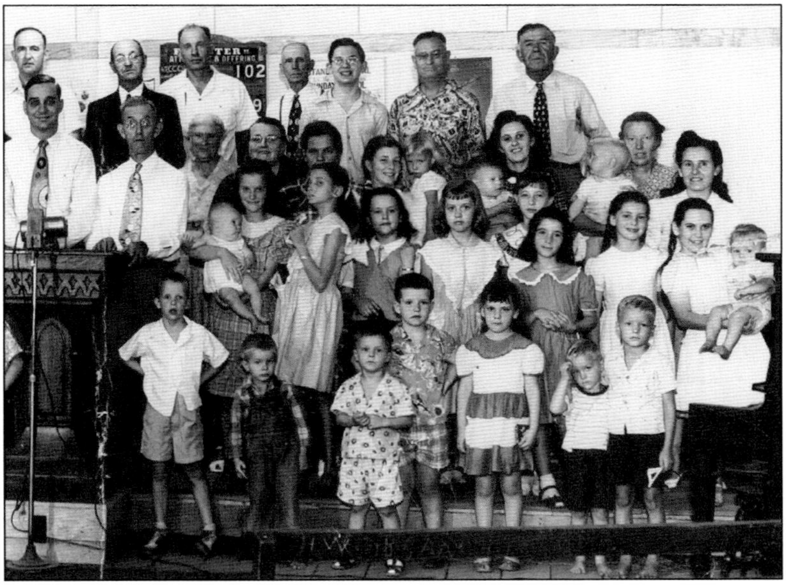

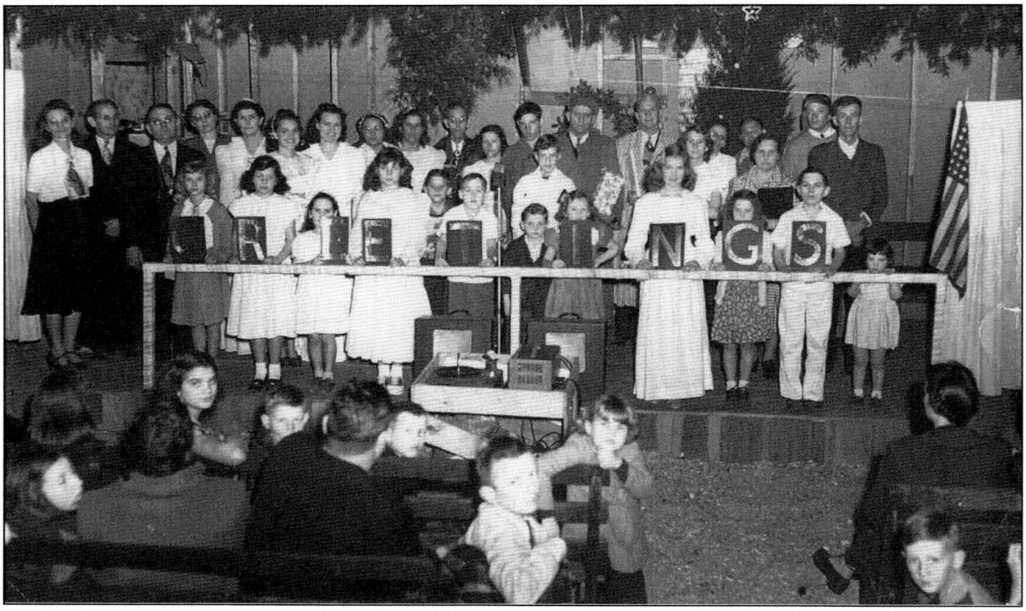

Clinton Tabernacle Church of God members identified in this photograph from about 1946 are the Reverend Walter Webb, Bertha Sargent, Imogene Jackson, Louella Farmer, Gladys Dotson, John Roach, Delores Lawson, Bonnie Holloway, Steve Jackson, Rowena Webb, Bill Holloway, Kay Duncan, Jeannette Webb, Ralph Garner, James Charles Farmer, Anderson Garner, Linda Garner, Edward Webb, Marilyn Webb, Homer Copeland, Bob Copeland, and Eula Mae Copeland. (Courtesy of Robert Copeland.)

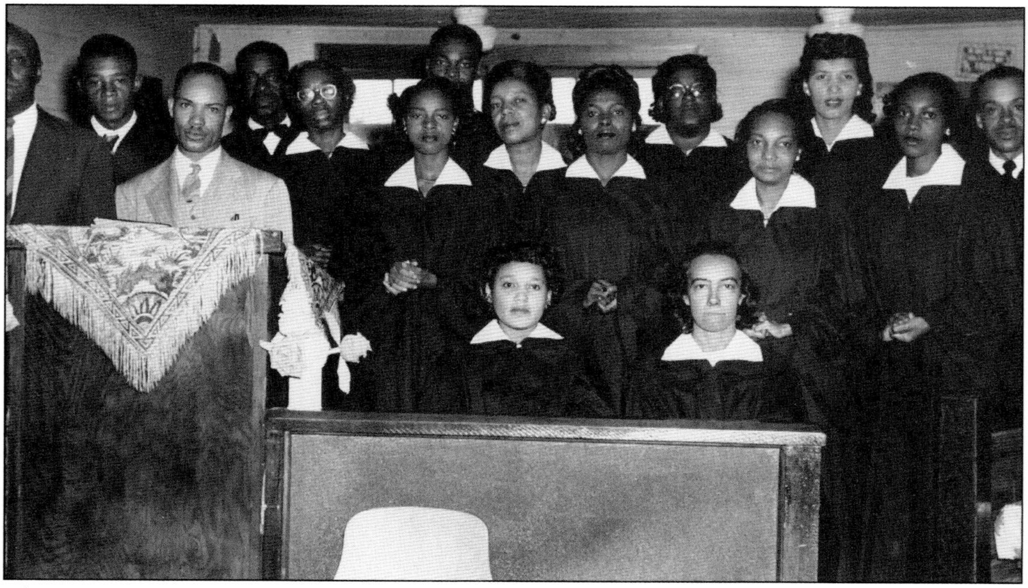

The Mount Sinai Baptist Church choir was a show choir that was invited to perform in churches all over Anderson County, Knoxville, and beyond. Members of this 1950s choir were photographed with the Reverend Orville Willis, head pastor of Mount Sinai (in the light-colored suit behind the pulpit), and the Reverend George Iker, associate pastor of Mount Sinai. (Courtesy of Jo Ann Allen Boyce.)

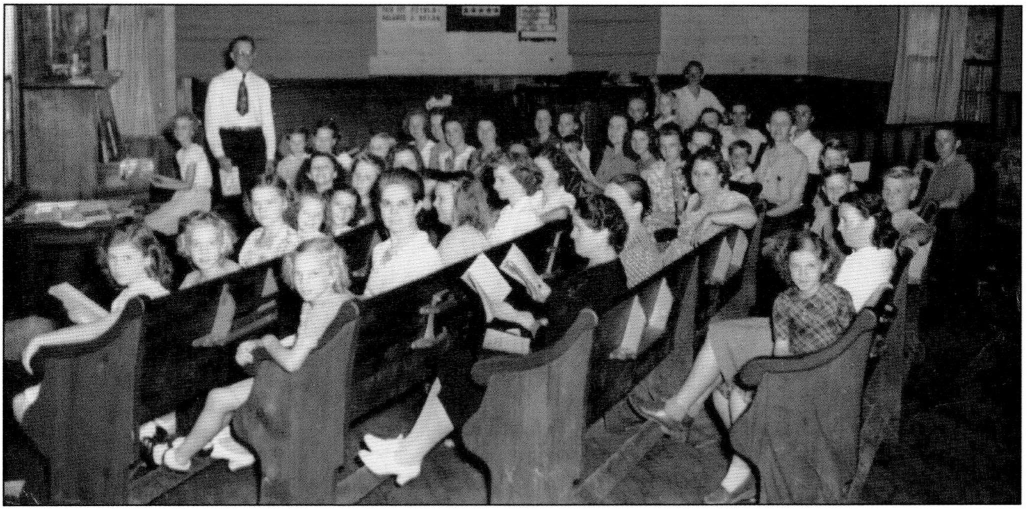

In the 1940s and early 1950s, church musicians and singers traveled the county conducting schools that taught shape note singing in an attempt to keep the tradition alive. In this photograph from about 1945, Daily O. "D.O." Wright, from Black Oak Baptist Church, is teaching a class at the South Clinton Baptist Church. Maxine Meade Holbrook is pictured playing the piano. (Courtesy of Maxine Meade Holbrook.)

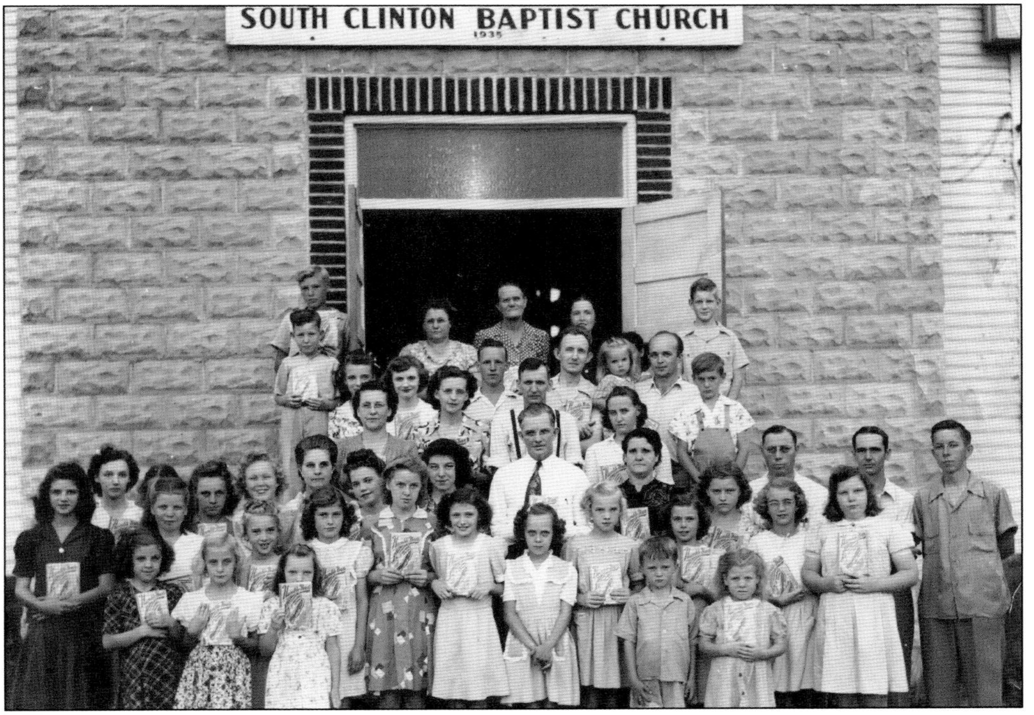

The same class that was photographed inside the church in the previous image posed outside of South Clinton Baptist Church with their *Humble Hearts* songbooks. The class was taught as part of that summer's vacation Bible school. Identified in the picture are Mr. Wright (center of second row, in dark tie) and Maxine Meade Holbrook, who served as pianist for the class (second row, second from left). (Courtesy of Maxine Meade Holbrook.)

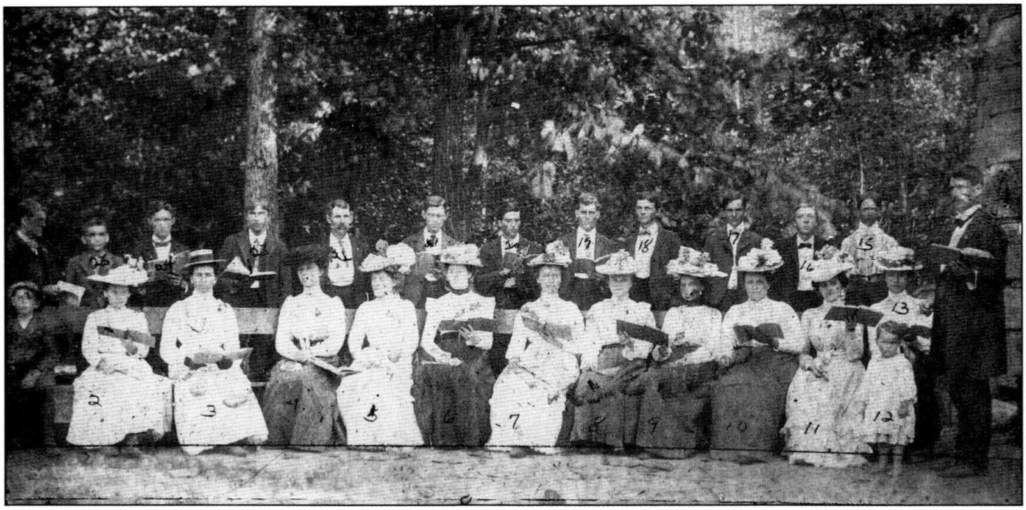

Members of the Mount Vernon Methodist Church congregation and their pastor posed with their Bibles during a dinner on the grounds at an all-day service in this photograph from about 1910. The church, also known as Dunaway's Chapel, was located on Mount Vernon Road in Bethel Valley. (Courtesy of Mary Elkins Barker.)

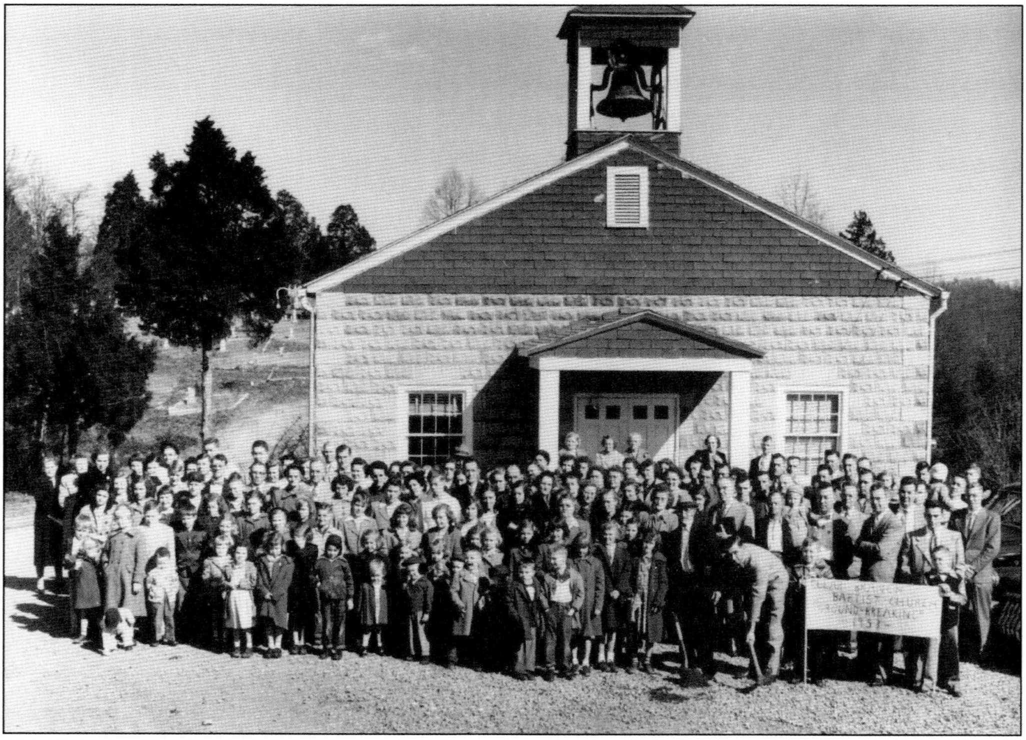

Members of the Clear Branch Baptist Church, located on Clear Branch Road, posed outside their former church building during the 1953 ground-breaking ceremony for their current building. Clear Branch Baptist Church is a member of the Clinton Baptist Association, the Tennessee Baptist Convention, and the Southern Baptist Convention. Behind the church is the Leach Cemetery. (Courtesy of Charles Hugh Abner.)

Three

Schools

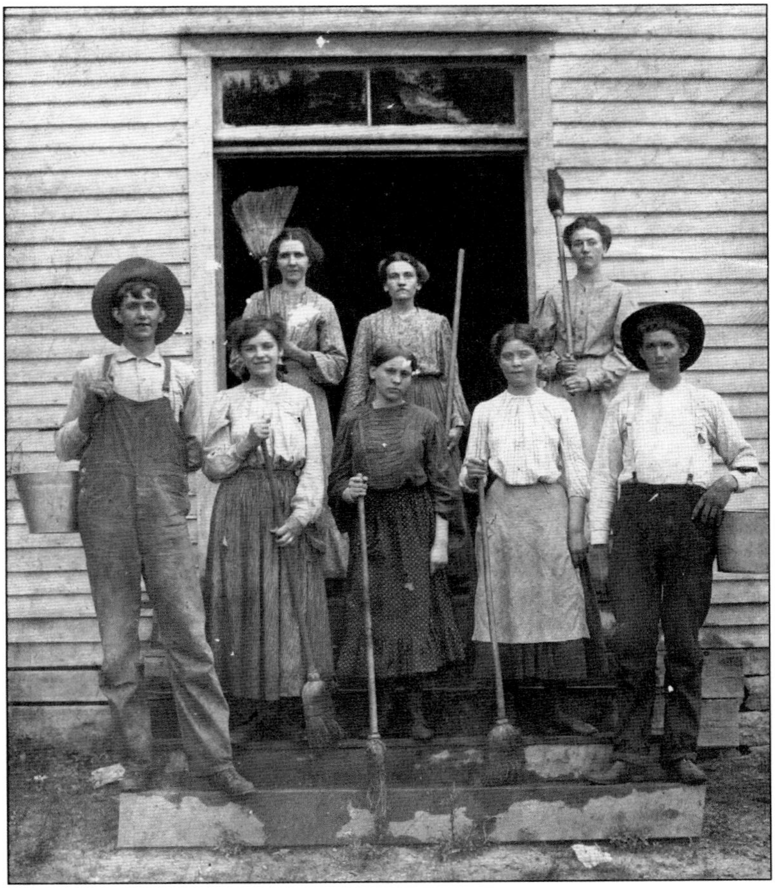

Birdie Worthington (second row, center) and friends pose on the steps of the Lupton School in this photograph from about 1900. Birdie married Henry Duncan. Lupton School was located south of the Clinch River on the side of Emory Valley Road near its intersection with what is Fairbanks Road today. (Courtesy of Judy Duncan Blakely.)

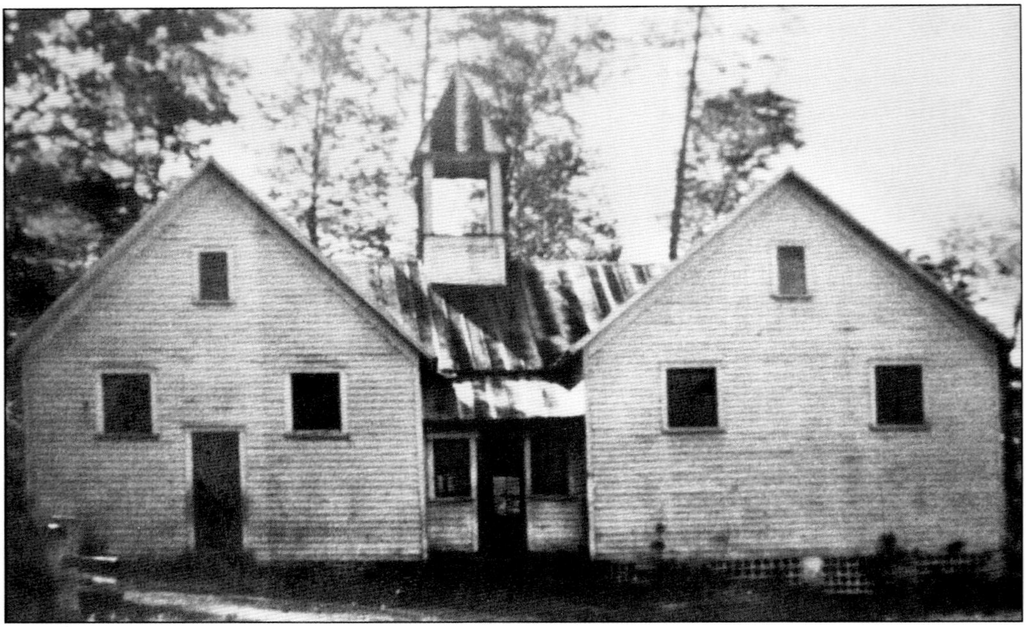

Knapp School was built in 1913 at Knapp Station in what is now the Medford community. It was a two-room frame building located on what is now US Highway 25W near Cane Creek. It was replaced by the Medford School, a brick structure built on the opposite side of the highway. (Courtesy of Mary Harris.)

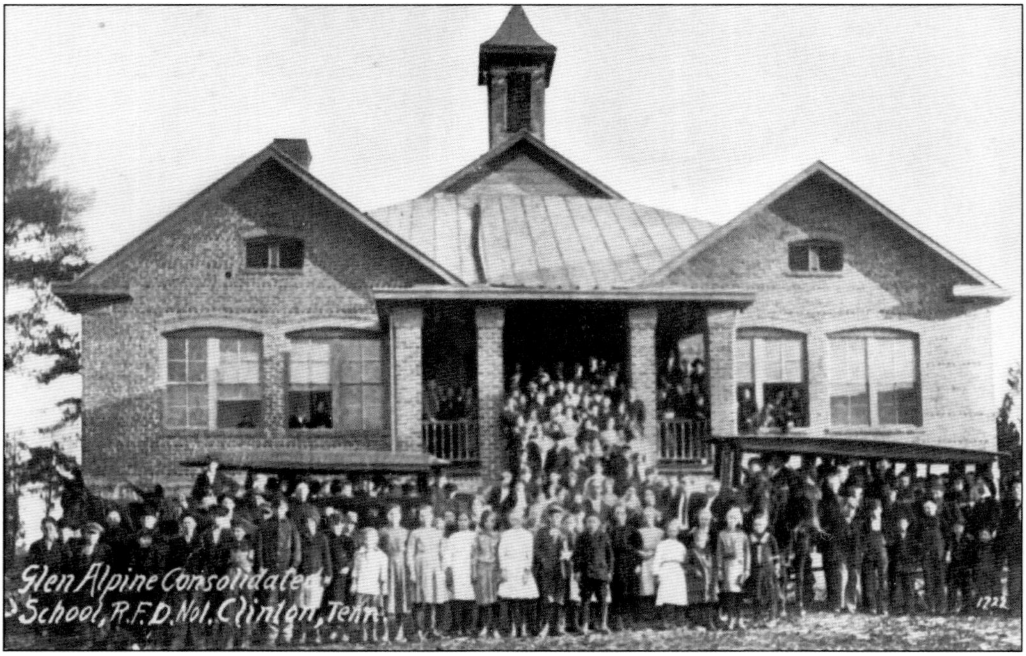

The Glen Alpine Consolidated School was built in 1913 of frame construction but was later bricked. Prior to consolidation, it had been known as Bethel School. Glen Alpine was the first consolidated school built in the county. Pictured behind the children are the horse- and mule-drawn covered school wagons used before school buses. (Courtesy of Mary Harris.)

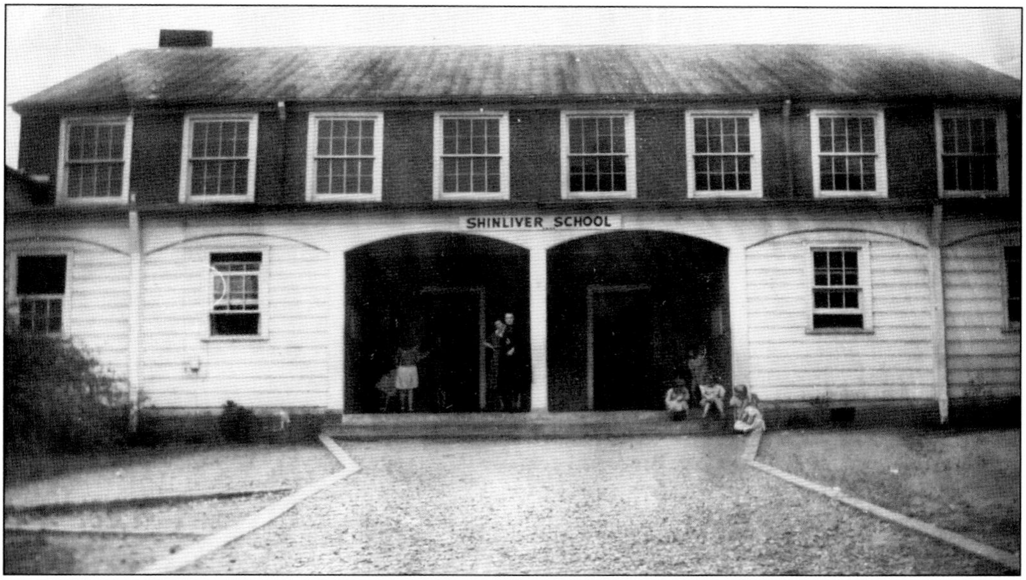

The old Shinliver School is located on Sulphur Springs Road between its intersections with Carroll Hollow and Laurel Roads. This photograph was taken in the 1950s. After the school closed, it became private property, and part of it is now used as a private home. (Courtesy of Carolyn Spessard Braden.)

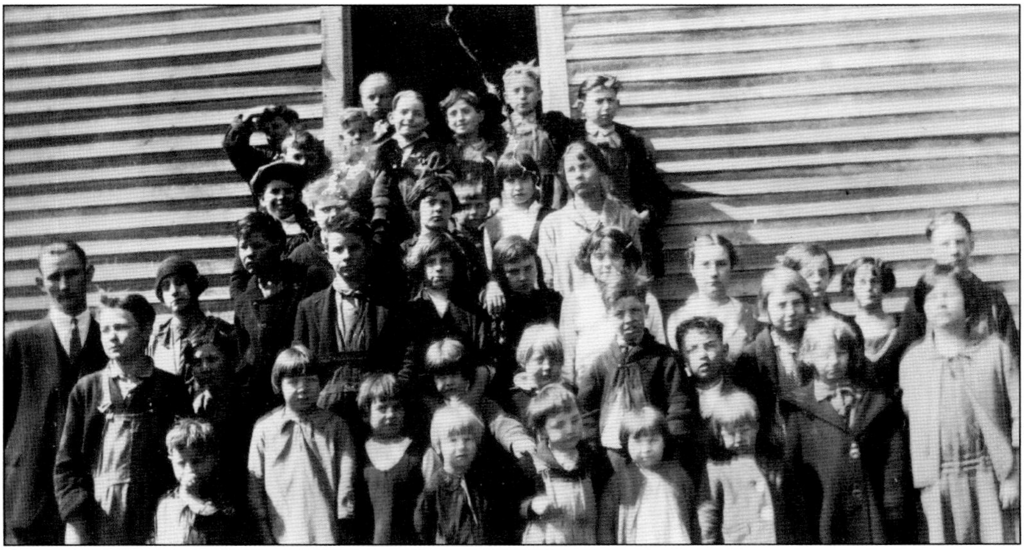

Students at the Fowler School in Dutch Valley posed with their teacher in 1924. The Fowler School was built in 1905 by Samuel Patton Fowler, who also taught at the school. It burned in the late 1920s, and the students transferred to Coal Creek School. George Fowler, son of Samuel Patton and Mary Lee Robertson Fowler, is identified fourth from right in the top row. (Courtesy of Susan Fowler.)

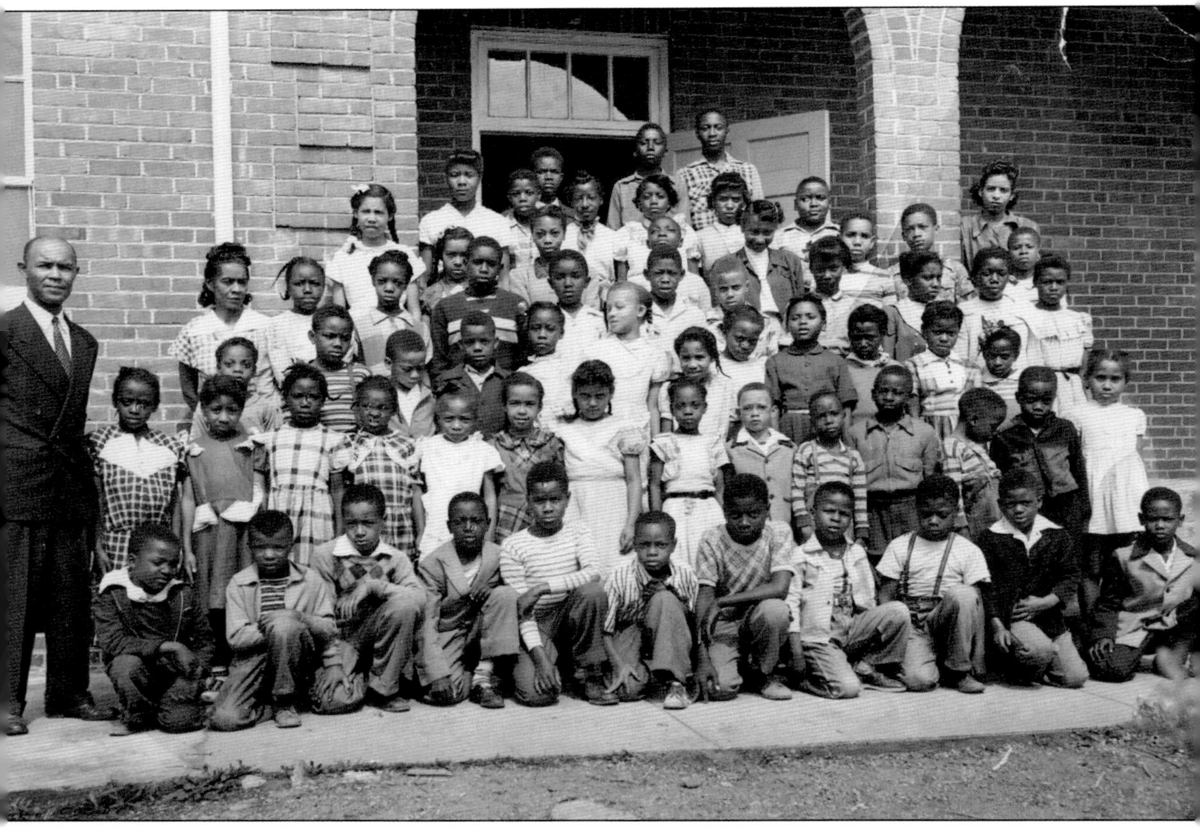

Students of the Green McAdoo Elementary School in 1953 pose with their principal (second row, far left) and teacher Theresa Blair (fourth row, far left). The Green McAdoo School was the only school in Clinton for African American children prior to integration. Students wanting to attend school after the eighth grade were bused to Vine Middle School and Austin East High School in Knoxville. Busing cost per student, and it was this inconvenience and extra expense that prompted the parents of Alvah McSwain to file suit to allow African American students to attend Clinton High School. That lawsuit led to the integration of the high school in 1956 by the Clinton Twelve and to the bombing of the school in 1958. The Green McAdoo School is now the Green McAdoo Cultural Center and a memorial to the Clinton Twelve and the integration of Clinton High School. (Courtesy of Jo Ann Allen Boyce.)

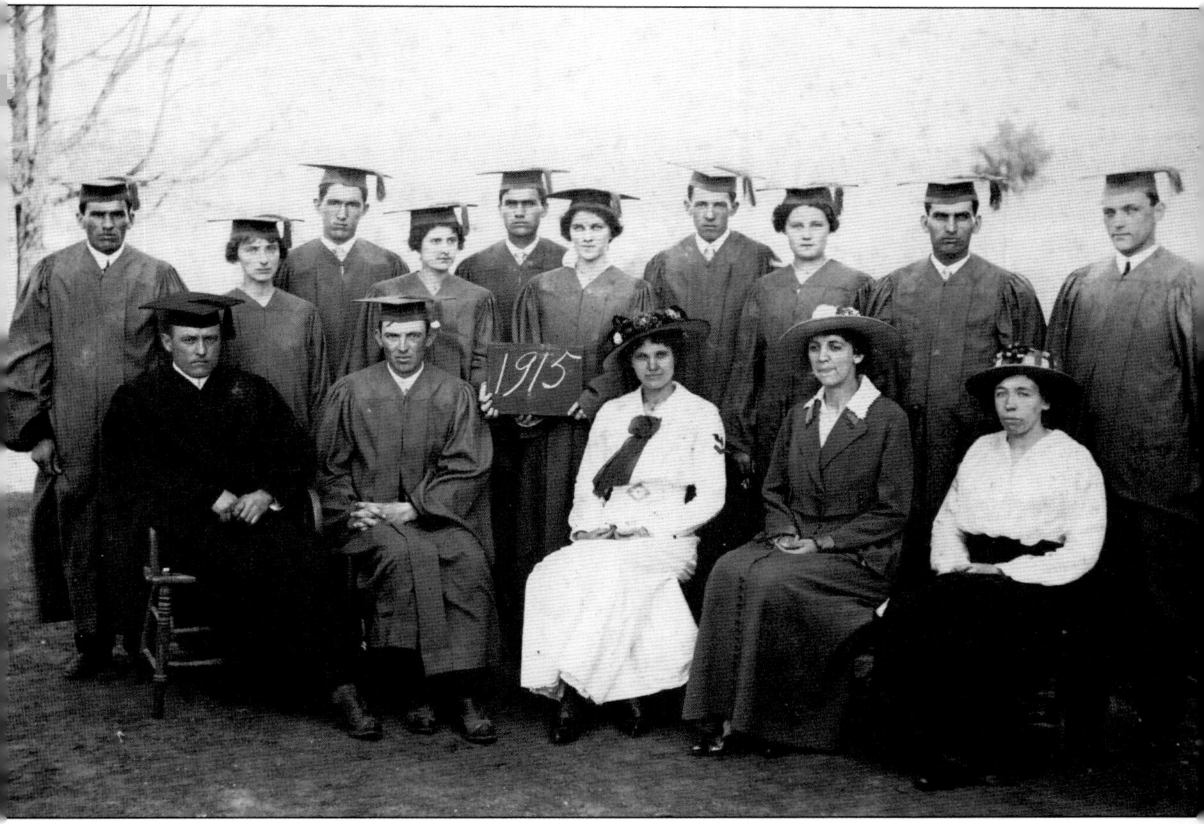

Posed on the grounds of the Andersonville Institute are members of the graduating class of 1915 with the principal and teachers. From left to right are (first row) Principal W. H. Miller, G.W. Ridenour, music teacher Esta Carden, Ella Miller (G.W. Ridenour's date), and elementary teacher Bonnie Wallace; (second row) Carrie Ridenour, Blanche Shumate, Della Carden, and Sallie Weir; (third row) Lee Sharp, Mirma Miller Wallace, Gip Sharp, Frank W. Wallace, Moss Sharp, and Moss Humphrey. Andersonville Institute grew out of two prior schools in the area. Big Valley Academy was in existence a few years prior to 1873 and taught primarily grammar school subjects. A need for high school courses for some of its students was recognized by some members of the Baptist churches in the area. Around 1897, the Baptist Associational High School was formed, and out of it grew Andersonville Institute. (Courtesy of Kay Crowell Davis.)

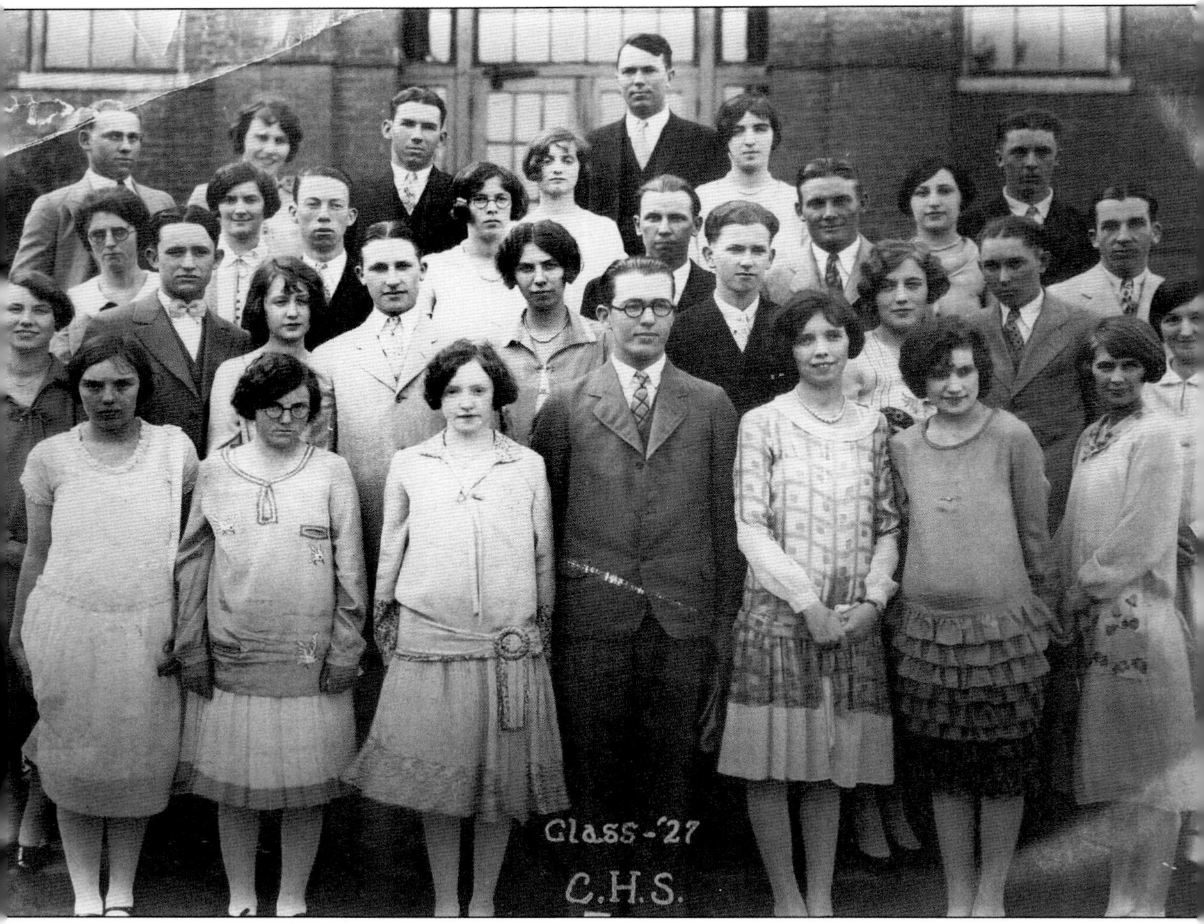

After the State of Tennessee passed a law requiring each county to operate at least one high school, the City of Clinton consolidated Clinton High School and contracted with Anderson County to operate it. A new school for high school students was built, and the old Clinton Public School was used as a grammar school. The new high school was dedicated in late 1927. Posed in front of the old public school are the members of Clinton High School class of 1927, the last graduates of the old school. Official school records listing the graduates are not in existence. A.H. Graybeal was the principal. A native of Mountain City and a graduate of Peabody College, he served two years as principal at Clinton High School (1925–1926 and 1926–1927) before moving to Maryland, where he taught until his retirement. (Courtesy of Robert Copeland.)

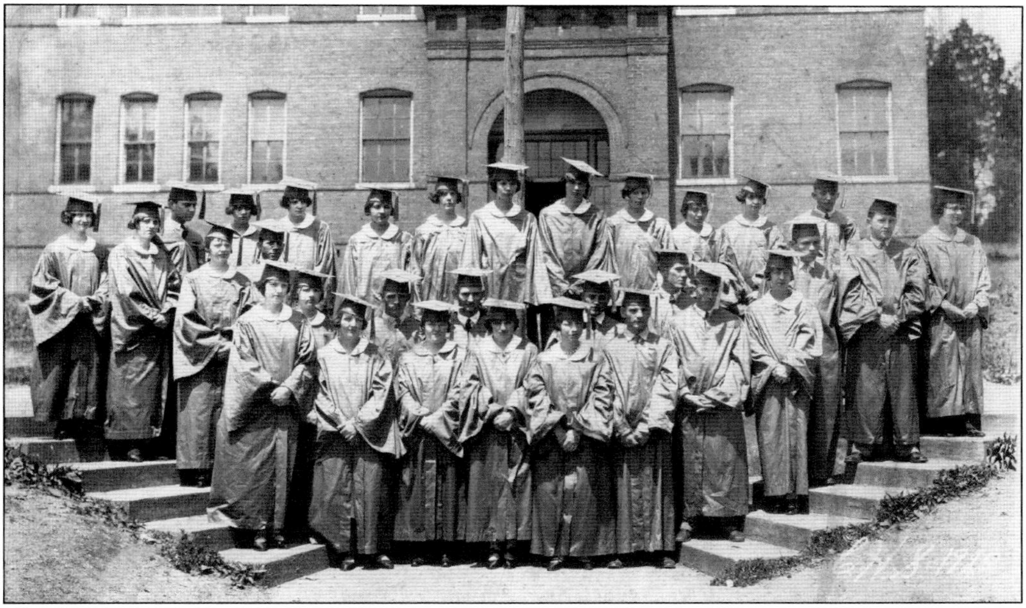

Members of Clinton High School's graduating class of 1925 pose on the steps of the Clinton Public School. Clinton High School did not begin publishing annuals until 1928, and official rosters of faculty and students for the high school do not exist. However, it is known that C.C. Justus was principal from the fall of 1923 through the spring of 1925. (Courtesy of Maxine Meade Holbrook.)

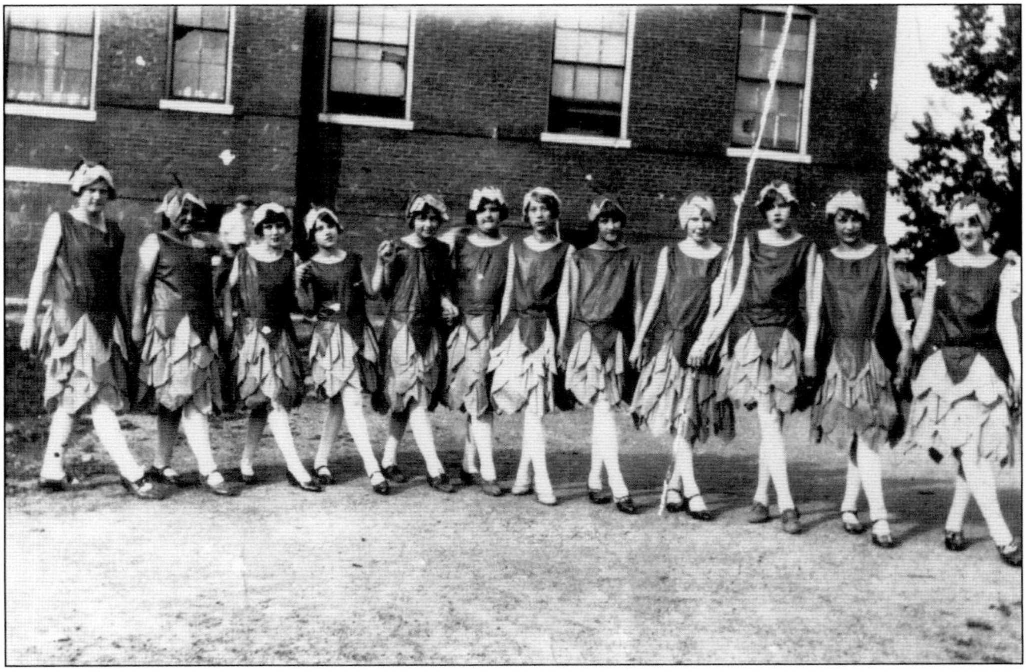

The seventh-grade dance class of the Clinton Grammar School posed in their costumes for this photograph in 1926. The members of this class have not been identified. The Clinton Grammar School was the brick public school built in 1903 as the successor to Union Academy. (Courtesy of Mary Harris.)

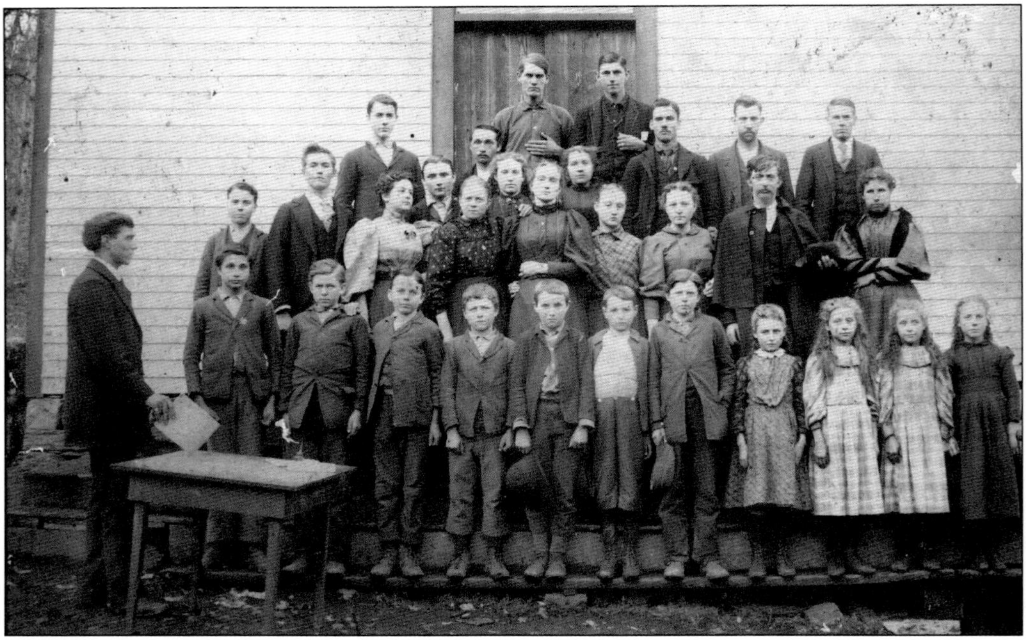

Students of the Robertsville School and their teacher posed for this photograph about 1890. Will King is identified second from right in the second row, wearing the caped coat and holding his hat. Will King, who was born in 1873 and died in 1957, was the father of Ethel King Holbrook. (Courtesy of Maxine Meade Holbrook.)

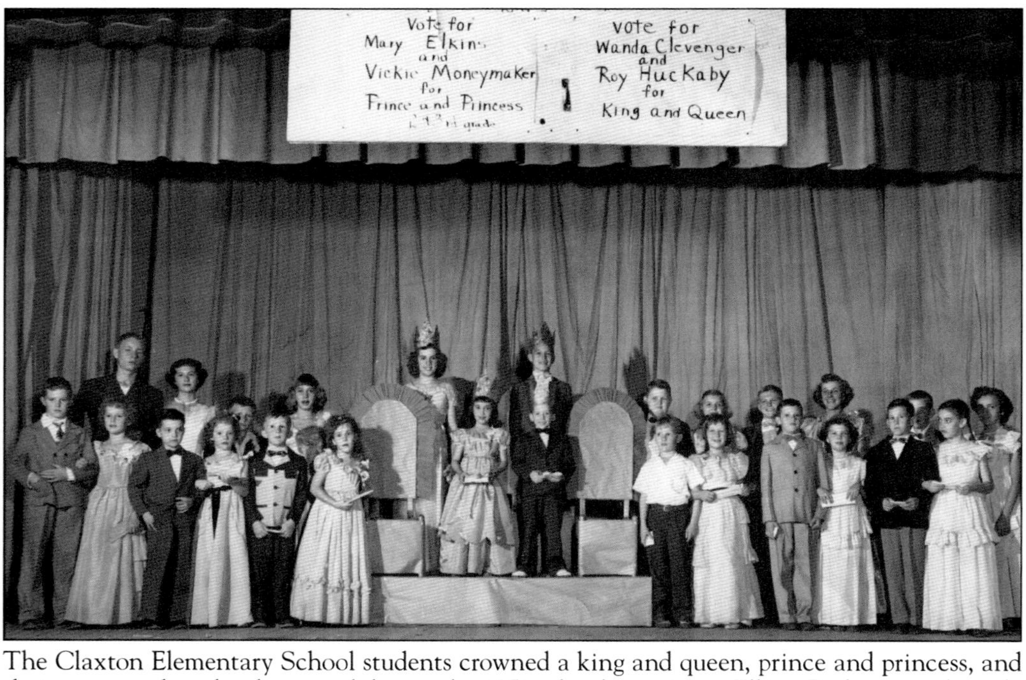

The Claxton Elementary School students crowned a king and queen, prince and princess, and their court at the school carnival during the 1951 school year. Mary Elkins Barker won the title of princess. Mary attended Claxton Elementary School from the first through the eighth grades before starting Clinton High School. (Courtesy of Mary Elkins Barker.)

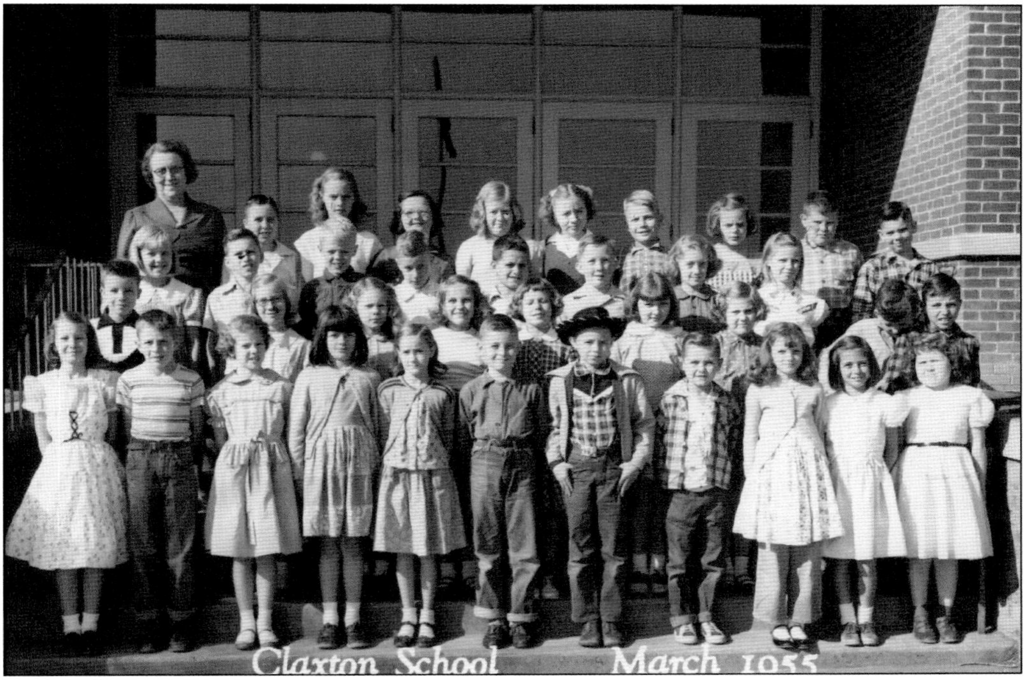

Some of the students of Miss Moneymaker's 1954–1955 fourth-grade class at Claxton Elementary School are identified as Pat Fox, Lynn Carroll, Mary Elkins, Martha Gray, Doris Linkus, Doris Cooper, Harry Lamb, Mike Ledbetter, Shirley Cooper, Margaret McBee, Doug Petroski, and Mary R. Herrell. (Courtesy of Mary Elkins Barker.)

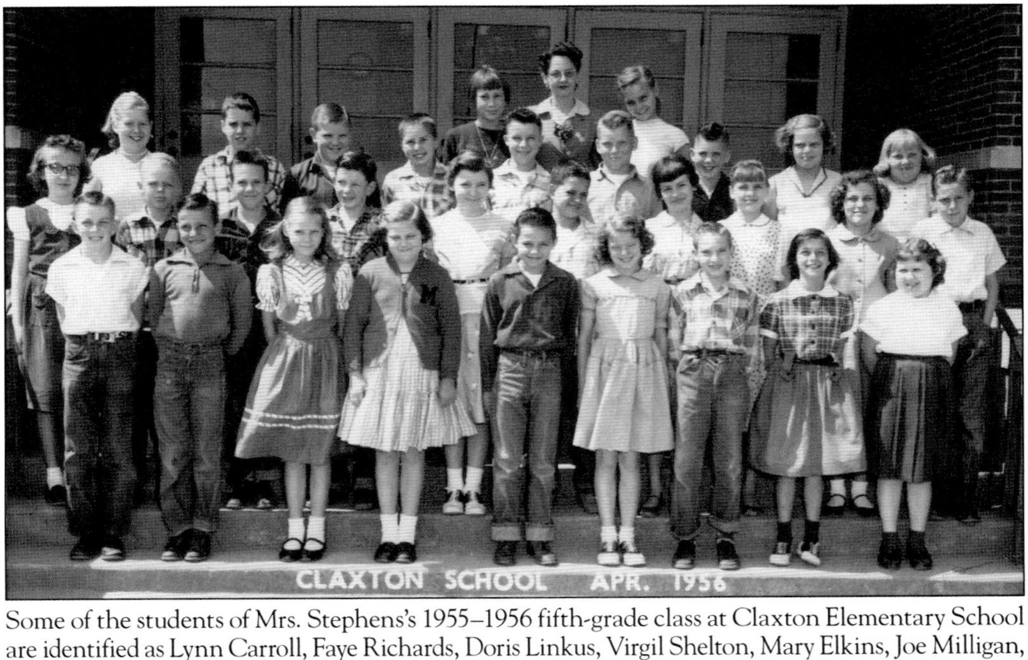

Some of the students of Mrs. Stephens's 1955–1956 fifth-grade class at Claxton Elementary School are identified as Lynn Carroll, Faye Richards, Doris Linkus, Virgil Shelton, Mary Elkins, Joe Milligan, Billy Foust, Eugene Armstrong, Martha Gray, Judy Webb, Richard Minor, Mike Ledbetter, Billy Jo Gibson, Mary R. Herrell, and Doris Cooper. (Courtesy of Mary Elkins Barker.)

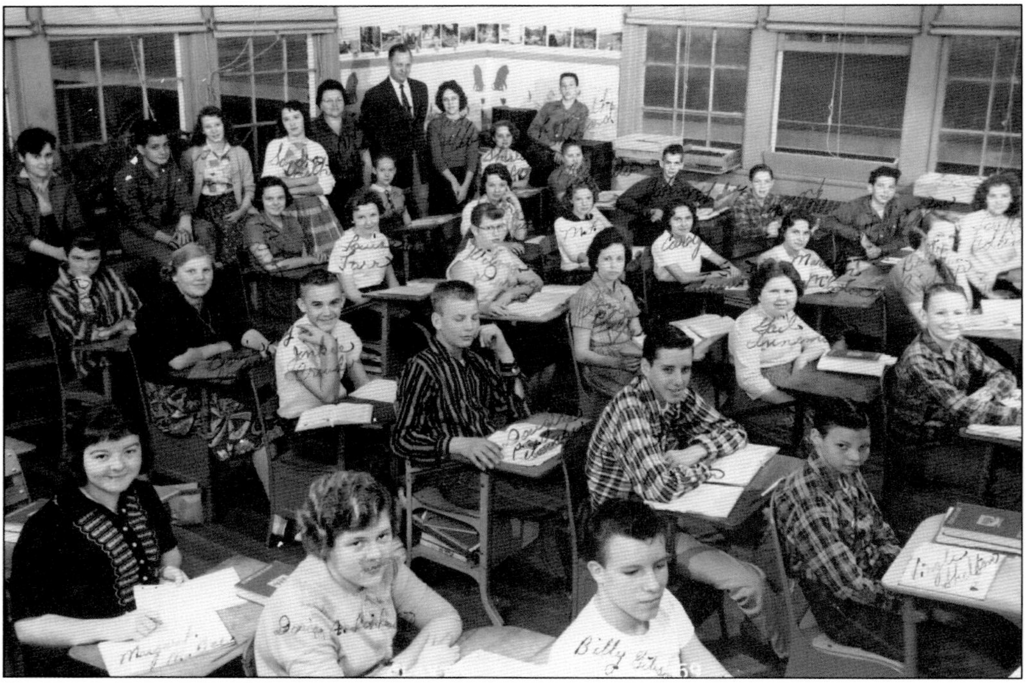

Some students in Opal Fritts's 1958–1959 eighth grade class at Claxton Elementary School are identified as Margaret McBee, Doris Linkus, Billy Gibson, Janice Phelps, Louise Farr, Judy Webb, Virgil Shelton, Douglas Petroski, Sandra Smith, Kenneth Shepard, Betty Bishop, Marilyn Minton, Mike Ledbetter, and Loretta Collins. (Courtesy of Mary Elkins Barker.)

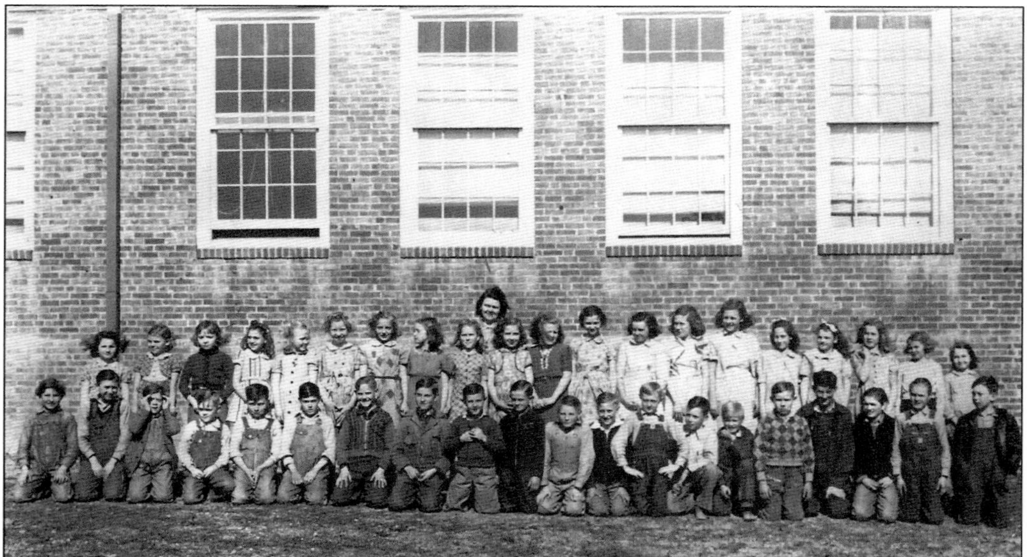

The students of Scarboro School's class of 1941–1942 posed outside the school. This was the next-to-last class to attend Scarboro School. In 1943, when the federal government seized the land to build the city of Oak Ridge as part of the Manhattan Project, Scarboro was a thriving community with a school, churches, businesses, and homes. (Courtesy of Robert Copeland.)

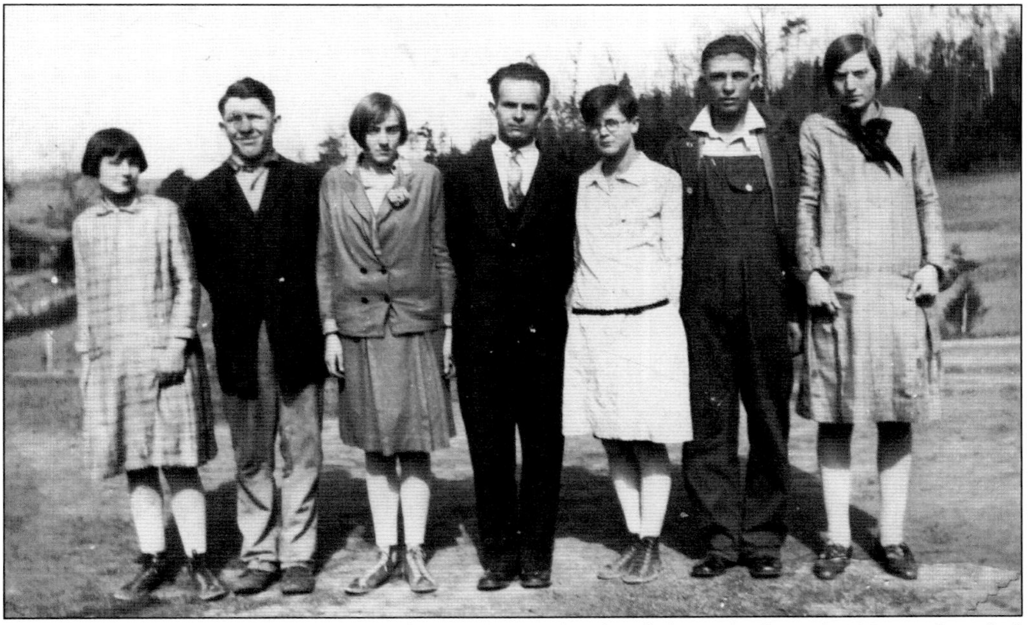

In the photograph above, members of the Scarboro School eighth-grade class of 1928 are identified as, from left to right, Anna Ruth Jones Offutt, Herman Grills, May Dean Holloway, teacher and principal Glen I. Tuttle, Clarice Jones, Tolbert Taylor, and Ruth Moore. In the photograph below are members of the Andersonville School class of 1940. Students are, from left to right, (first row) Lucy Hudson, June Irwin, Barbara Longmire, Grace Womack, Lucille Hudson, Ruth Womack, Dorothy Reynolds, and Hope Owens; (second row) Lonas Hunley, Bud Rutherford, J.C. Walker, Eugene Miller, Claude Atkins, Marshall Duncan, and Bill Johnson. Andersonville now has only an elementary school; middle school students attend Norris Middle School, and high school students now attend Anderson County High School. (Above, courtesy of Mary Elkins Barker; below, courtesy of Mary Harris.)

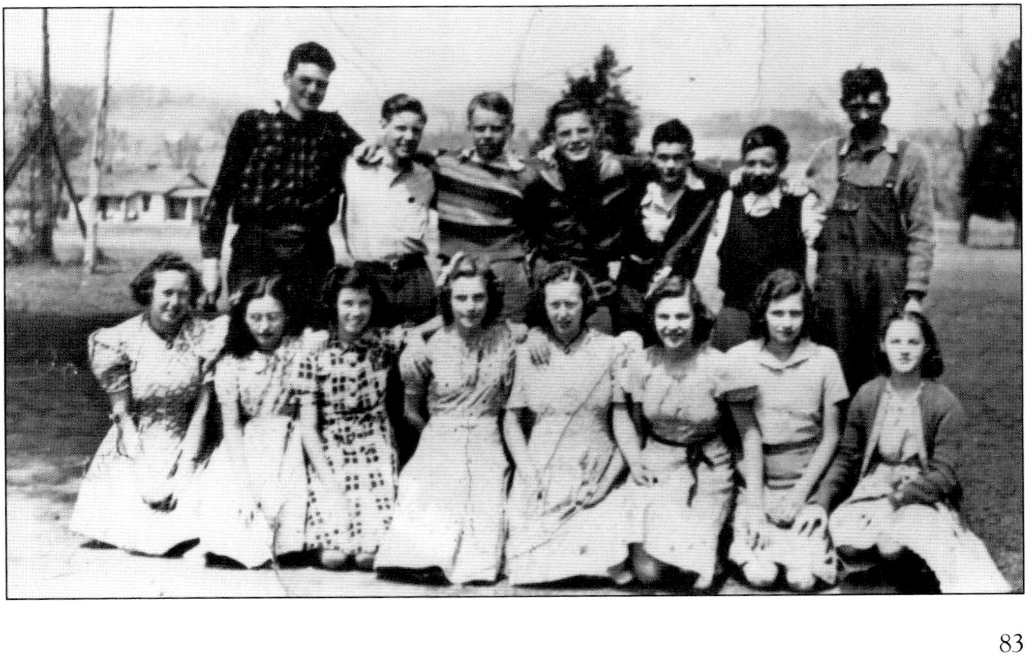

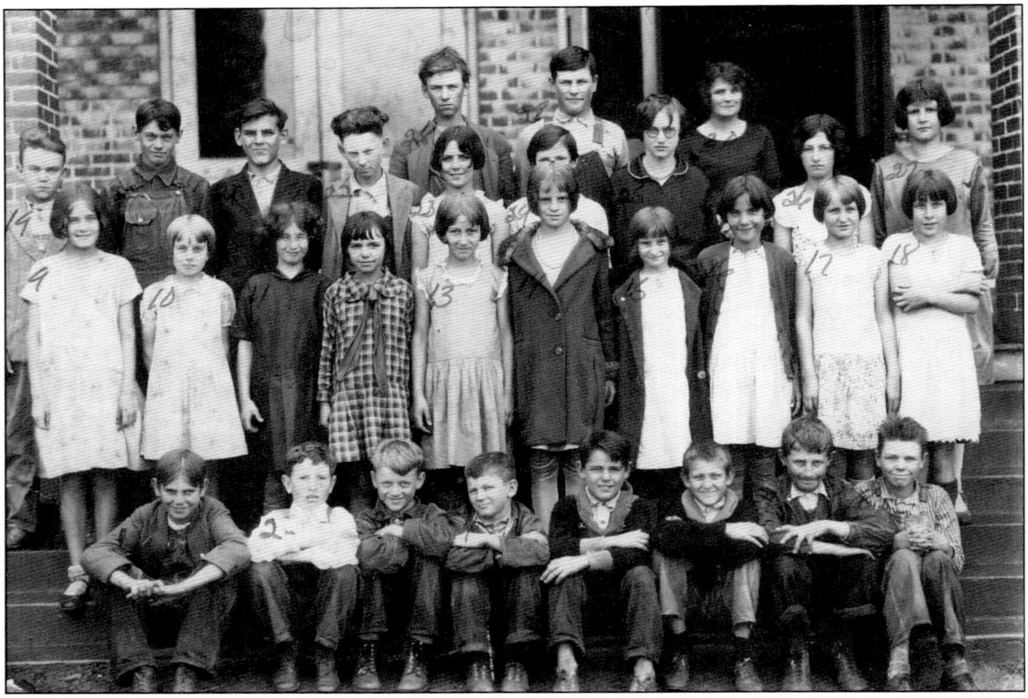

The 1928 class of the Robertsville School is pictured in the photograph above. They included, from left to right, (first row) Harris Hill, James Copeland, Herbert Walters, Glen Scarbrough, Melton Jones, Clarence Clough, unidentified, and Frank Scarbrough; (second row) Ruth Wise, Dorothy Peck, Ruth Turnbill, Imogene ?, Pauline Brummett, Gladys Duncan, Sarah Pyatt, Zetta Shetterly, Pauline Foster, and Ruth Brock; (third row) George Anderson, Johnny Miller, John Burgess, Bill Steele, Cloda Nelson, Lois Elkins, Dolly Sharp, Frances Brummett, and Lorene Braden; (fourth row) Burrell Austin stands in the middle, and the students on either side of him are unidentified. The Robertsville High School gym is pictured below. It stood where the Robertsville Middle School stands today in Oak Ridge. (Both, courtesy of Mary Elkins Barker.)

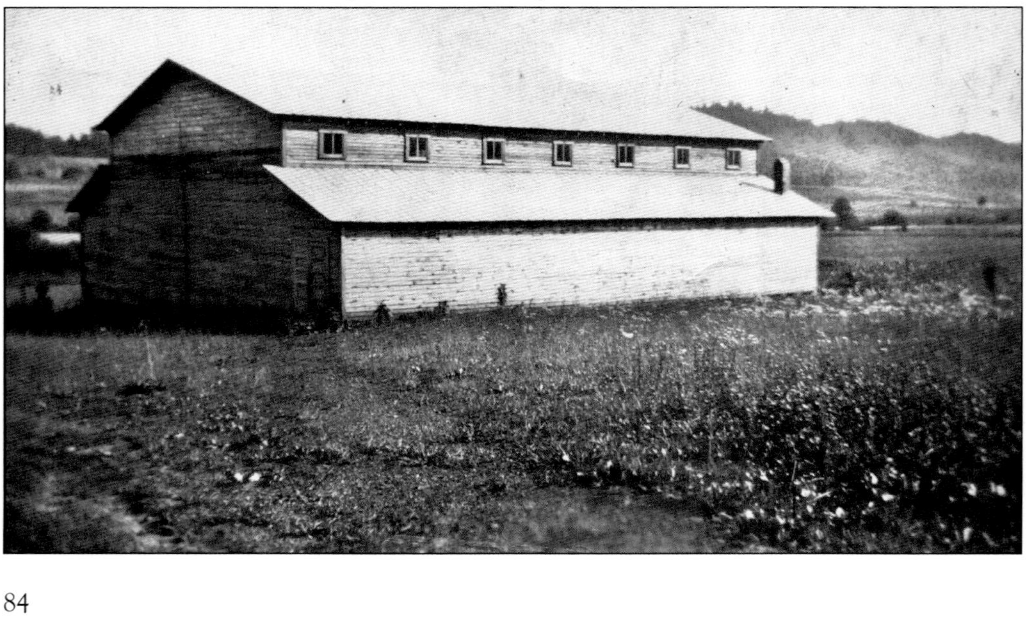

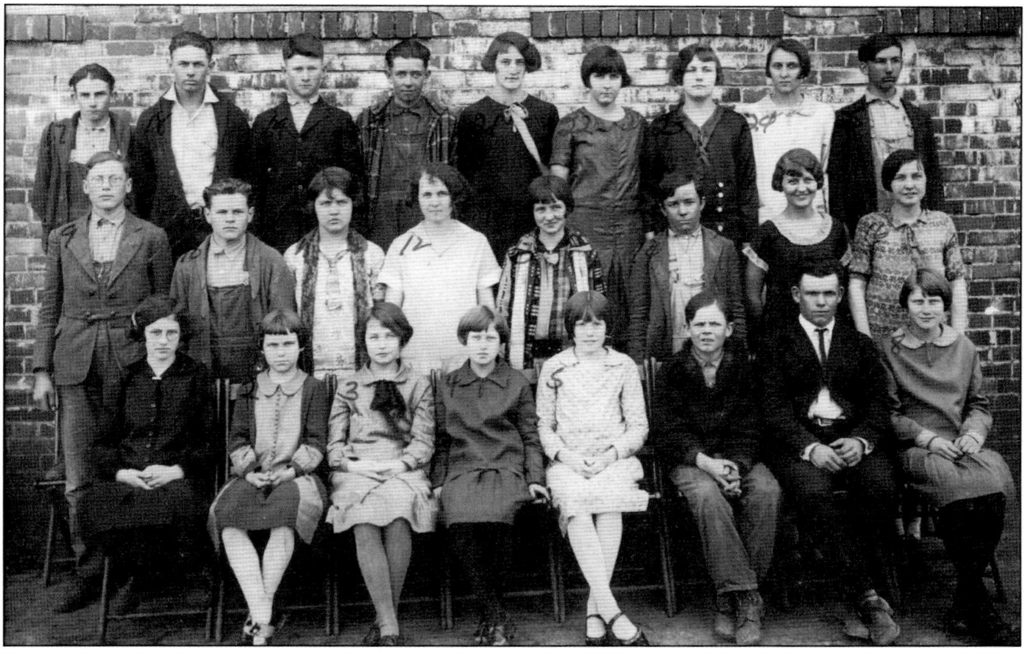

Pictured in the above photograph are members of the 1926 class of the Robertsville School. The Robertsville community was located where the city of Oak Ridge is today. In 1943, when the federal government took the land for the Manhattan Project, the Robertsville community was a thriving one. Families were forced to move, many with less than a week's notice. The school, churches, businesses, and homes were all torn down, and the "secret city" of Oak Ridge was built. Those students identified are, from left to right, (first row) Lola Hatcher, Neva Meek, Lorene Smith, Mildred Peck, Volena Foster, Sam Tadlock, Dennis Elkins, and Irene Peck; (third row) Ralph Pyatt, Herman Miller, Raymond Garrison, Willie Keith, teacher Pearl Huff, Beulah Burgess, Annie Austin, Bonnie French, and Charles Elkins. Students in the second row are not identified. The new consolidated Clinton High School was completed in 1927. It appears in the photograph below as it did in 1928. (Above, courtesy of Mary Elkins Barker; below, courtesy of Jerry Patterson.)

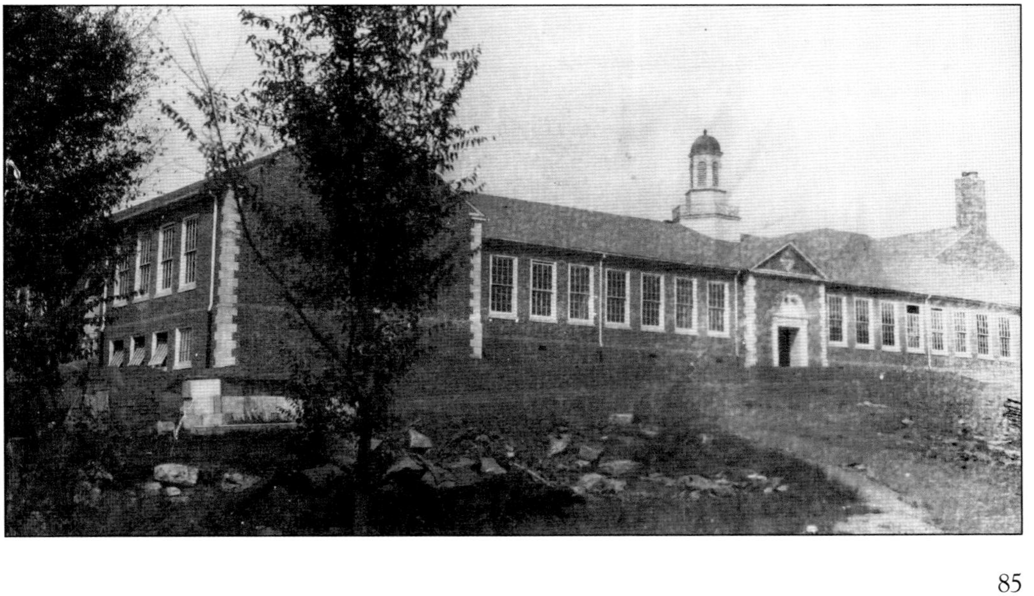

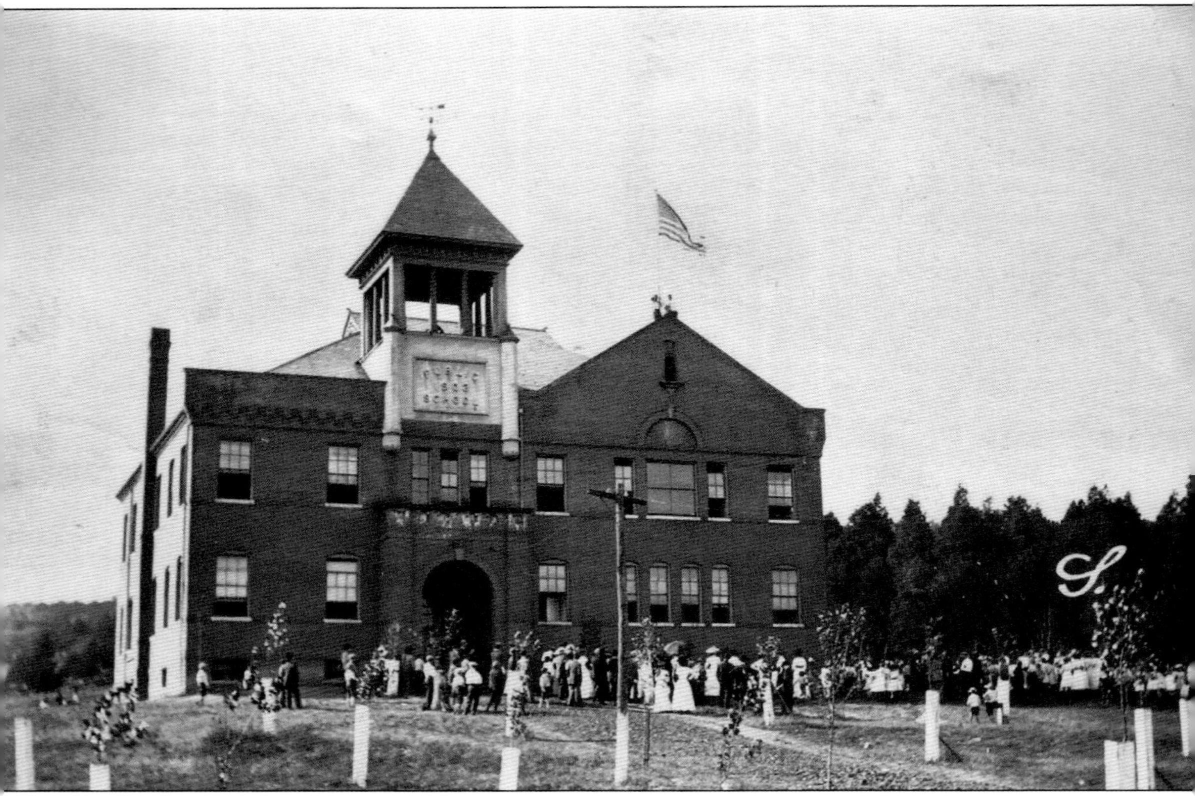

The General Assembly of the State of Tennessee established Union Academy in 1806 by naming its first board of trustees. These trustees were Arthur Crozier, Benjamin Parker, Jesse Roysden, Hugh Barton, and Samuel Frost. However, it was several years before the frame building known as Union Academy was built in Clinton. It was destroyed during the Civil War. No records of teachers or students exist, but a few principals are known from other sources. Charles Y. Oliver, son of Revolutionary War veteran and early Anderson County settler Douglas A. Oliver Sr., taught and was principal at the academy. The Reverend Nelson Roberts, his brother the Reverend Samuel Roberts, and William G. McAdoo are known to have been principals of the academy. A new frame Union Academy building was erected after the war, and it stood until replaced by the brick Clinton Public School in 1903. In this photograph, the grounds of the public school were the scene of a Labor Day celebration and the raising of the flag. (Courtesy of the Pellissippi Genealogical and Historical Society.)

Four

Sports

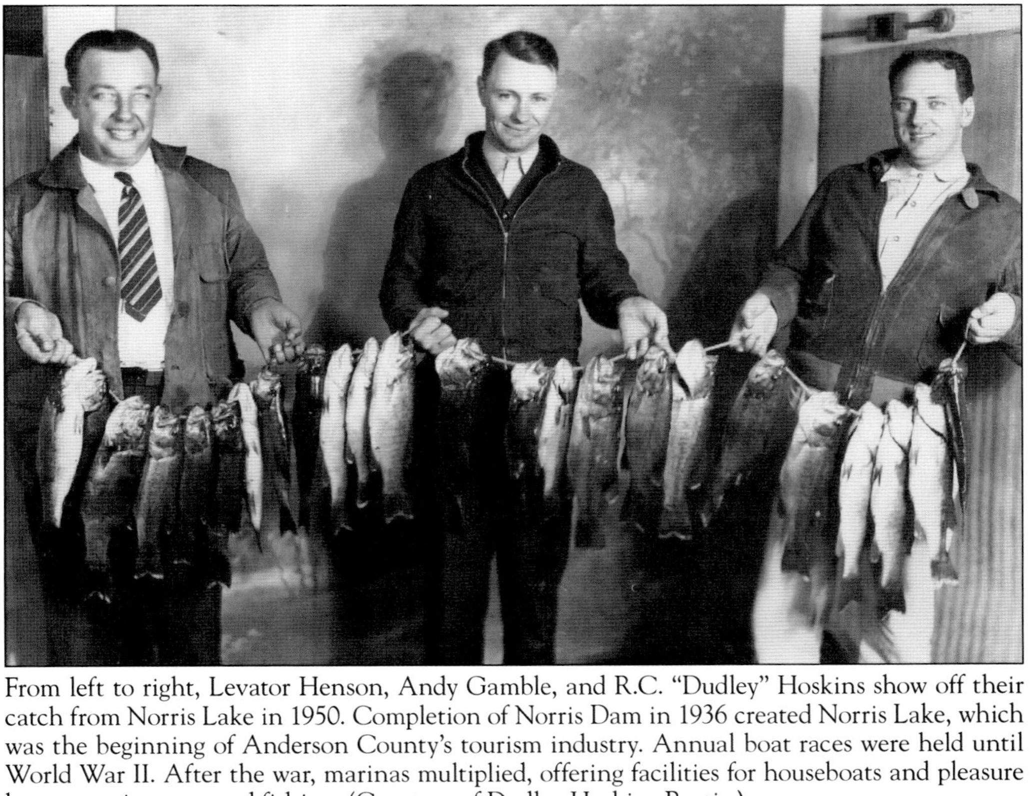

From left to right, Levator Henson, Andy Gamble, and R.C. "Dudley" Hoskins show off their catch from Norris Lake in 1950. Completion of Norris Dam in 1936 created Norris Lake, which was the beginning of Anderson County's tourism industry. Annual boat races were held until World War II. After the war, marinas multiplied, offering facilities for houseboats and pleasure boats, scenic tours, and fishing. (Courtesy of Dudley Hoskins Bostic.)

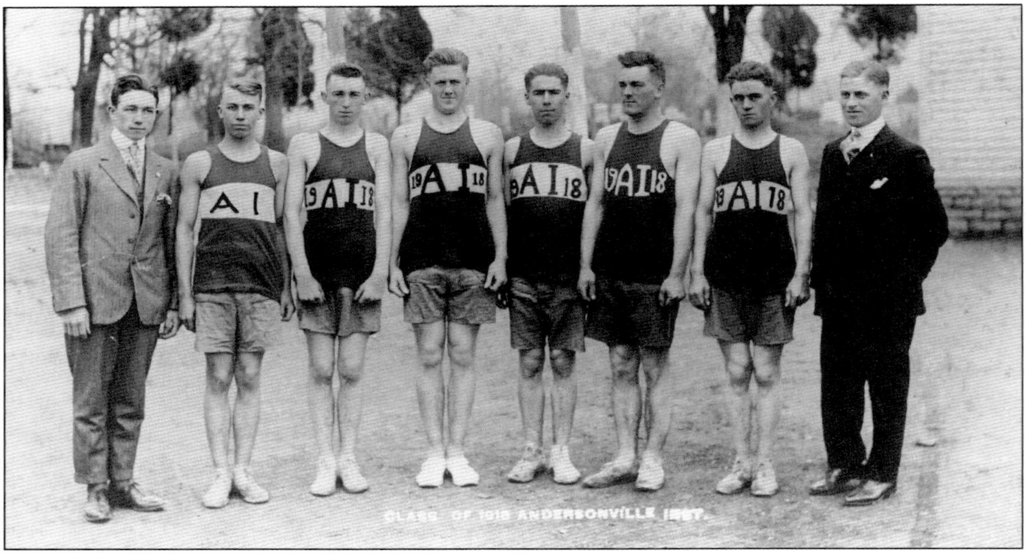

Andersonville Institute's class of 1917–1918 boys' basketball team is pictured above. The institute was dissolved in 1917 and ceased operation at the end of that school year. The 1916–1917 boys' basketball team is pictured below. Members of the teams are not identified. A church-sponsored private school, Andersonville Institute was established in 1898 as a feeder school for Mossy Creek (now Carson-Newman) College. Many graduates of the institute later became teachers in Clinton and Anderson County. The members of the original board of trustees for the institute were Frank P. Rutherford, J.K.P. Wallace, J.M. Carden, J.W. Williams, J. Allen Carden, W.H. Rutherford, S.W. Tindell, J.W. Key, J.M. Andrews, G.W. Wendling, J.C. Johnson, J.S. Lindsay, J.A. Anderson, Rice Snodderly, Parlie Hill, B.L. Stanfill, J.F. Miller, and G.P. McCloud. (Both, courtesy of Emily Wallace Haverkamp.)

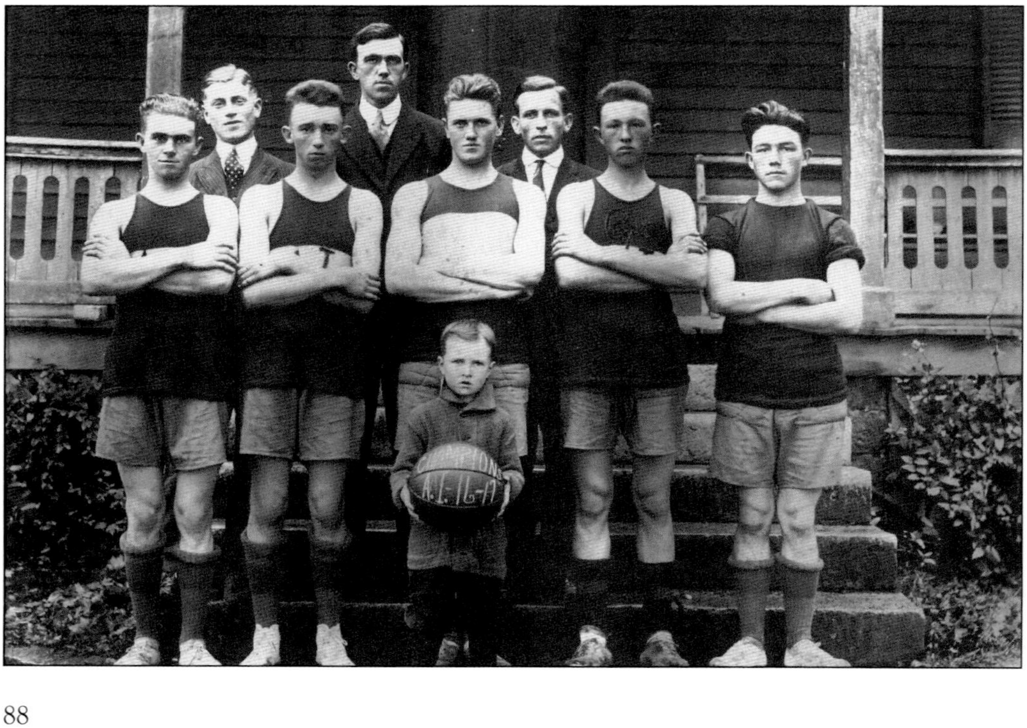

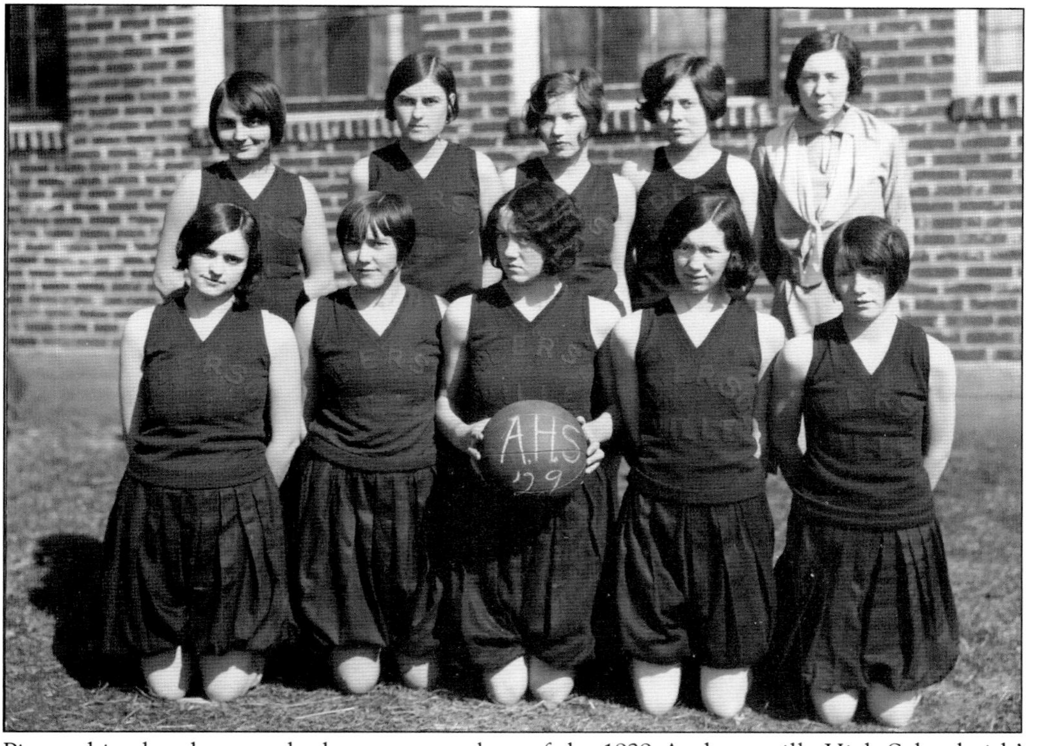

Pictured in the photograph above are members of the 1929 Andersonville High School girls' basketball team. Team members were not identified, but among them are Hazel and Helen Wallace, twin daughters of J. Shields and Nora Murray Wallace. Hazel Wallace married Homer Lambert, and Helen Wallace married Claude E. Sharp. On the right in the back row is coach Anna Ruth Wallace, who married Hansford DeFoe. Pictured in the photograph below are the members of an Andersonville Institute baseball team from about 1915. The members are not identified, but some of the young men appear in other photographs of the class of 1915. (Both, courtesy of Kay Crowell Davis.)

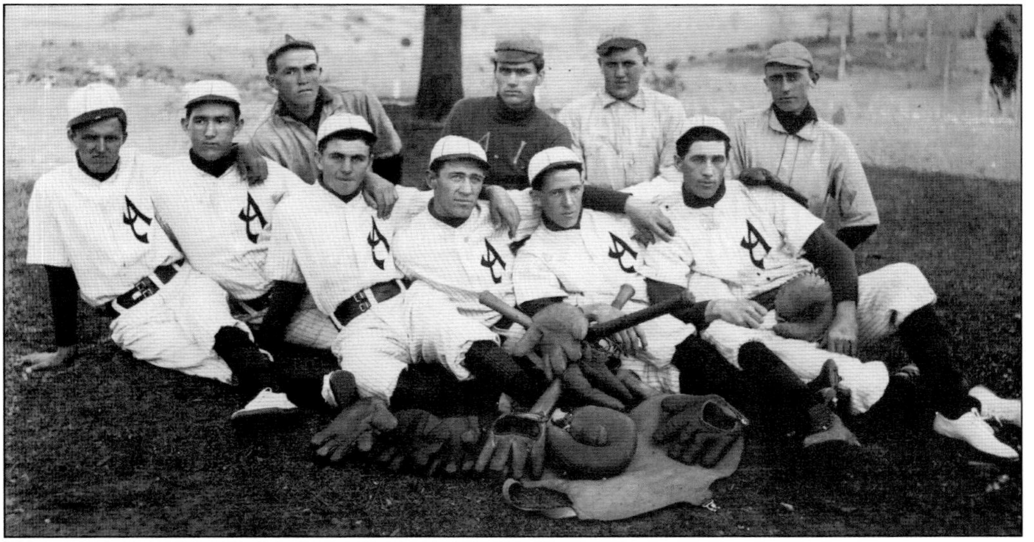

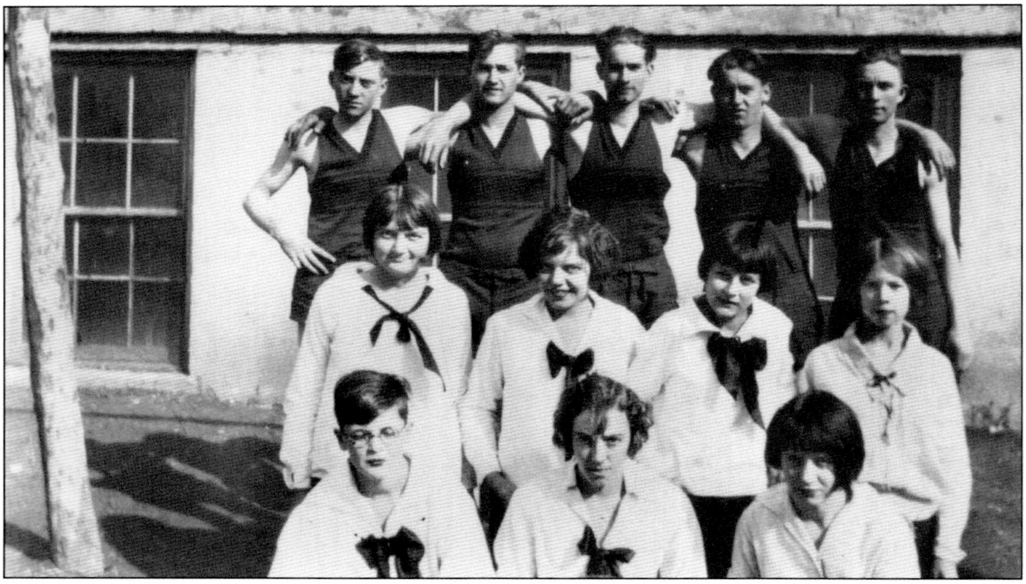

Members of the boys' and girls' basketball teams of Scarboro School are pictured in the above photograph. The photograph is undated, but the boys' team members are, from left to right, (third row) Boyd Moore, Evert Grills, Mack Hackworth, Leroy Gray, and Tolbert Taylor. The girls' team members in front are identified as Gladys Raby, Edna Holloway, Anna Ruth Jones Offutt, Jamie Hackworth, Clarice Jones, and Nadine Holloway. In the photograph below are members of Clinton High School's first football team in 1923. Known as the Clinton Tornadoes, they were James Williams, Ernest Harmon, Carvel Hoskins, Wallace Carden, Revon Johnson, Vaughn Disney, James Scruggs, Frank Underwood, Rufus Goins, Cecil Miller, S. Sharp, Fletcher "Granny" Sweet, Harry Miller, Amos Offutt, Roscoe Hendrickson, Edward Daniels, Earl Goins, Roy Underwood, and L.B. Harvell. They posted a 6-2-0 season. (Both, courtesy of Mary Harris.)

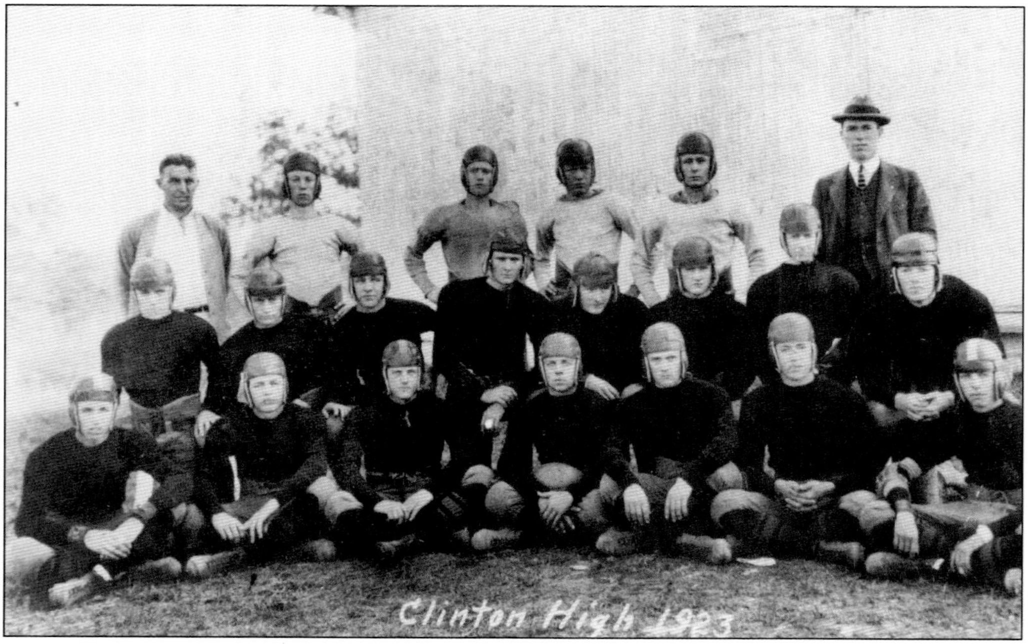

Five

Homes

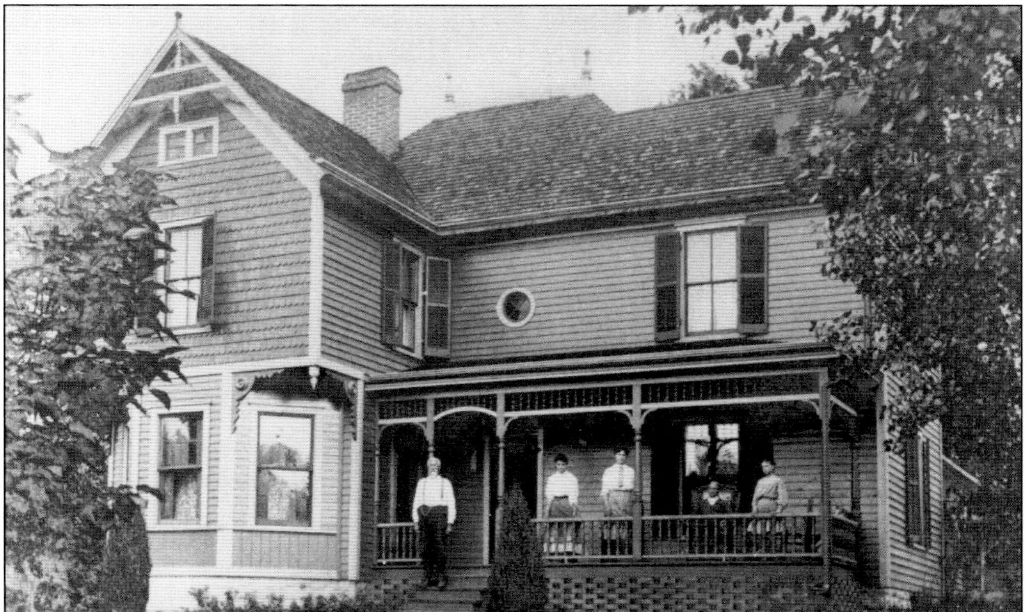

This is the Rutherford home in Andersonville about 1910. A classic example of the Victorian-era style of the second half of the 19th century, the house has clapboard siding, spindle banisters, a bay window, and elaborate gingerbread trim. The house was typical of many homes in the area. (Courtesy of Mary Harris.)

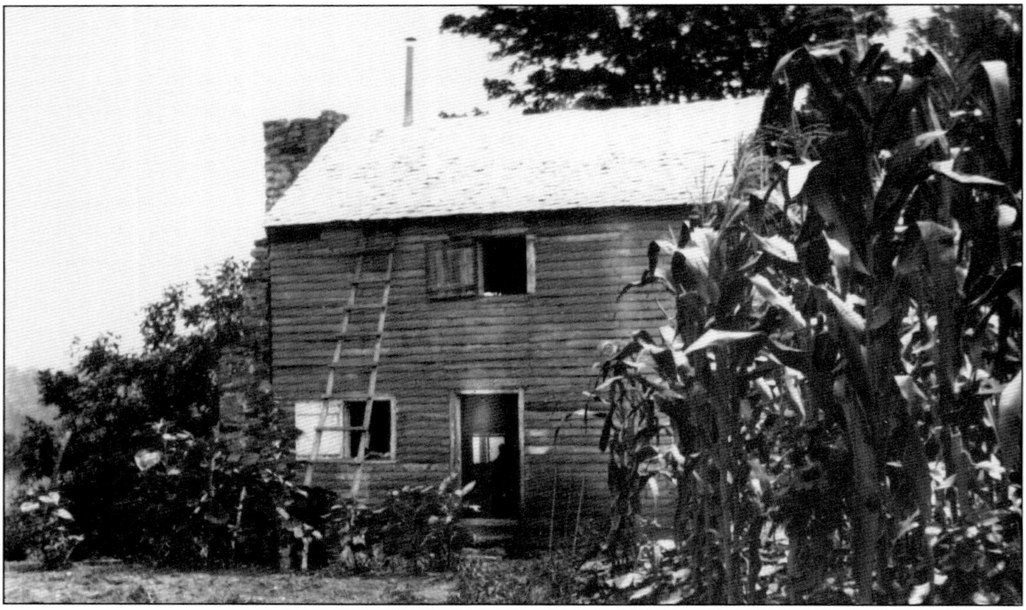

In the photograph above, the David Hall cabin appears as it was discovered by Elizabeth Thomason Bumgardner, granddaughter of Walter Scott and Nannie Thomason, in 1996. The cabin was built about 1799 by David Hall, a Revolutionary War veteran who settled in southern Anderson County. The cabin is located on Old Edgemoor Road and was originally a dogtrot with a single story attached to the side of this two-story section, which was run by David Hall as a tavern and inn. He and his family lived in the single-story section. In the photograph below, the cabin appears as it did when in use as the tavern and inn. The Bumgardners have restored the cabin to its original state by adding a single-story period cabin and reconstructing the dogtrot to join the two cabins. (Both, courtesy of Elizabeth Thomason Bumgardner.)

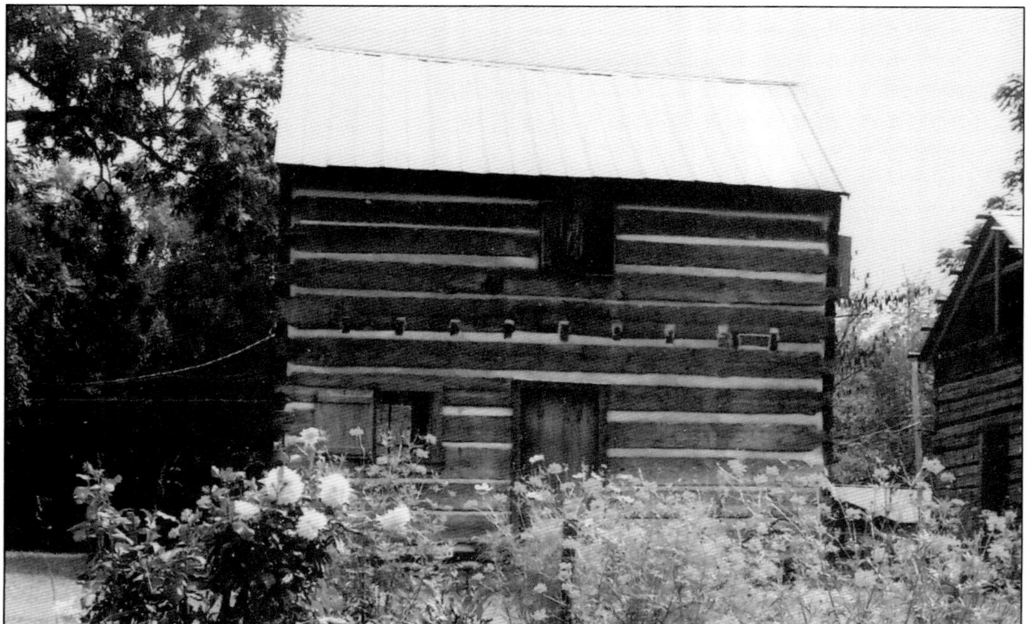

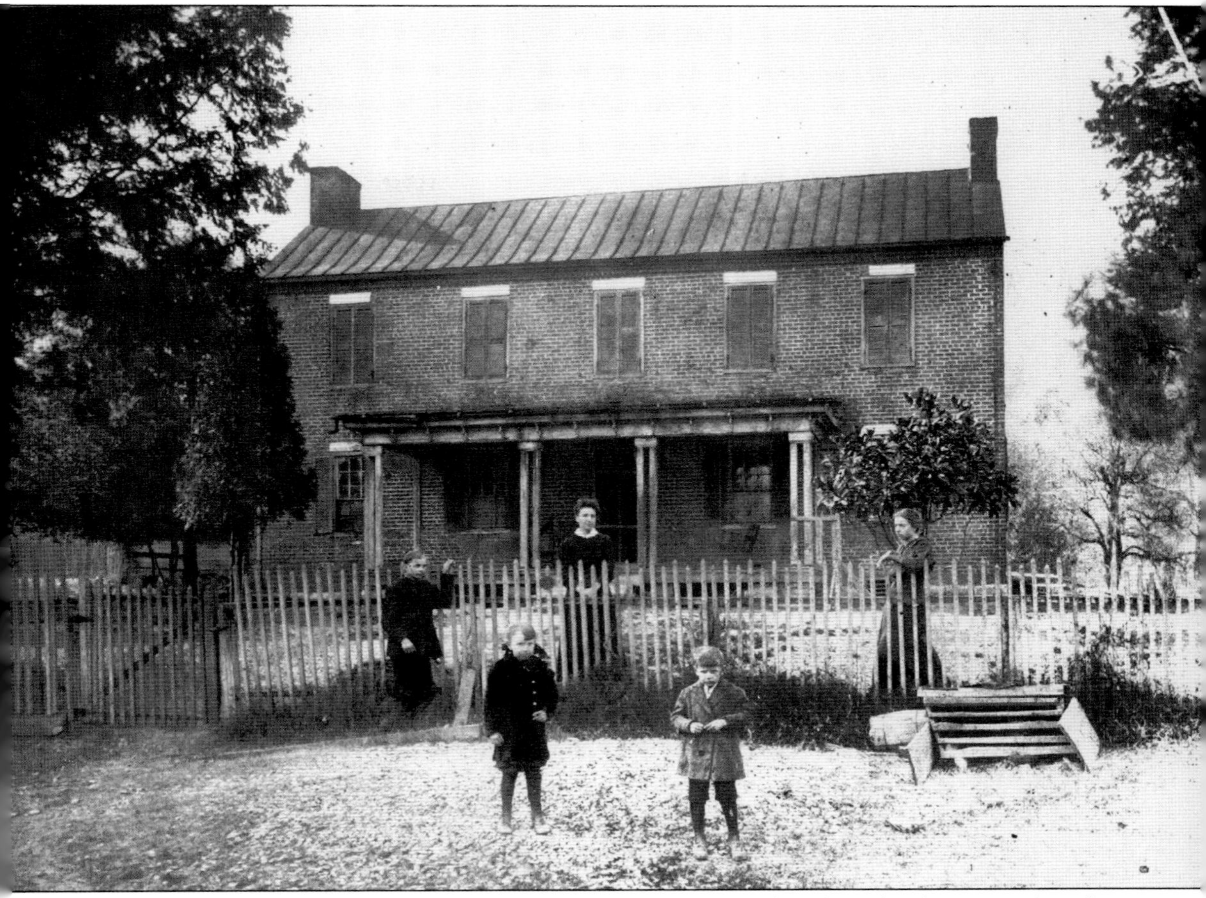

The Hemlocks was built in the 1830s by E.C. and Niecy Ross Edwards on land given to them by her father, James Ross. Ross was an early settler and large landowner and slave owner who had settled in Anderson County about the time it was created. The house is located in Dutch Valley at the intersection of Old Dutch Valley Road and Old Lake City Highway. Bricks for the house's construction were handmade on the property. The house has two rooms on the second floor, originally built as slave quarters. Samuel Patton Fowler bought the house and surrounding acreage about 1900, when he joined his brother James A. Fowler in the East Tennessee Nursery Co. He soon moved his growing family out from Knoxville to live on the farm. Pictured are Mary Lee Robertson Fowler (left, behind the fence), wife of Samuel Patton Fowler, and four of their children. The Hemlocks is listed in the National Register of Historic Places. (Courtesy of Susan Fowler.)

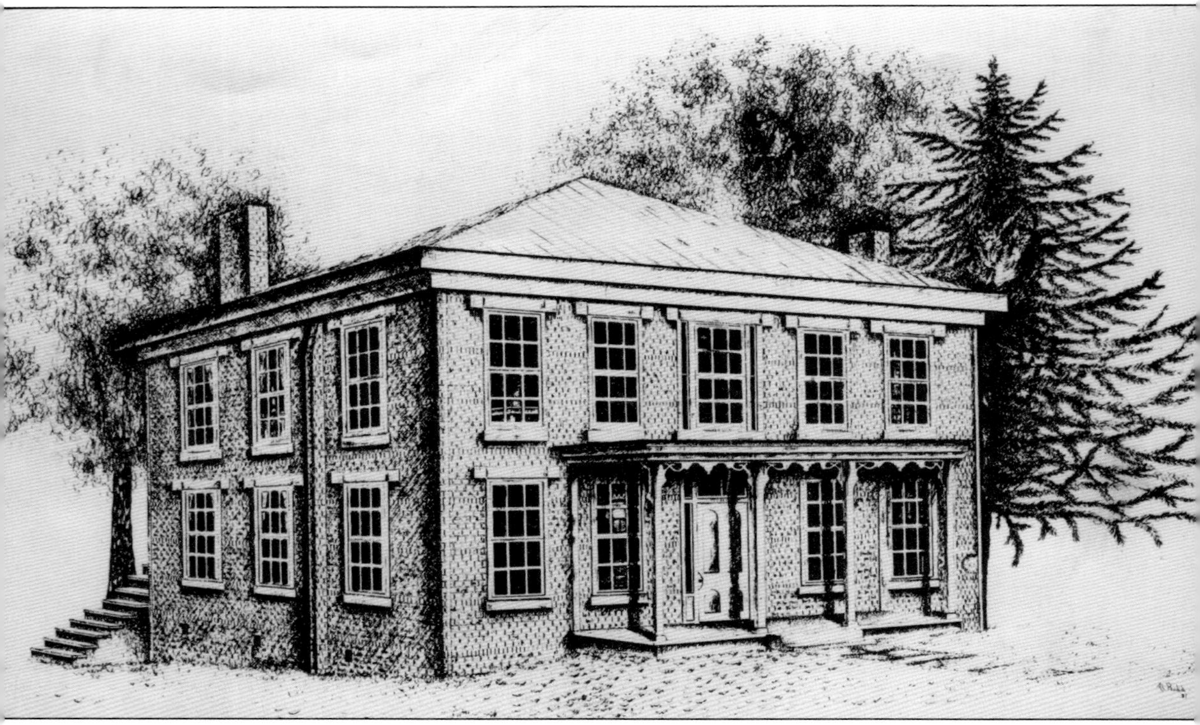

The Jarnigan-Peak House, also known as the "Jarnigan Brick," is believed to have been built in 1839 by John Jarnigan as part of a 200-acre plantation that straddled both sides of the Clinch River. Located at the corner of North Main and East Broad Streets, directly across from the Anderson County Courthouse, it was built facing the old Jacksboro Pike (now North Main Street), which was the stagecoach road and main north-south route from Knoxville to Jacksboro. The bricks for the construction were made on the property, and the building was constructed using slave labor. The last owner of the house was C.W. Peak, who bought it in 1924. He died in 1962, and the house was torn down in 1984 because of the high cost of renovation. Bank of America now occupies the lot. (Drawing by Al Rodd; courtesy of Mary Harris.)

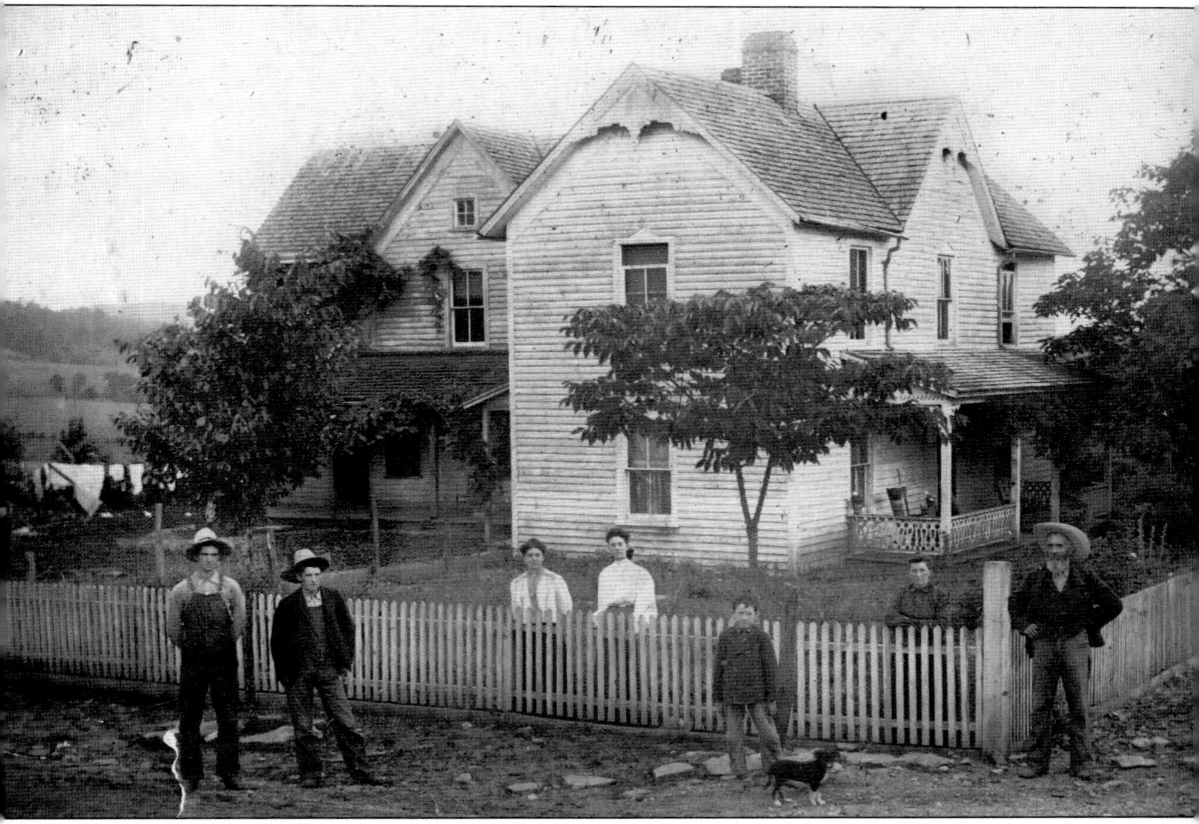

The James Knox Polk Wallace house was located on the family's farm near Andersonville. In this photograph dated 1900 are, from left to right, J. Shields Wallace, Lawrence Wallace, Mayme Wallace, Laura Wallace, Frank Wallace, Laura Caledonia "Callie" McKinney Wallace (Mrs. J.K.P.), and James Knox Polk Wallace, who was known as J.K.P. The house formerly stood about a quarter of a mile southwest of Andersonville on a slight hill. The current property owners have replaced the house with a brick rancher. In 1927, J.K.P. Wallace tracked down the school bell that had been discarded when the Andersonville Institute was torn down. The bell is now installed at Andersonville Elementary School. (Courtesy of Kay Crowell Davis.)

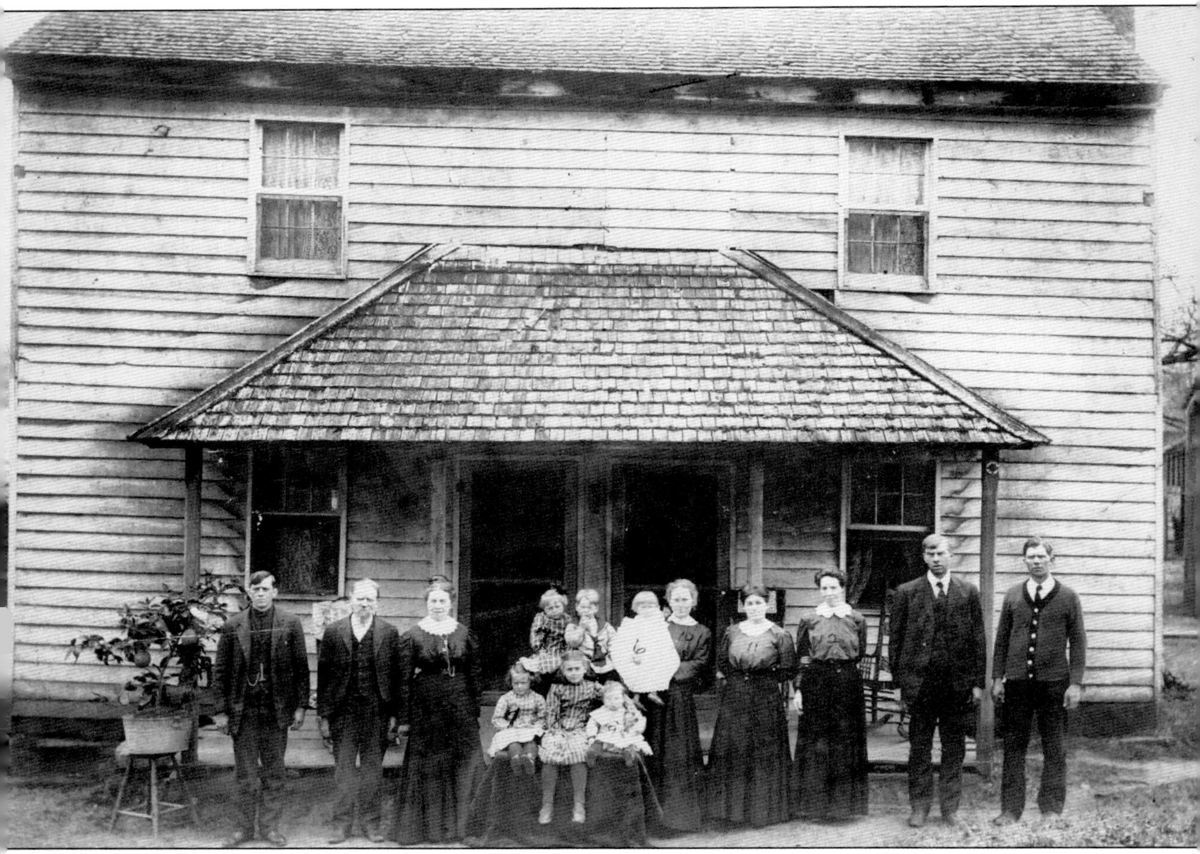

Pictured in this photograph from about 1900 are members of the Chiles family, standing outside the home of Col. John Coffee Chiles, a veteran of the Civil War and an early landowner along the Clinch River in the Edgemoor area of Anderson County. From left to right are (sitting) Callie Moore Webb, Myrtle Moore Edington, and Robert Moore; (standing) James Moore, Robert H. Moore, Annie Chiles Moore (wife of Robert H.), Gladys Moore Grelb, Carl Moore, Mary Harrington Moore holding Mable Moore Webb, Rose Foster Moore, Ida Florence Gammon Moore (wife of A.C.), Algernon Carl "A.C." Moore, and John R. Moore. (Courtesy of Mary Elkins Barker.)

Six

Business and Industry

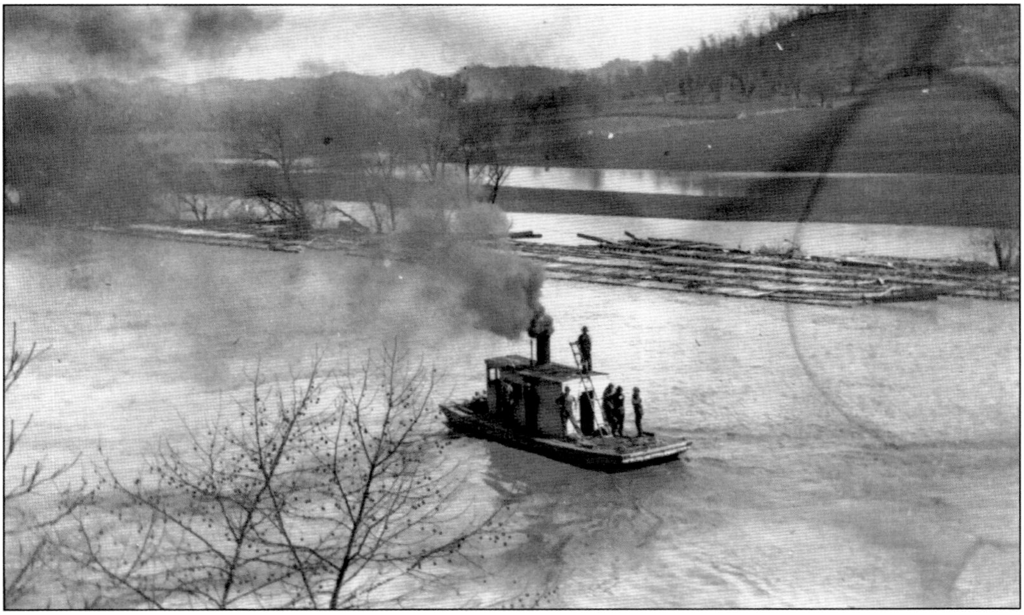

Prior to the construction of Norris Dam, rafting logs down the Clinch River was common practice, and furniture manufacturers lined Clinton's riverbank. Hunting mussels for Clinch River pearls was also a thriving business, and Clinton was a major pearl trading center. Completion of the dam caused lower water temperatures, which killed the pearl trade, and lower water levels, which prevented the rafting of logs. (Courtesy of Mary Harris.)

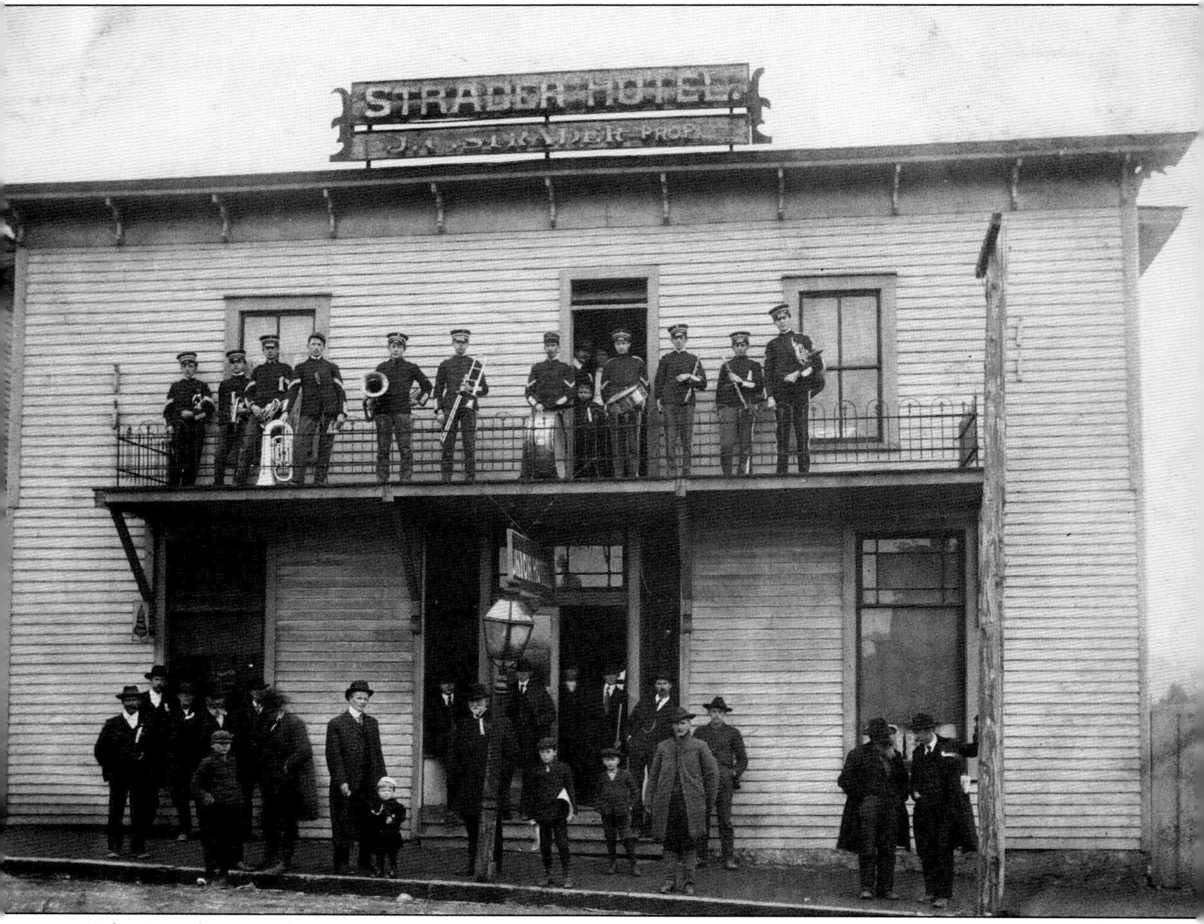

The Strader Hotel stood on Depot (now Market) Street, where the Market Street park gazebo is today. Convenient to the Southern Railway depot, it catered to pearl buyers who frequented Clinton during the pearling season from May through October. From 1880 until the completion of Norris Dam in 1936, the Clinch River pearl trade flourished in Clinton. Mussels that lived in the Clinch were prized for the size and luster of their pearls, and Clinton was one of the few places were the pearls could be harvested in quantity. Pearling was a seasonal occupation used to supplement summer incomes. As the county seat, Clinton was the marketplace for pearl dealers who made monthly visits to buy. Market day was a busy day, and it was common to see bands playing at the hotels. This picture was taken in 1905 by Bernie H. Shinliver, owner of Clinton Art Studio. Sam Hendrickson, a local pearl trader, is pictured standing to the left of the lamp, holding the small child by the hand. (Courtesy of the *Clinton Courier-News.*)

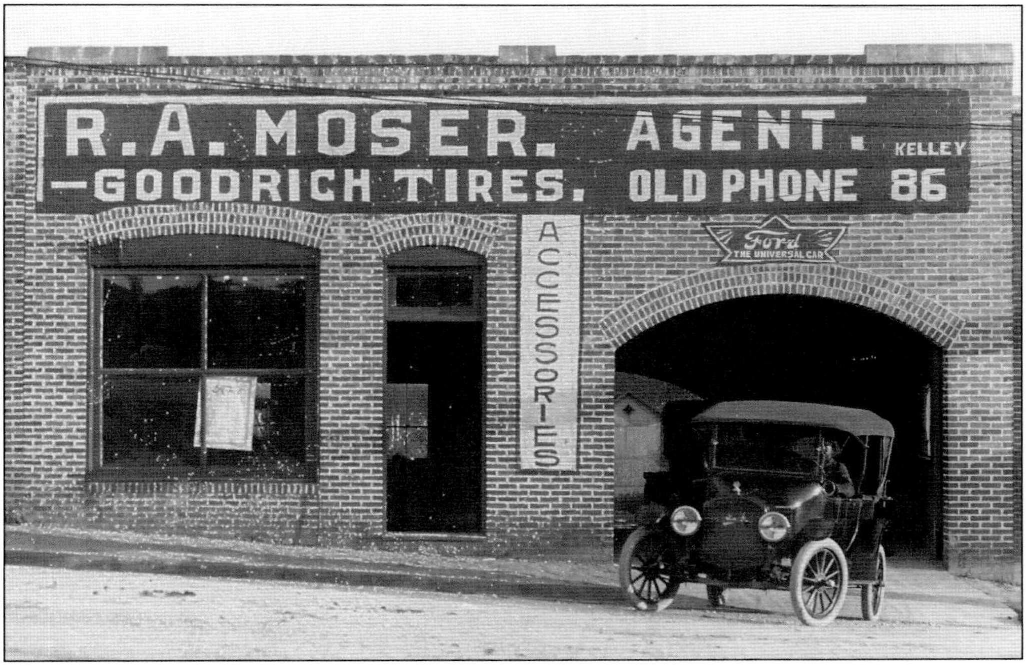

R.A. Moser was Clinton's first automobile agent. He represented the Ford Motor Company. Moser was a Presbyterian preacher, the pastor of two Presbyterian churches, and a principal of Clinton High School. The Moser Ford agency was located on Depot (now Market) Street. (Courtesy of the *Clinton Courier-News.*)

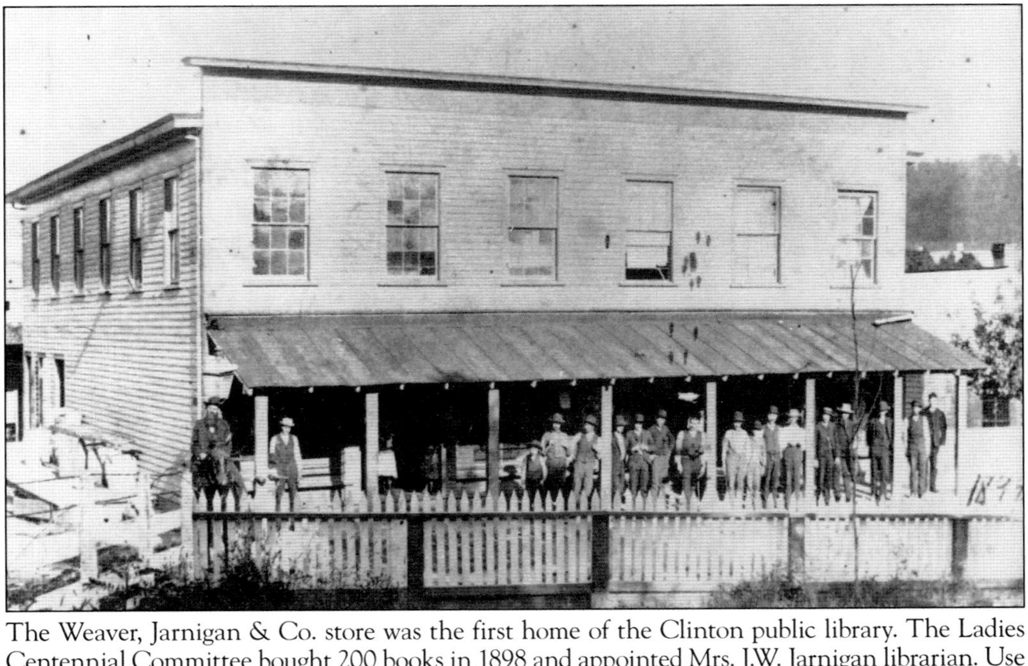

The Weaver, Jarnigan & Co. store was the first home of the Clinton public library. The Ladies Centennial Committee bought 200 books in 1898 and appointed Mrs. J.W. Jarnigan librarian. Use of the books was free to library members, and others could borrow the books upon payment of a fee. The books were housed on the second floor of the store. (Courtesy of the *Clinton Courier-News.*)

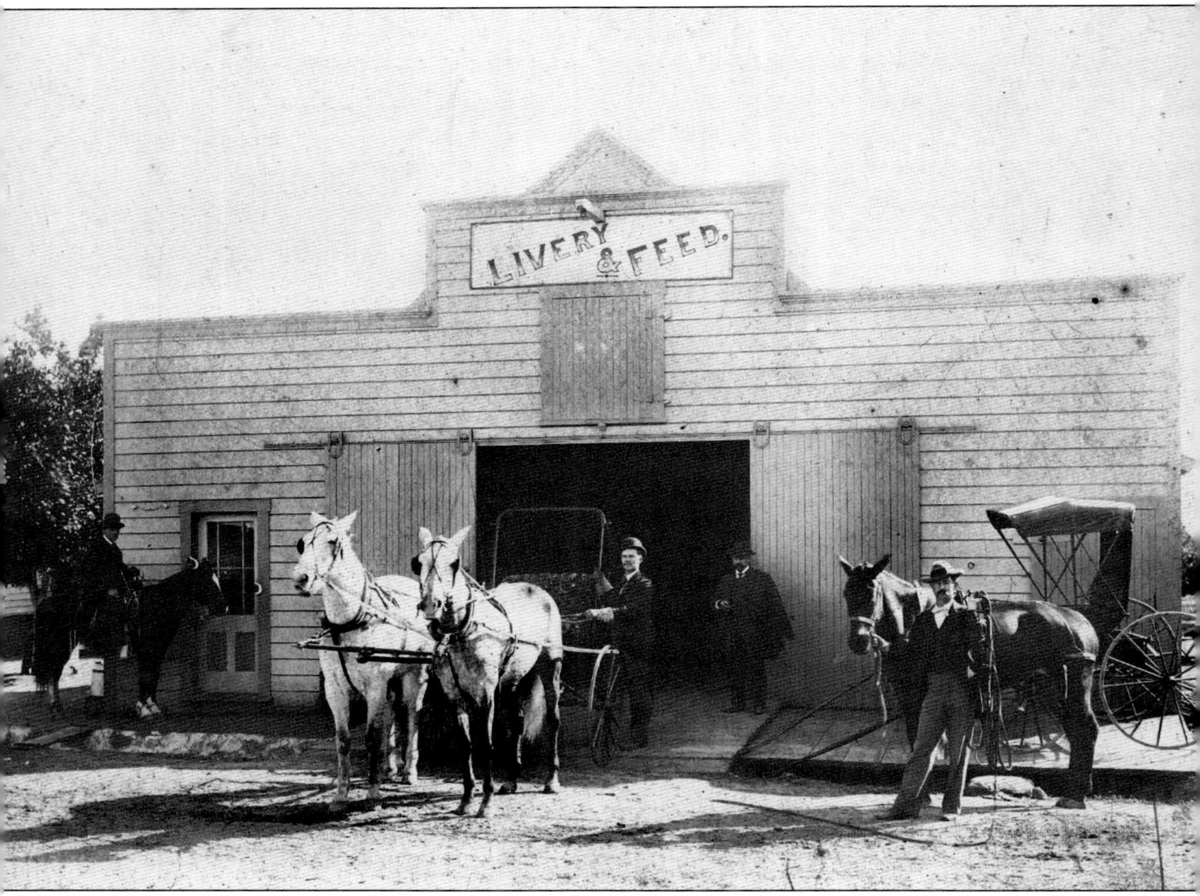

The Livery & Feed store was located on Depot (now Market) Street, where Freddy Fagan Way connects with Market Street. W.W. Underwood owned the store, and it was operated by Bill Young. Traveling salesmen who came in by train rented buggies from the livery to travel the countryside, drumming up business before catching the train to their next stop. After the livery was closed, the building housed a Chevrolet dealership owned by Lawrence Seeber and Clyde Peak. Next to use the building was the National Guard, which stayed until it was mobilized in 1941. Lake Jewelry store moved in and stayed until it closed in the 1970s. Kelly Goins's barbershop occupied the site until he closed his business in the 1980s. The site is now occupied by an antique store. This photograph was taken around 1905. (Courtesy of *the Clinton Courier-News.*)

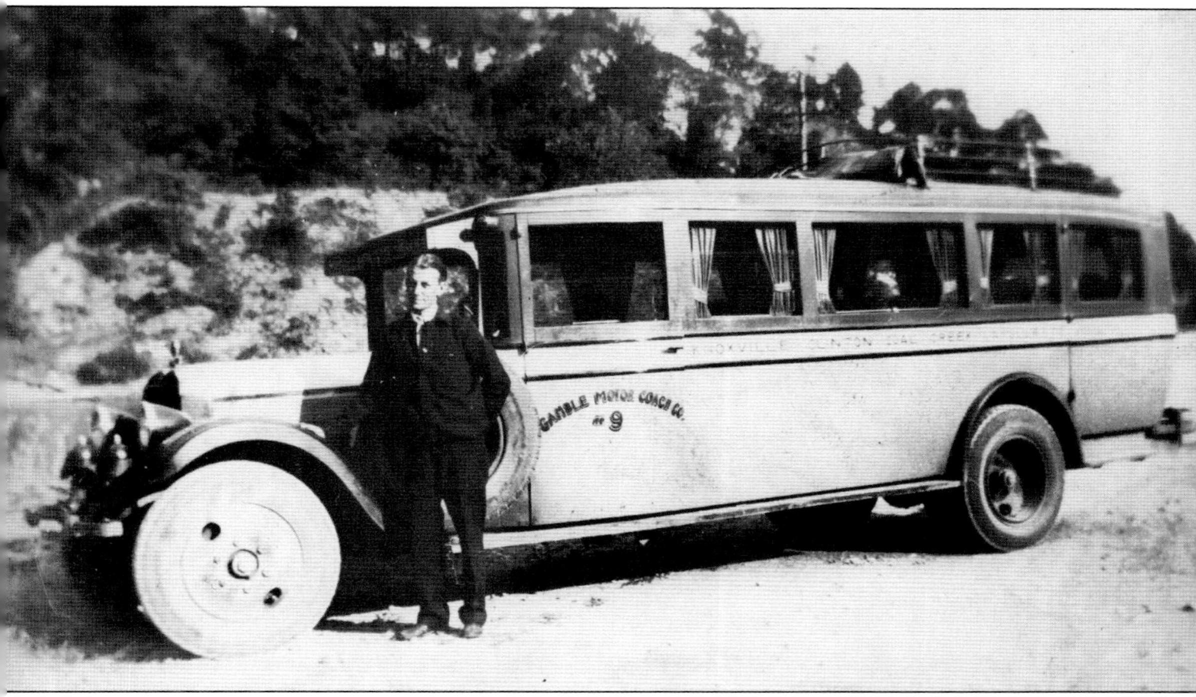

The Gamble Motor Coach Co. operated a bus line between Knoxville and Jellico with main stops in Clinton, Coal Creek (now Lake City), Jacksboro, and LaFollette. In 1926, the company's garage, located next door to the courthouse in Jacksboro, caught fire in the middle of the night and burned to the ground. In the early hours of the following morning, the Campbell County courthouse also caught fire and burned. It was never proved whether both fires were caused by the same catalyst, whether the garage fire caused the courthouse fire, or whether the courthouse fire started the garage fire and just took longer to spread. In later years, both Greyhound and Trailways bus lines served Clinton, and the bus stop was located on Main Street. This image dates to about 1925 and was taken outside the line's Clinton stop. (Courtesy of Jerry Patterson.)

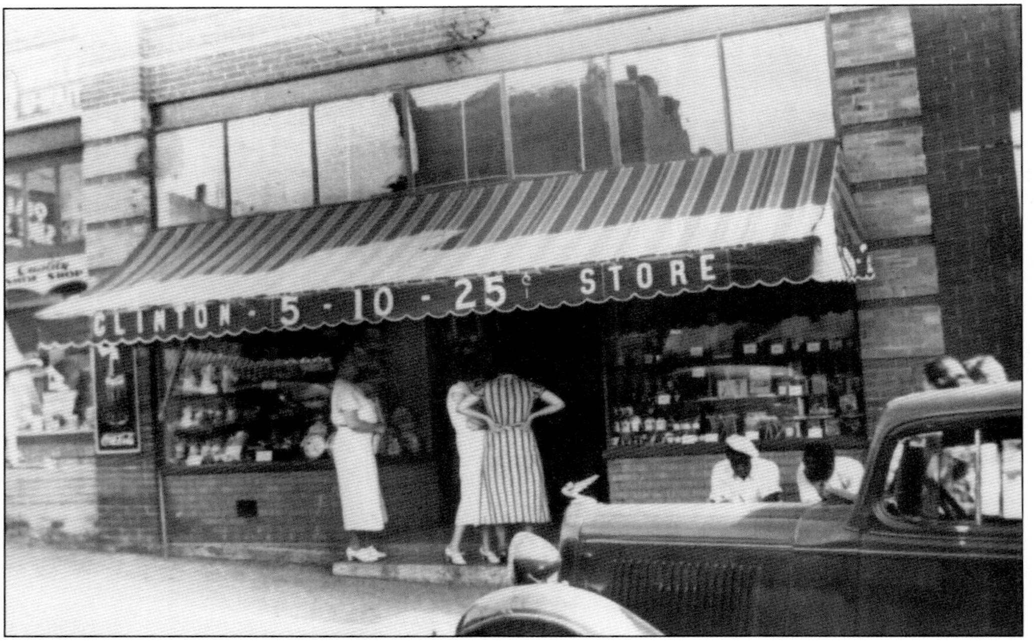

The Clinton 5-10-25¢ Store, Clinton's answer to Woolworth's, was located on Depot (now Market) Street in the same building as the Clinton Art Studio for many years. It would be impossible to name everyone who ever worked at the store, but many young ladies were employed there through the years. (Courtesy of Mary Harris.)

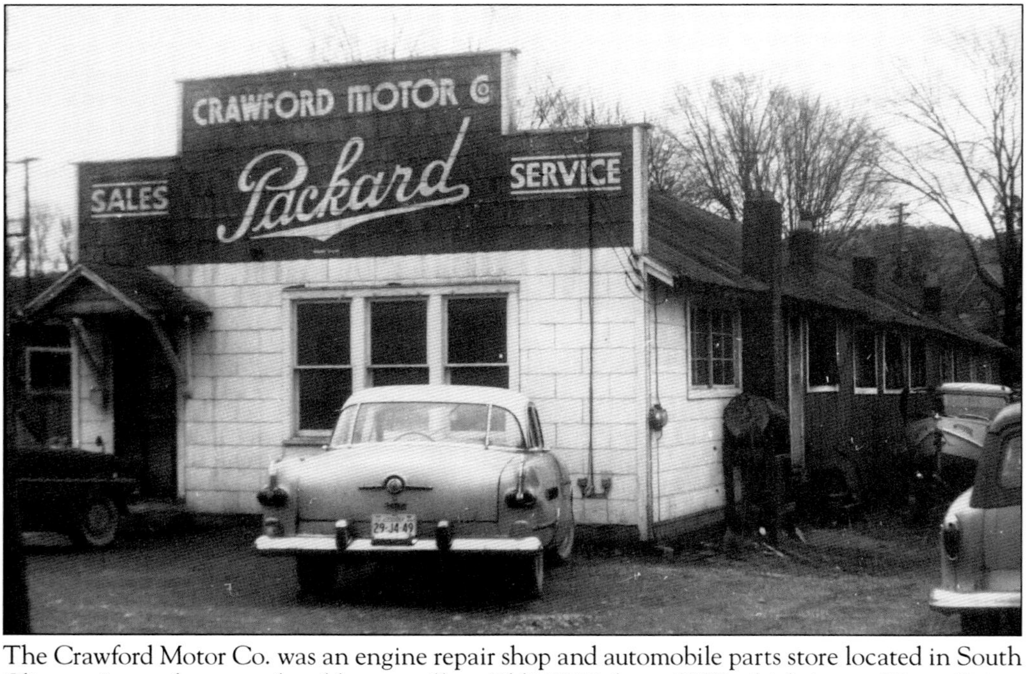

The Crawford Motor Co. was an engine repair shop and automobile parts store located in South Clinton. It stood next to the old corn mill on Old US Highway 25W, which is now Hiway Drive. The present South Clinton fire station is near the former Crawford Motor location. (Courtesy of Mary Harris.)

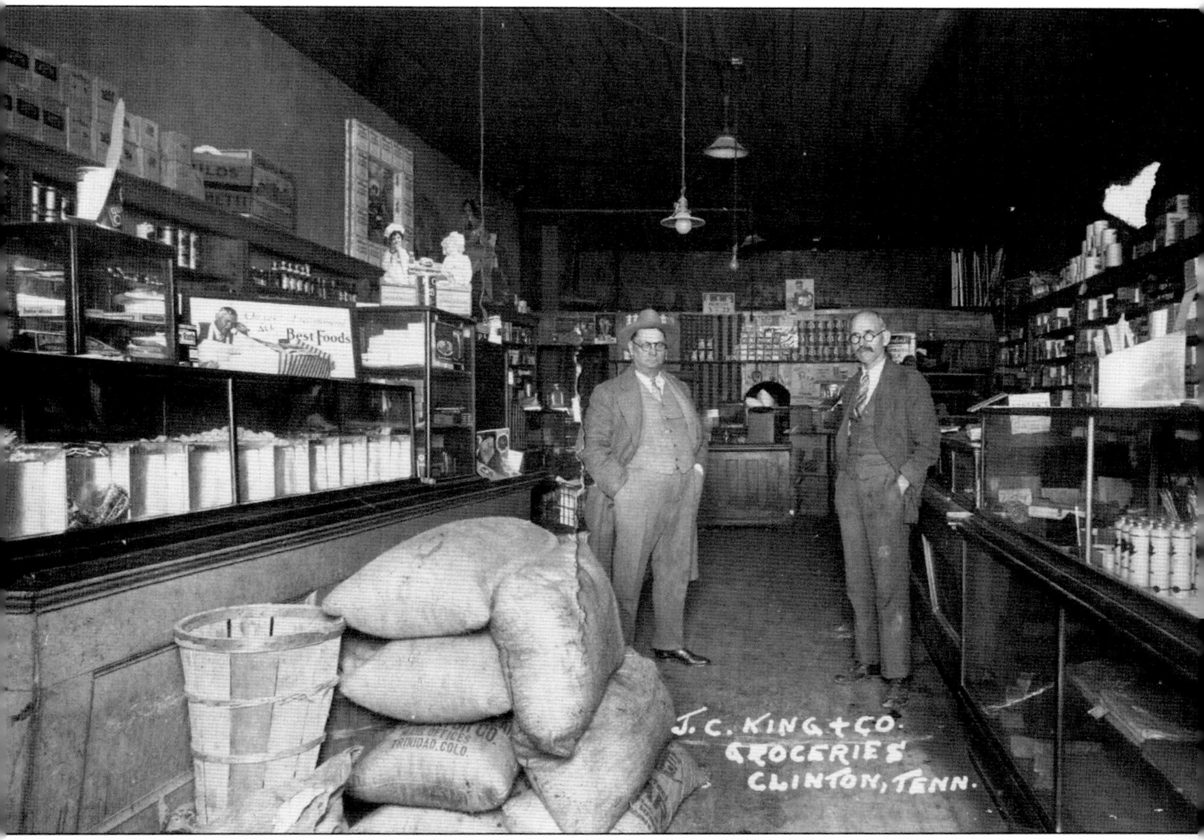

The J.C. King & Co. grocery store was owned by James Calvin King and located on Broad (now West Broad) Street, where the city's Memorial Recreation Center is located today. The store's layout was typical for its time, with a long, narrow design to maximize the town lot size and a short storefront to minimize street-front window exposure. It sold dry goods, which included everything from Shredded Wheat and Kellogg's Corn Flakes (top shelf on the left side) to Palmolive soap and Sauer's vanilla (center back shelves) and to Bruton's snuff and flour sacking material (right side shelves). This photograph is undated, but the men's dress and product advertising dates it to approximately the 1920s. (Courtesy of Charles Hugh Abner.)

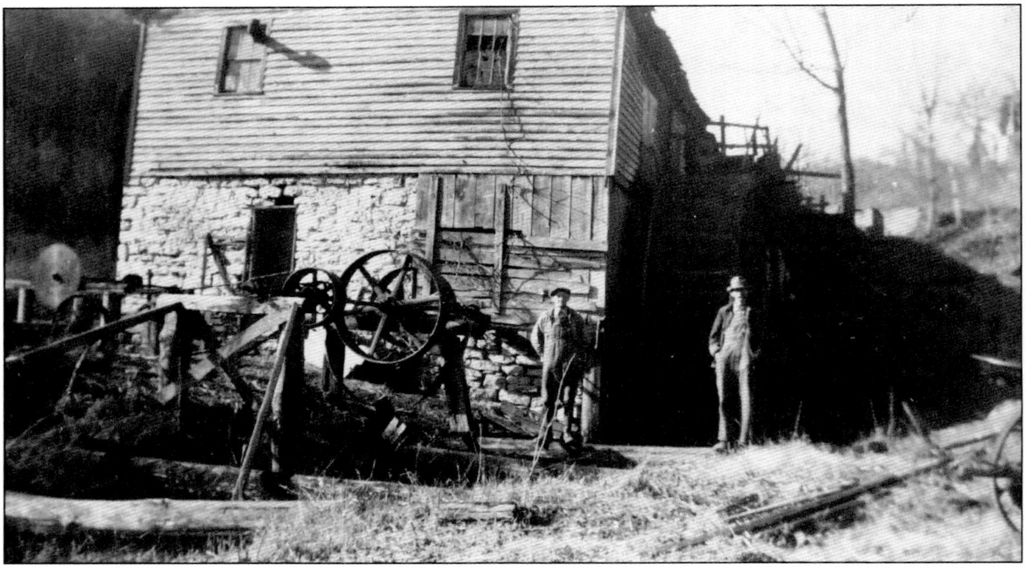

Sam Spessard operated a corn mill and a sawmill on his farm. To harness more power for his saws, he built his sawmill over the same stream that powered his corn mill and directly behind the mill. His daughter remembers playing on the logs laid across the stream and falling into the water. (Courtesy of Carolyn Spessard Braden.)

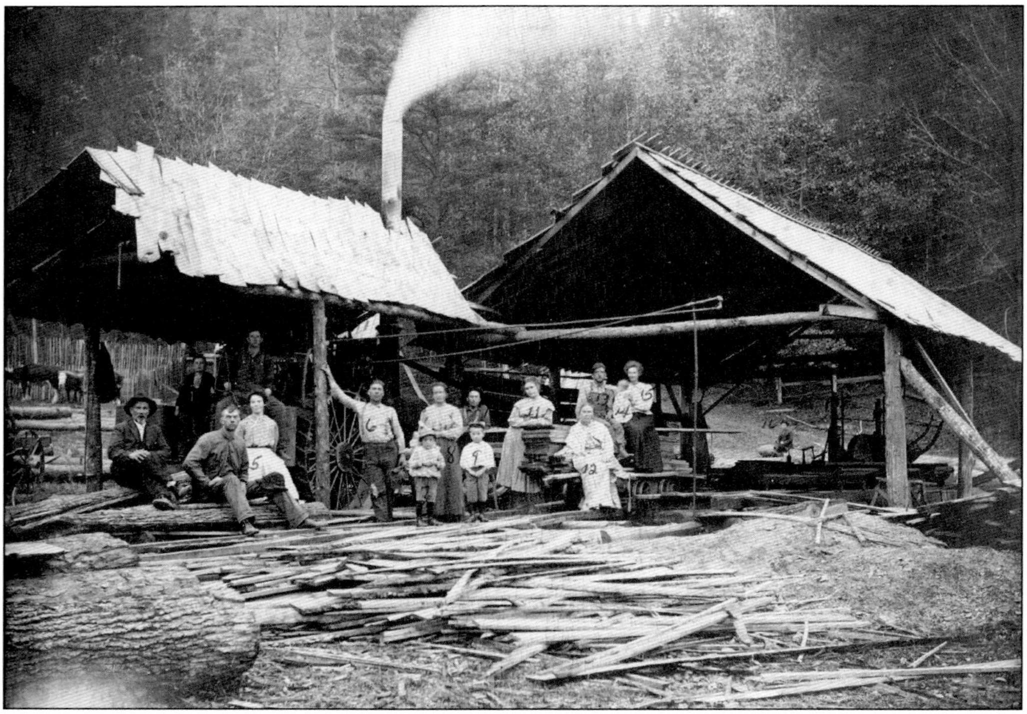

With timber plentiful and many creeks running through the area, sawmills were a common sight in the county at the turn of the century. In this photograph from about 1900, the women of the family share a picnic lunch with the men working at the sawmill. (Courtesy of Mary Elkins Barker.)

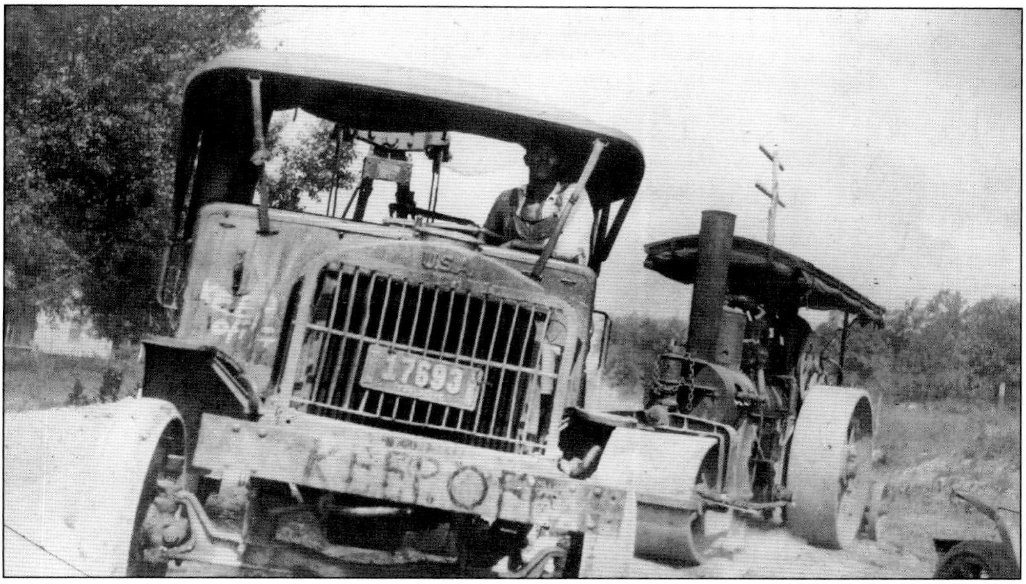

A.C. Moore was a farmer in the Edgemoor area and an entrepreneur who contracted roadwork not only in Anderson County but also on the Cumberland Plateau and in Illinois. In this photograph, he is shown operating his road grading equipment somewhere on the plateau. (Courtesy of Mary Elkins Barker.)

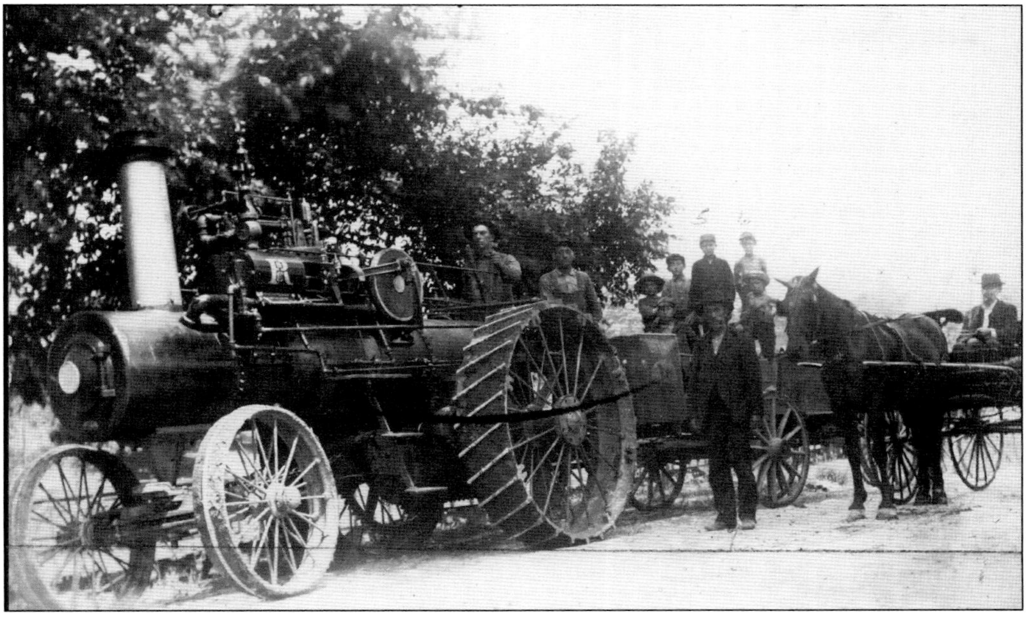

As well as being a farmer and road contractor, A.C. Moore traveled around the county and contracted with farmers to thresh their crops. In this photograph, he is shown operating his threshing machine while a neighboring farmer and a group of fascinated young men look on. (Courtesy of Mary Elkins Barker.)

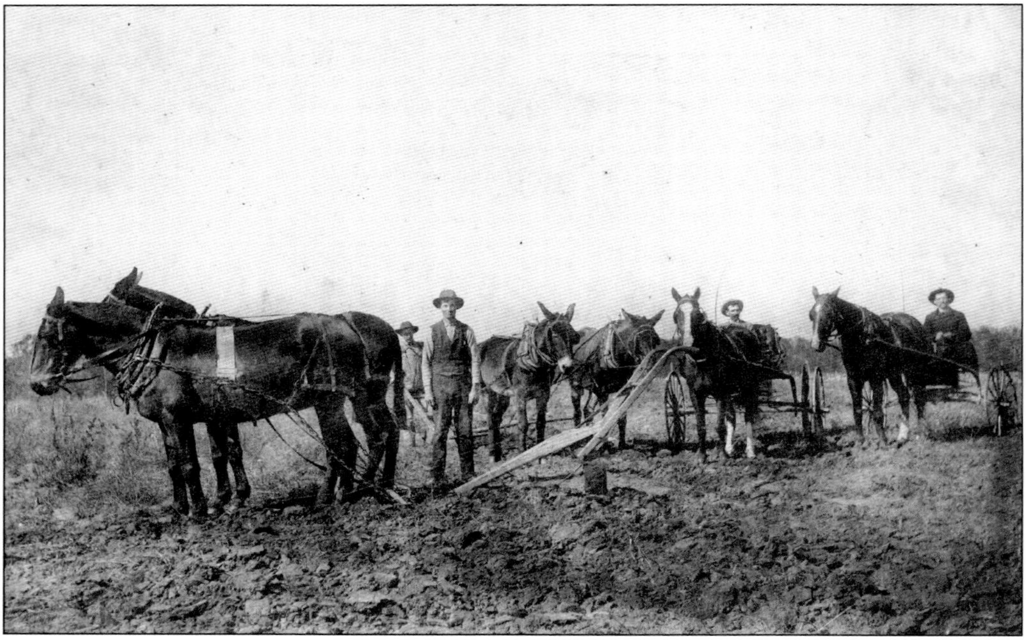

Gibb Stanley and a field hand stand behind wooden plows in the fields of the East Tennessee Nursery Co. while two nursery agents sit in their sulkies. The nursery sold plants and trees nationwide through a mail order catalog and shipped them from the railroad depot in Coal Creek (now Lake City). (Courtesy of Susan Fowler.)

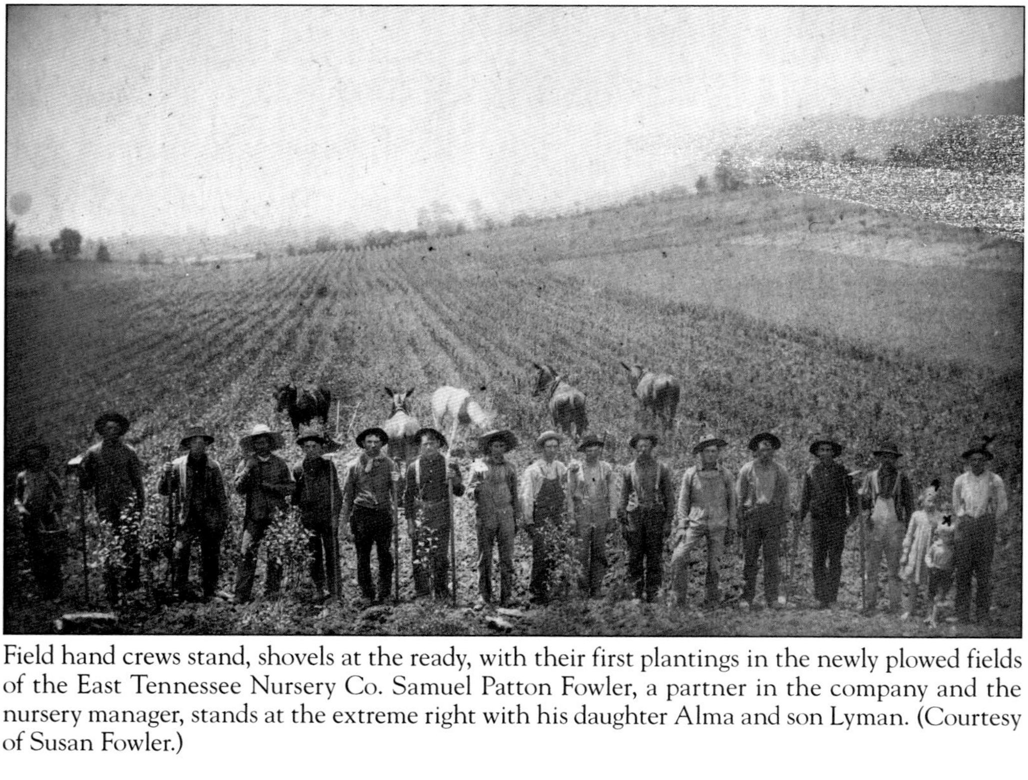

Field hand crews stand, shovels at the ready, with their first plantings in the newly plowed fields of the East Tennessee Nursery Co. Samuel Patton Fowler, a partner in the company and the nursery manager, stands at the extreme right with his daughter Alma and son Lyman. (Courtesy of Susan Fowler.)

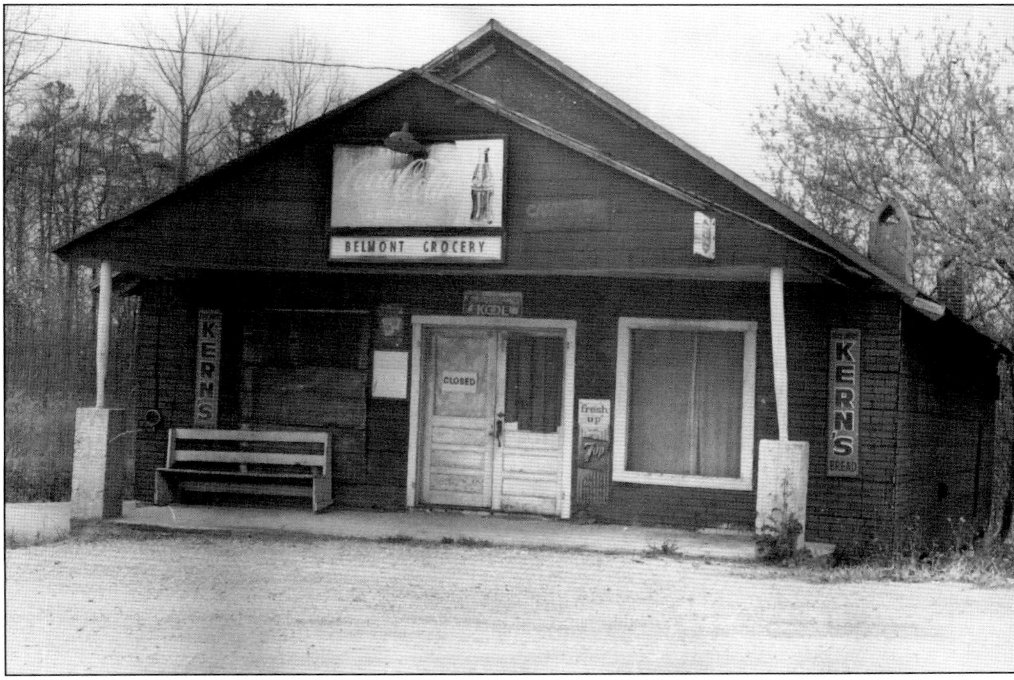

The John Wesley Stooksbury Store, located in the Belmont community above Andersonville, was called the Belmont Grocery. In the late 1950s, it was operated by H.H. Ridenour. John Wesley Stooksbury was the son of Robert and Harriet Melton Stooksbury, and he married Maggie Poston. (Courtesy of Mary Harris.)

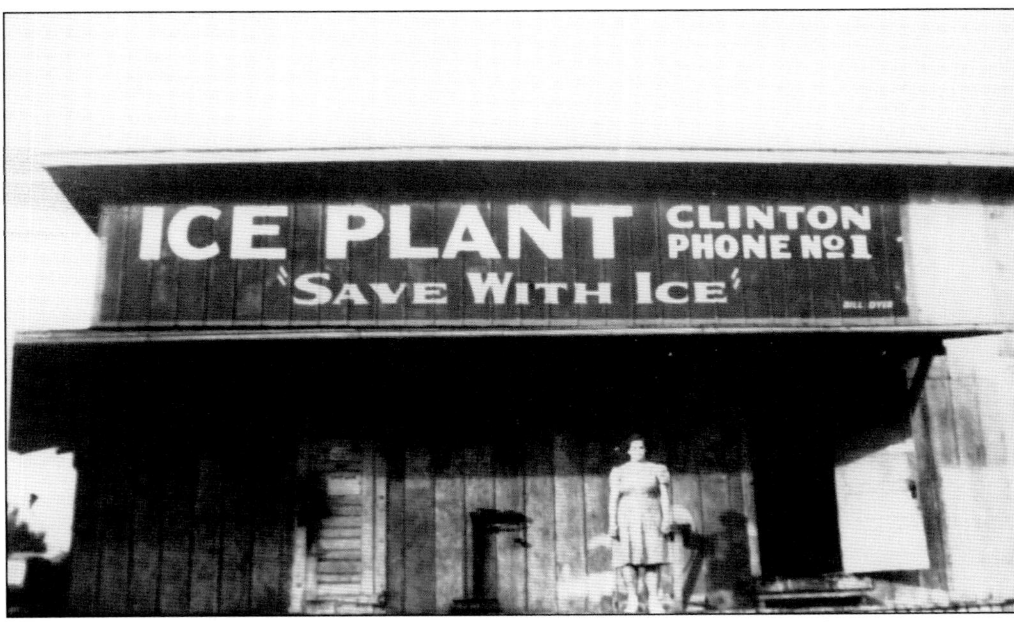

The Clinton Ice Plant was located on the same lot where the BP gas station and convenience store stands today, on North Main Street in front of the railroad yard. This photograph was taken in the 1950s, and the ice plant went out of business in the 1960s. (Courtesy of Mary Harris.)

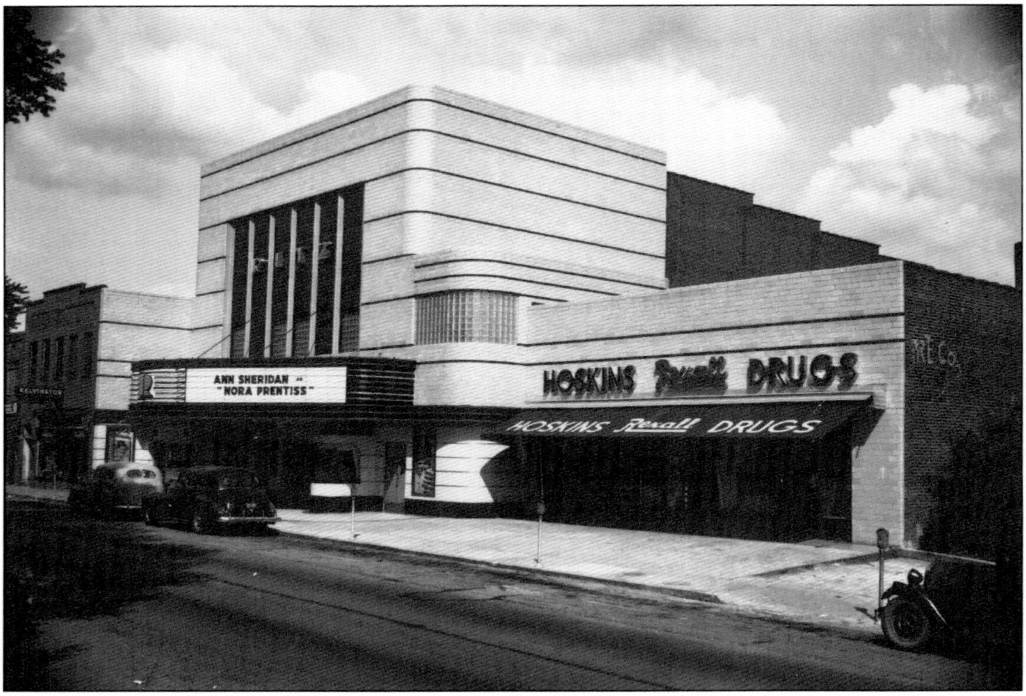

The Ritz Theatre and Hoskins Drug Store building was built in 1942. This photograph is undated but must have been taken about 1947, as the movie *Nora Prentiss* is showing at the theater. The Ritz building is now listed in the National Register of Historic Places. (Courtesy of Dudley Hoskins Bostic.)

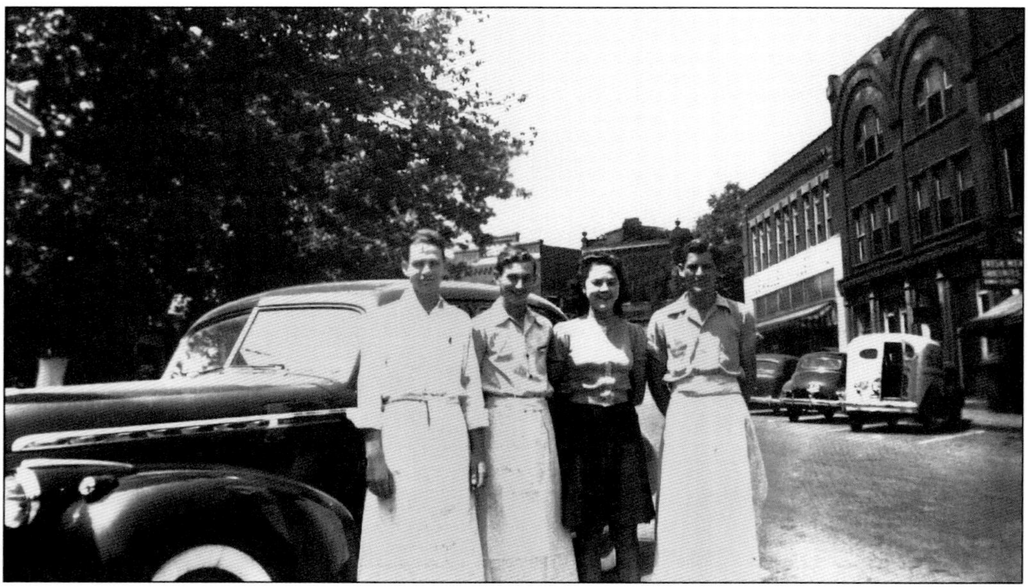

Katherine Hoskins, wife of R.C. "Dudley" Hoskins, owner of Hoskins Drug Store, stands with the soda fountain crew outside their store on Depot (now Market) Street around 1947. The old Clinton Hardware Co. building that was torn down in 1961 can be seen directly behind Mrs. Hoskins's head. (Courtesy of Dudley Hoskins Bostic.)

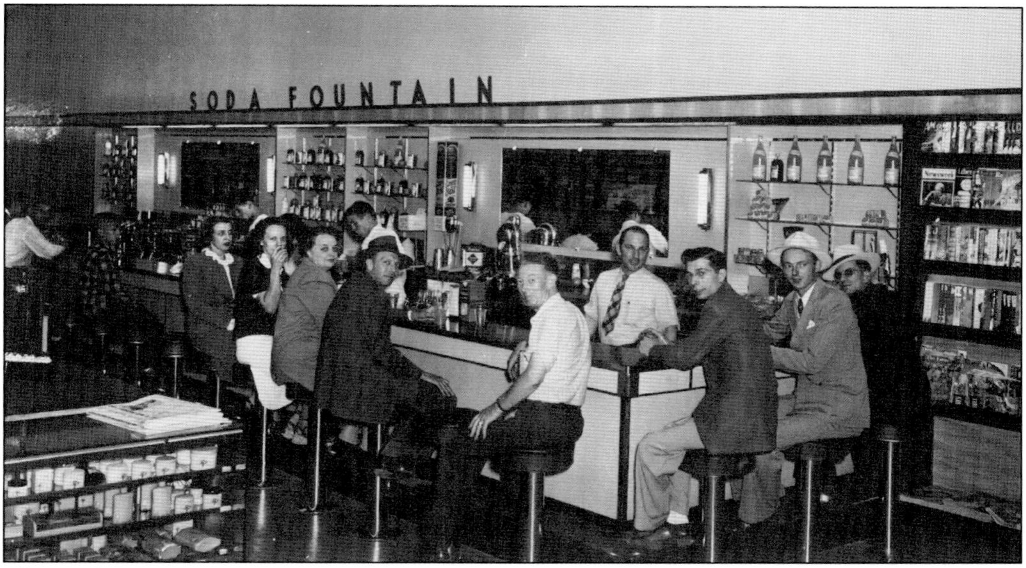

The Hoskins Drug Store soda fountain and lunch counter has been the place to go to hear the news since the store opened. Located directly across the street from the courthouse since about 1947, it is where county employees and politicians still go to eat lunch and talk with local businessmen and shoppers. (Courtesy of Dudley Hoskins Bostic.)

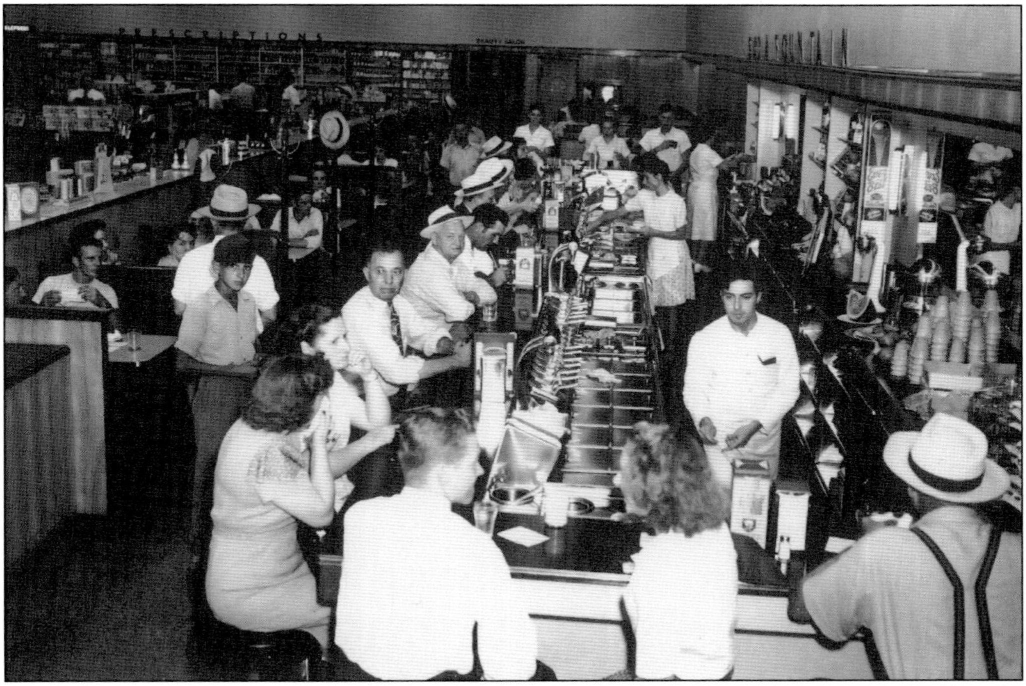

An interior view of Hoskins Drug Store about 1947 shows how busy the lunch counter and booths were when breakfast and lunch were being served. Hoskins was also the place where teenagers could stop on the way home from school for ice cream or an after-school snack. The door at the back of the store led to a beauty parlor and a private meeting room. (Courtesy of Dudley Hoskins Bostic.)

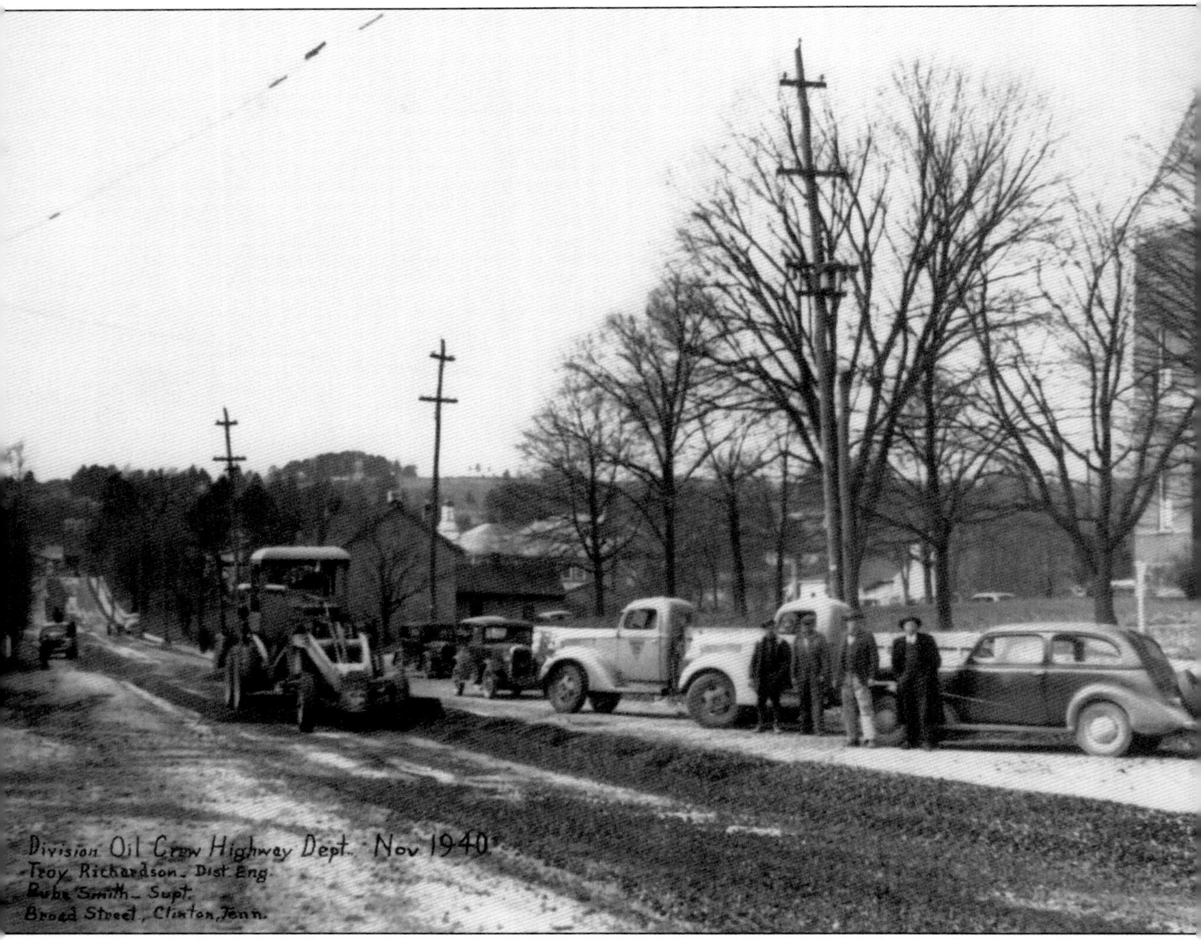

In November 1940, the Highway Department began paving Broad Street. The side of the courthouse can be seen at the right of this photograph. Behind Courthouse Square stands a house; today, this is where Clinton's city hall and police department take up the block between Bowling and North Hicks Streets. The first telephone lines were installed in Clinton around 1904, and electricity first came to the city in 1906. In 1922, Jacksboro (now North Main) Street became a part of the Dixie Highway system, the main north-south route from Miami to Detroit, but Clinton did not begin to pave the city streets until the 1940s. Broad Street began at the river, where the Old US Highway 25W entered Clinton from the old Clinch River Bridge. The highway turned north onto Jacksboro (now North Main) Street. (Courtesy of Mary Harris.)

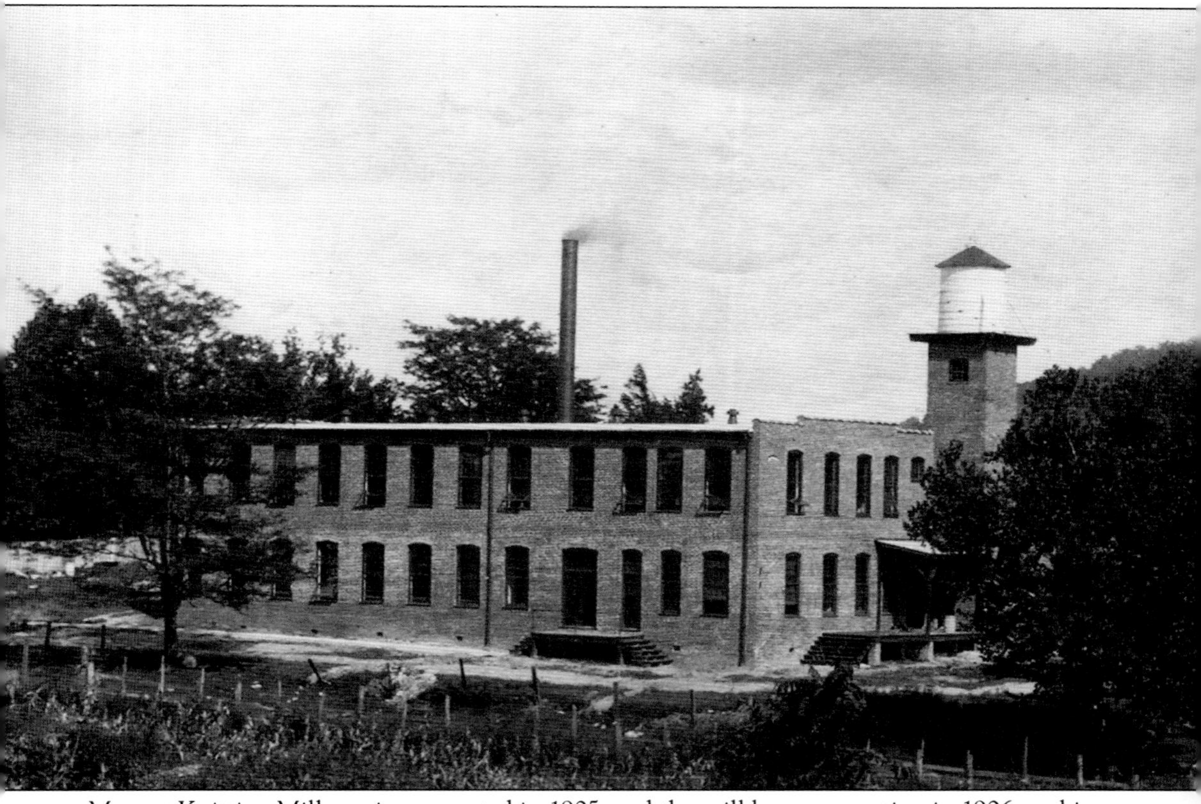

Magnet Knitting Mill was incorporated in 1905, and the mill began operation in 1906, making men's socks. Wanamaker's of New York was an early customer. International trade conditions in the early years gave Magnet the chance it needed to compete internationally and to grow. By 1910, Magnet employed 200 people. The first addition to the plant was built in 1916, and employment jumped to almost 500. In 1918, plants in Coal Creek (now Lake City) and LaFollette were opened. The LaFollette plant was closed after World War I ended. Another addition to the Clinton plant was built in 1924, followed by the largest and last addition in 1929. The mill was reorganized as Magnet Mills, Inc., and the company opened a sales office in the Empire State Building in New York City. The mill was sold to Prestige, Inc., in 1962. When a strike was called in 1967, the new owners closed the mill. This photograph shows the original mill building in 1906. (Courtesy of the *Clinton Courier-News*.)

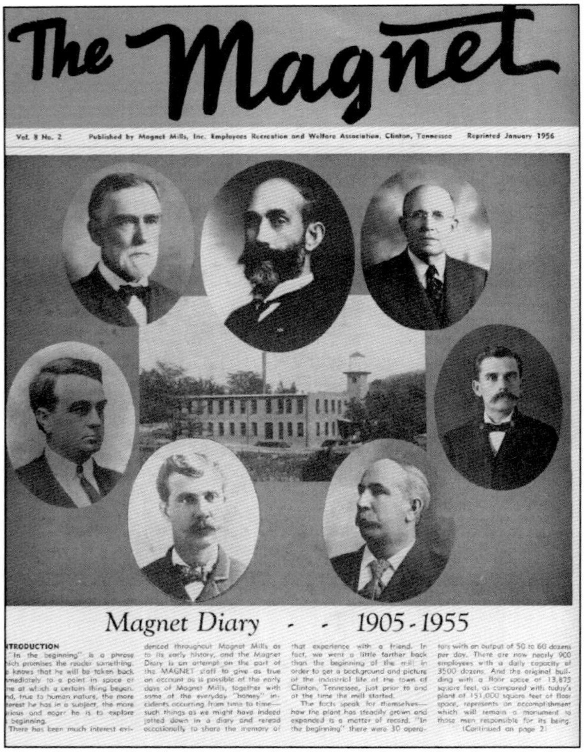

The Magnet

Vol. 8 No. 2 Published by Magnet Mills, Inc. Employees Recreation and Welfare Association, Clinton, Tennessee Reprinted January 1956

Magnet Diary - - 1905 - 1955

NTRODUCTION

"In the beginning" is a phrase hich promises the reader something. knows that he will be taken back mediately to a point in space or ne at which a certain thing began. nd, true to human nature, the more terest he has in a subject, the more rious and eager he is to explore beginning.

There has been much interest evidenced throughout Magnet Mills as to its early history, and the Magnet Diary is an attempt on the part of the MAGNET staff to give as true an account as is possible of the early days of Magnet Mills, together with some of the everyday "homey" incidents occurring from time to time—such things as we might have indeed jotted down in a diary and reread occasionally to share the memory of that experience with a friend. In fact, we went a little farther back than the beginning of the mill in order to get a background and picture of the industrial life of the town of Clinton, Tennessee, just prior to and at the time the mill started.

The facts speak for themselves—how the plant has steadily grown and expanded is a matter of record. "In the beginning" there were 30 operators with an output of 50 to 60 dozens per day. There are now nearly 900 employees with a daily capacity of 3500 dozens. And the original building with a floor space of 13,875 square feet, as compared with today's plant of 151,000 square feet of floor space, represents an accomplishment which will remain a monument to those men responsible for its being.

(Continued on page 2)

The *Magnet* was the plant publication for Magnet Mills, published by the Employees Recreation and Welfare Association. This issue was a January 1956 reprint of the 1955 edition celebrating the plant's 50th anniversary, and it contained a history of the plant and employee news and anecdotes. Katherine Baker Hoskins was editor of the *Magnet* during her 25 years with the mill. (Courtesy of the *Clinton Courier-News*.)

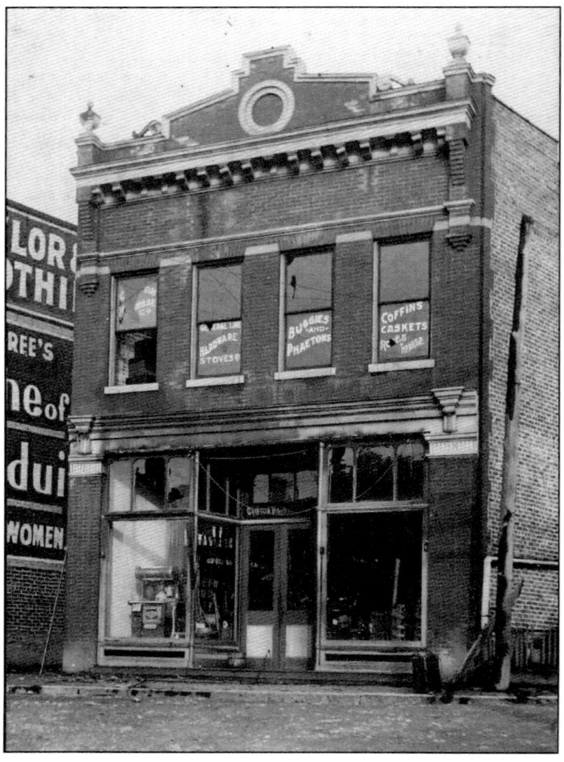

This building once stood on Main Street at the head of Depot (now Market) Street. It was built in about 1890 and was occupied successively by E.C. Cross's Clinton Hardware Co., Bernard's, the A&P Store, J.R. Daugherty's, and Sharp's Supply Co. It was torn down in 1961 to make way for the parking area between today's Corner Antiques and Memorial United Methodist Church. (Courtesy of the *Clinton Courier-News*.)

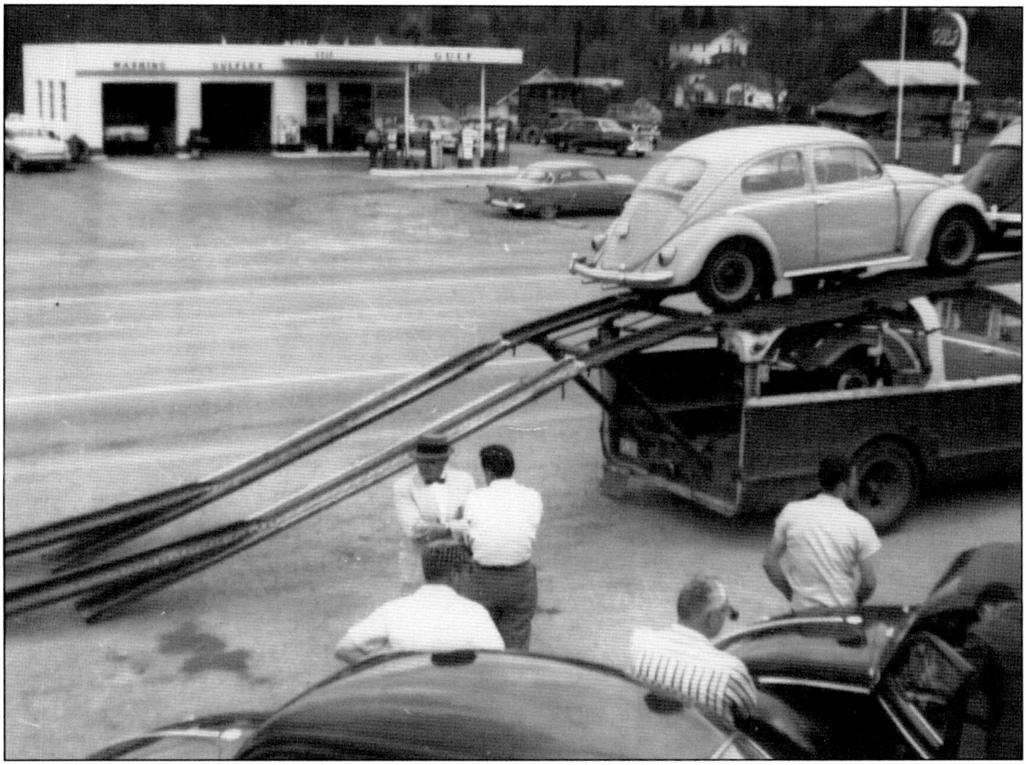

This 1964 photograph shows Volkswagen Beetles being unloaded at the first Holbrook Motors location on US Highway 25W in South Clinton. The Volkswagens were shipped by train to the Clinton depot and trucked across the Clinch River to the lot. The Gulf service station across the highway would later be remodeled into Holbrook's fourth and final location. (Courtesy of Maxine Meade Holbrook.)

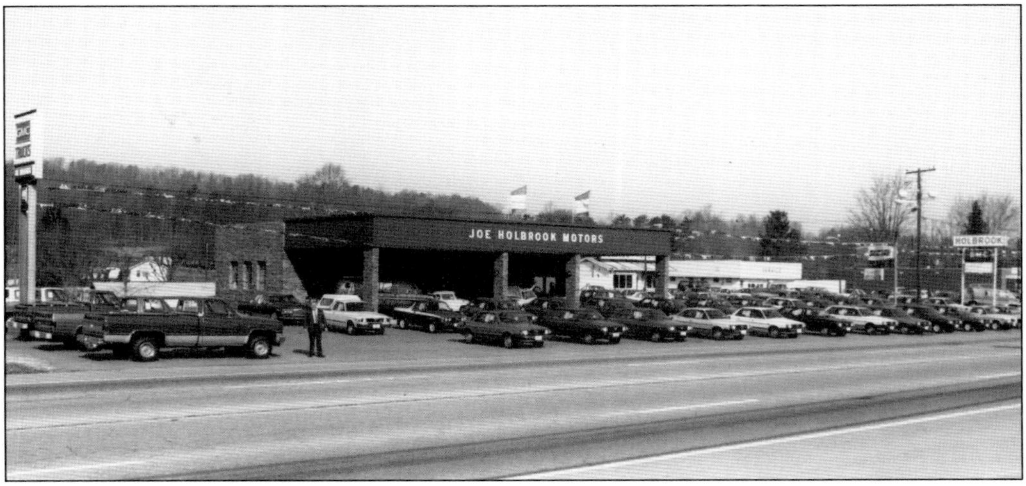

Joe Holbrook Motors' fourth and final location is pictured. The company survived two fires at this location before this building was constructed. Holbrook Motors specialized in luxury cars and was the area's DeLorean dealer. Holbrook owned 12 dealerships before the company closed. (Courtesy of Maxine Meade Holbrook.)

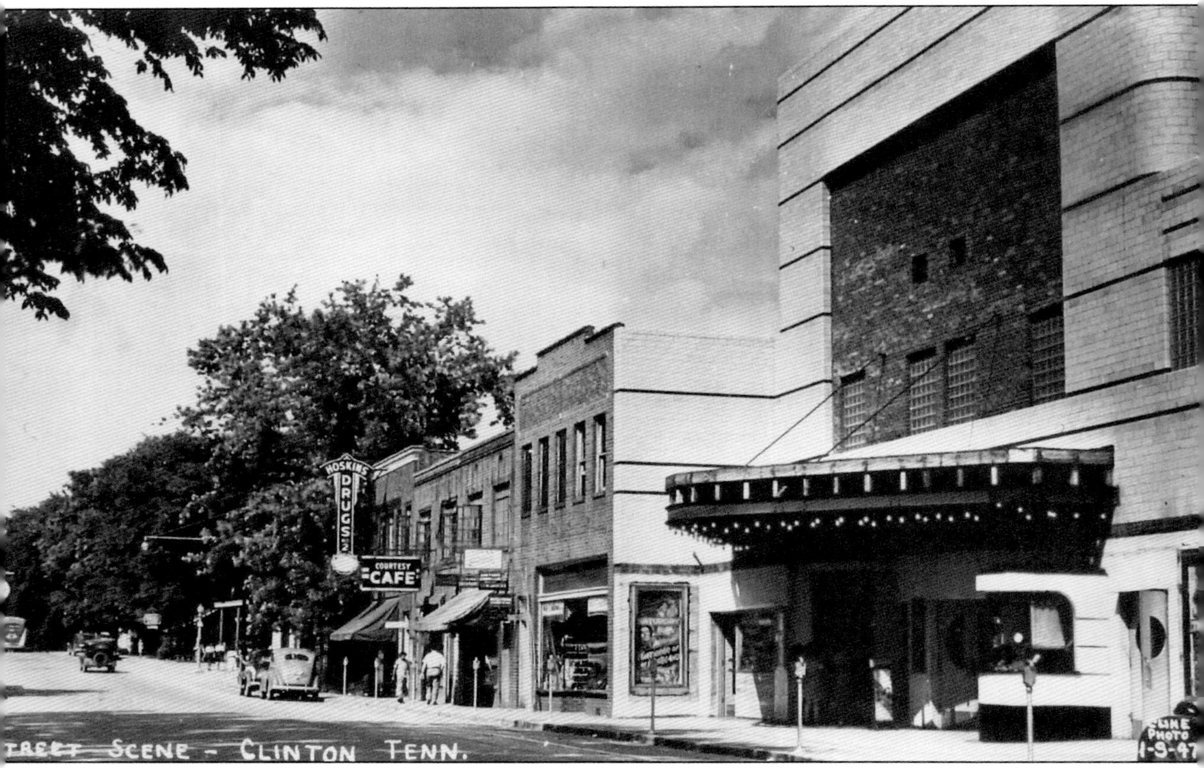

This real photo postcard view of Jacksboro (now Main) Street shows the Ritz Theatre before the neon lights and marquee lights were installed around 1947 and before Hoskins Drug Store relocated into the building from its first location farther down the street. US Highway 25W, which ran through Clinton on Main Street, was part of the Dixie Highway system, the main north-south route from Miami to Detroit. All highway traffic passed through Clinton on a two-lane road. Businesses lined the road and thrived. When Interstate 75 was completed and traffic was rerouted to the interstate road system, local businesses suffered. That was all in the future, and 1947, when this photograph was taken, was still the era of mom-and-pop stores with local ownership and management. (Postcard by Cline Photo; courtesy of Dudley Hoskins Bostic.)

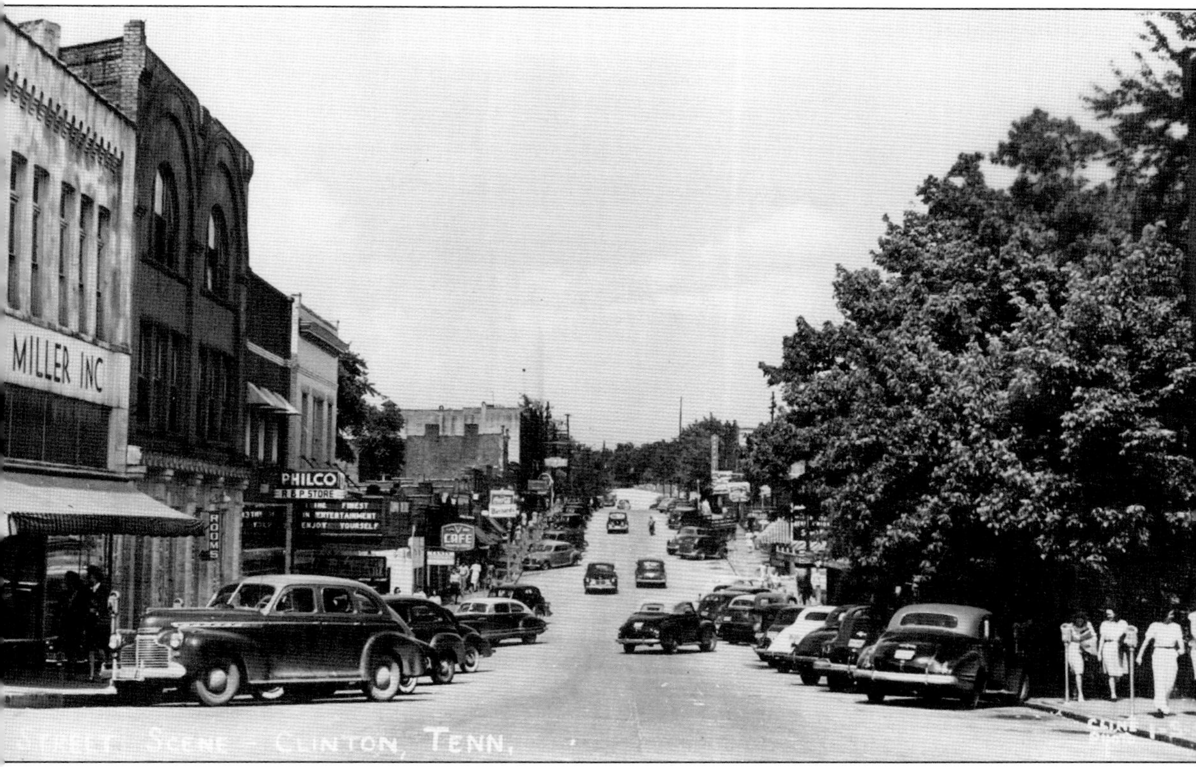

This real photo postcard view of Depot (now Market) Street, from about 1945, looks toward the Clinch River from the head of the street where it intersects with Main Street. Crowds of shoppers line the tree-shaded street, creating an idyllic view of the quiet country town Clinton was during the 1940s. On the left are, from left to right, the Lewallen-Miller store; the Jacob Leinart building, advertising rooms for rent; the A&P store, advertising the Philco brand; and the theater with advertising posters for *The Gay Senorita*. Farther down the street on the same side are the V Café and Bernard's. On the right edge of the photograph are the windows of the Clinton bank, and at the far end of the same side of the street is the vertical Park Hotel sign. (Postcard by Cline Photo; courtesy of Dudley Hoskins Bostic.)

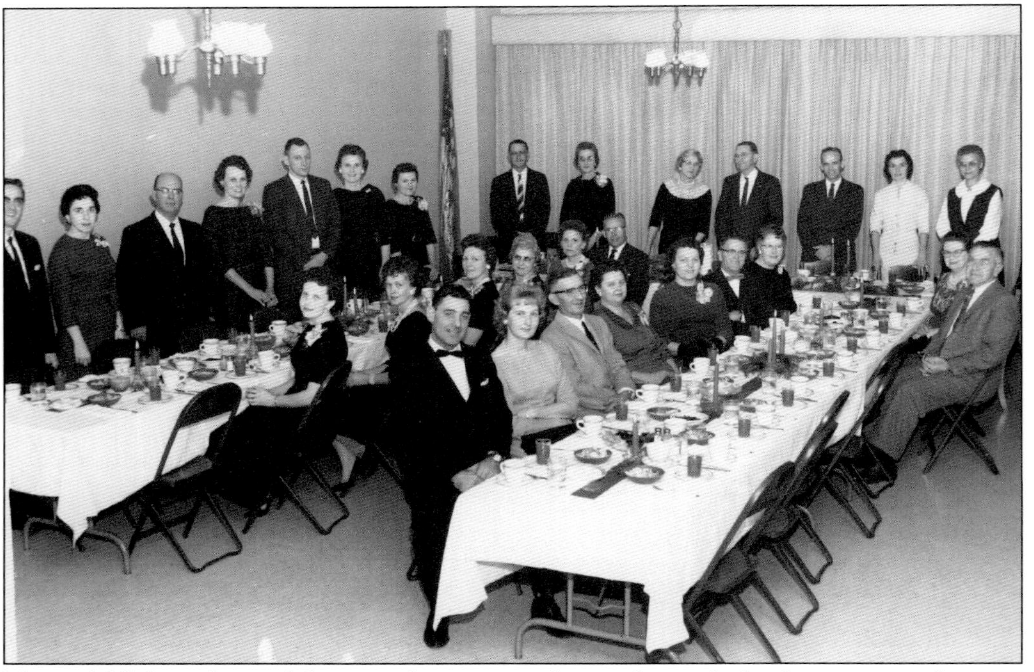

Magnet Mills hosted annual dinners to honor its employees who reached milestone years of service. This dinner was held at the Park Hotel in the 1950s. Charles B. and Ethel King Holbrook are seated at the right of the right-hand table. Both were members of the employees' 30-Year Club. (Courtesy of Maxine Meade Holbrook.)

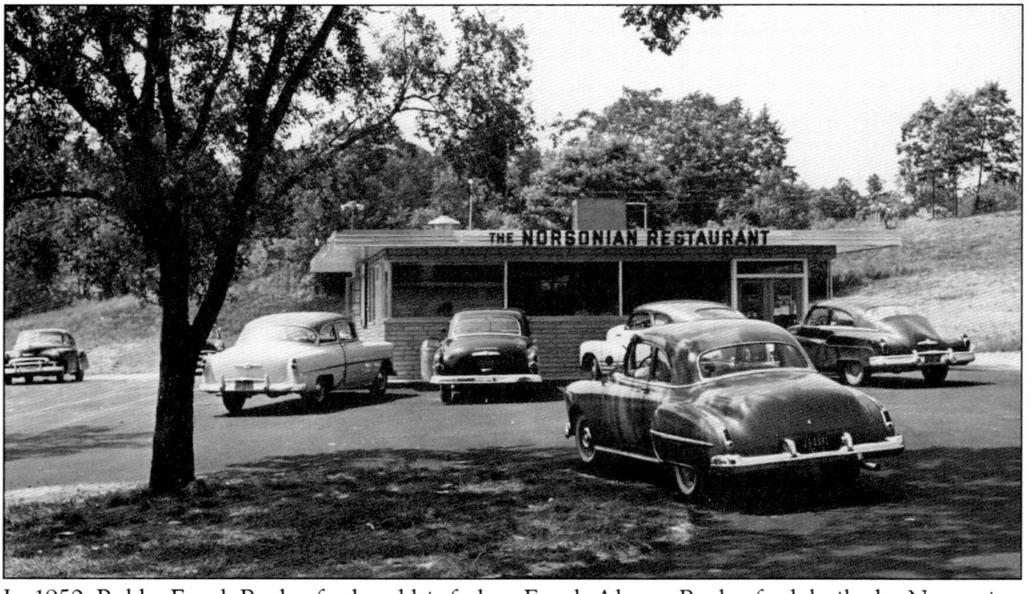

In 1950, Bobby Frank Rutherford and his father, Frank Alonzo Rutherford, built the Norsonian Restaurant across the street from the Norris town center. It was located in the building that is now occupied by Benchmark Physical Therapy. The Norris Police Department was a later addition. The Rutherfords owned the restaurant until 1973; Frank Rutherford stayed on as manager under the new owners until his death in 1976. (Courtesy of Doug Rutherford.)

Seven

SCENES

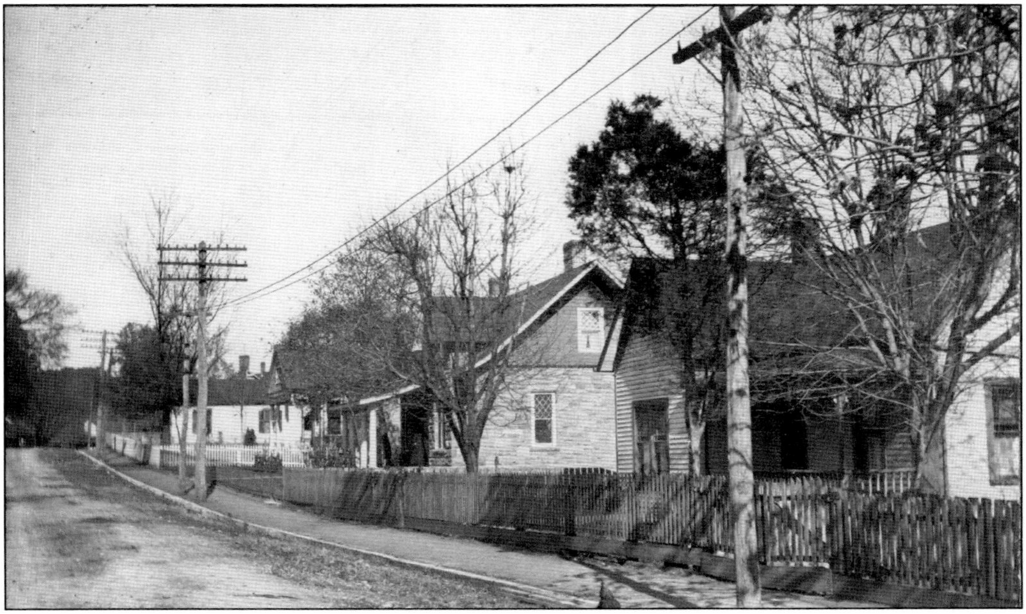

A real photo postcard from 1919 shows a picture of a quiet Jacksboro (now Main) Street lined with houses. Although Jacksboro (now Main) Street became part of the Dixie Highway system in 1922, Clinton did not start paving its streets until about 1940, and cows were allowed to graze the Courthouse Square to keep the grass down. (Courtesy of the *Clinton Courier-News*.)

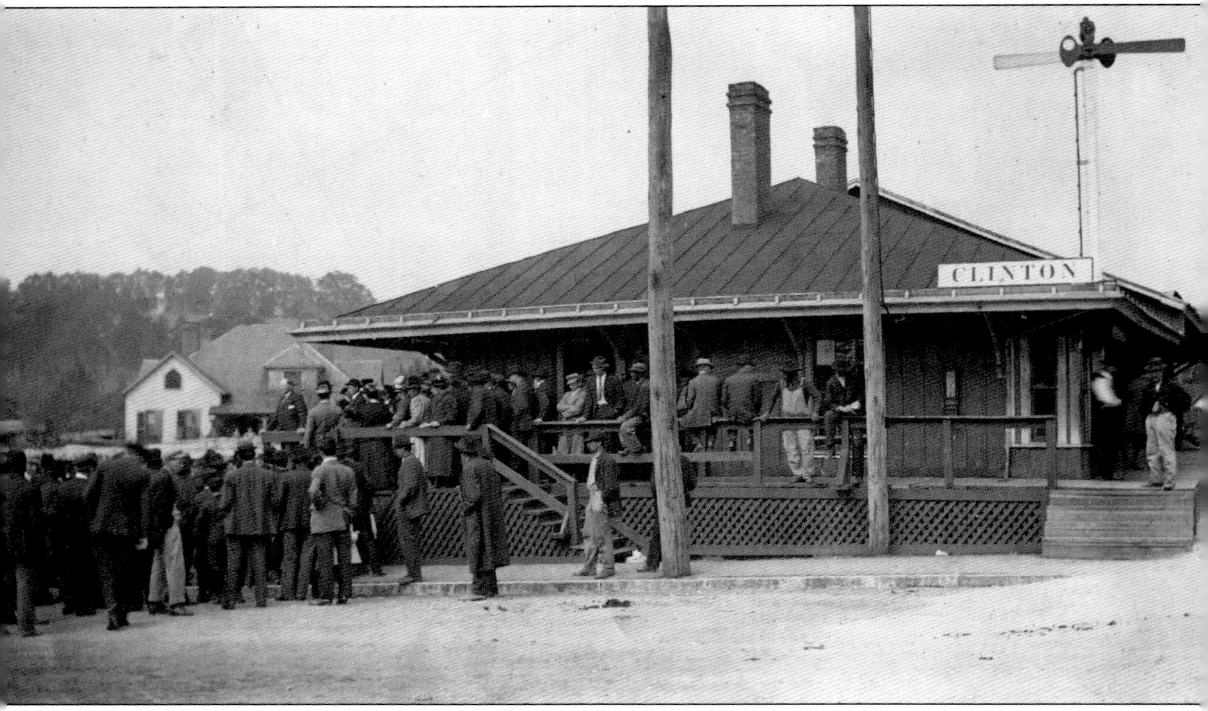

This Southern Railway depot was replaced by the current one in 1914. At the turn of the century, the depot was a favorite of drummers and stump speakers, and crowds gathered to listen and debate. In the early 1900s, eight passenger trains a day came through Clinton as well as about 40 freight trains. Rail traffic has ebbed and flowed with the mining and timbering industries, but Clinton has had rail service since the old Knoxville & Kentucky Railroad was established there in the 1860s. The Knoxville & Kentucky became the Knoxville & Ohio after the Civil War. A few years later, it became the Southern. When the line was built from Harriman to Clinton, Clinton became a junction; this increased its traffic, and it became a water and refueling station. Although both Southern Railway and the Louisville & Nashville laid track through Clinton, only Southern chose to build a depot. The rail lines and depot are now owned by Norfolk Southern. (Courtesy of the *Clinton Courier-News*.)

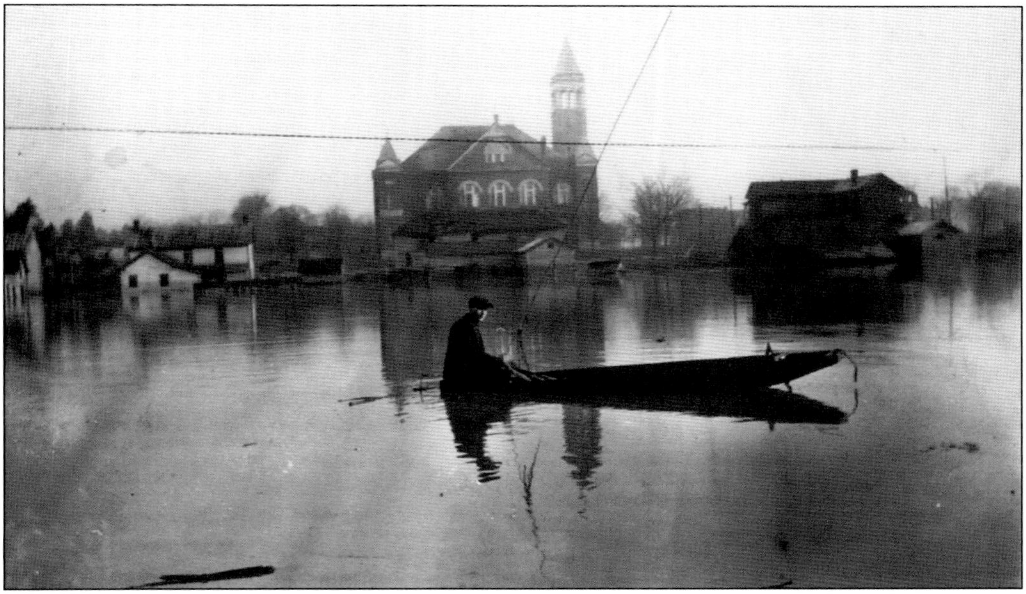

In March 1929, the Clinch River reached its highest recorded flood stage, and downtown Clinton was flooded. In this photograph, the Anderson County Courthouse Square can be seen standing above the water, while homes and businesses along Broad Street are under water. Residents traveled around town by boat until the waters receded. (Courtesy of the Pellissippi Genealogical and Historical Society.)

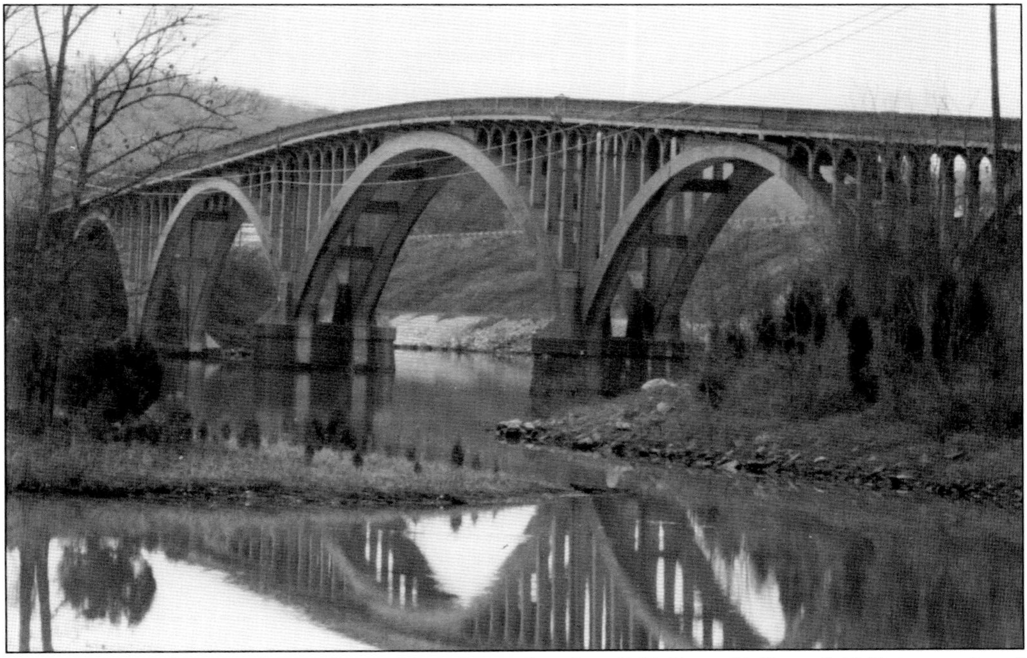

The Solway Bridge was designed in 1929 and completed in 1931. From 1943 until 1949, it was closed except to military traffic. It was reopened when the gates of Oak Ridge were opened in 1949. In 1976, the Tennessee Valley Authority decided it was too close to the new Pellissippi Parkway bridge to allow for safe navigation under both, and it was destroyed. (Courtesy of Mary Elkins Barker.)

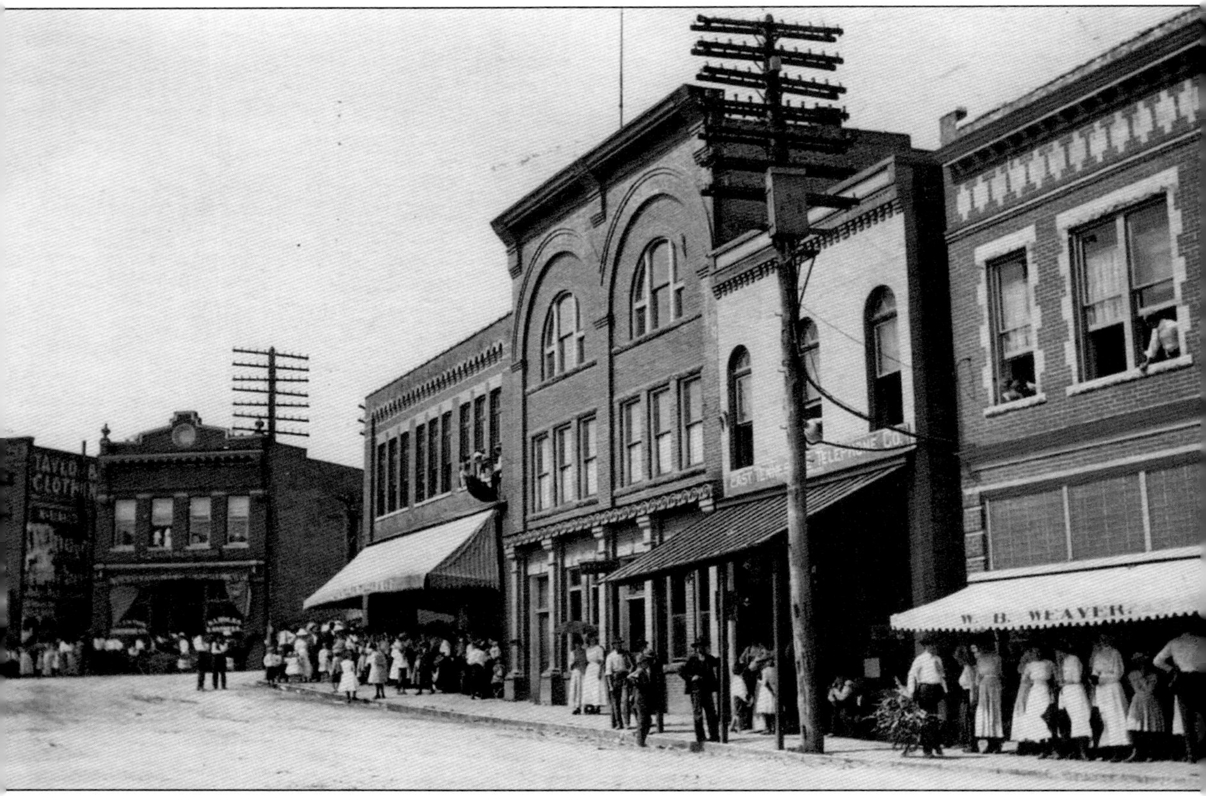

In this real photo postcard view from 1919, a Labor Day crowd lines Depot (now Market) Street with a view towards Jacksboro (now Main) Street. From the right and moving left are the W.B. Weaver store, the East Tennessee Telephone Co., the Jacob Leinart building, and Lewallen-Miller, Inc. From the left moving right are the Odd Fellows building and the old Clinton Hardware Co. building, which was torn down in 1961. The old Clinton Hardware Co. building had been home to Bernard's, the A&P store, and J.R. Daugherty's before it was demolished. The Jacob Leinart building was temporarily home to the Clinton Public Library. Lewallen-Miller, Inc., was known as "the Macy's of Clinton," and shoppers came all the way from Knoxville. Its millinery department was famous and employed milliners from Chicago to guarantee the latest style in hats. It sold the Famous and Buster Brown lines of footwear. (Courtesy of the Pellissippi Genealogical and Historical Society.)

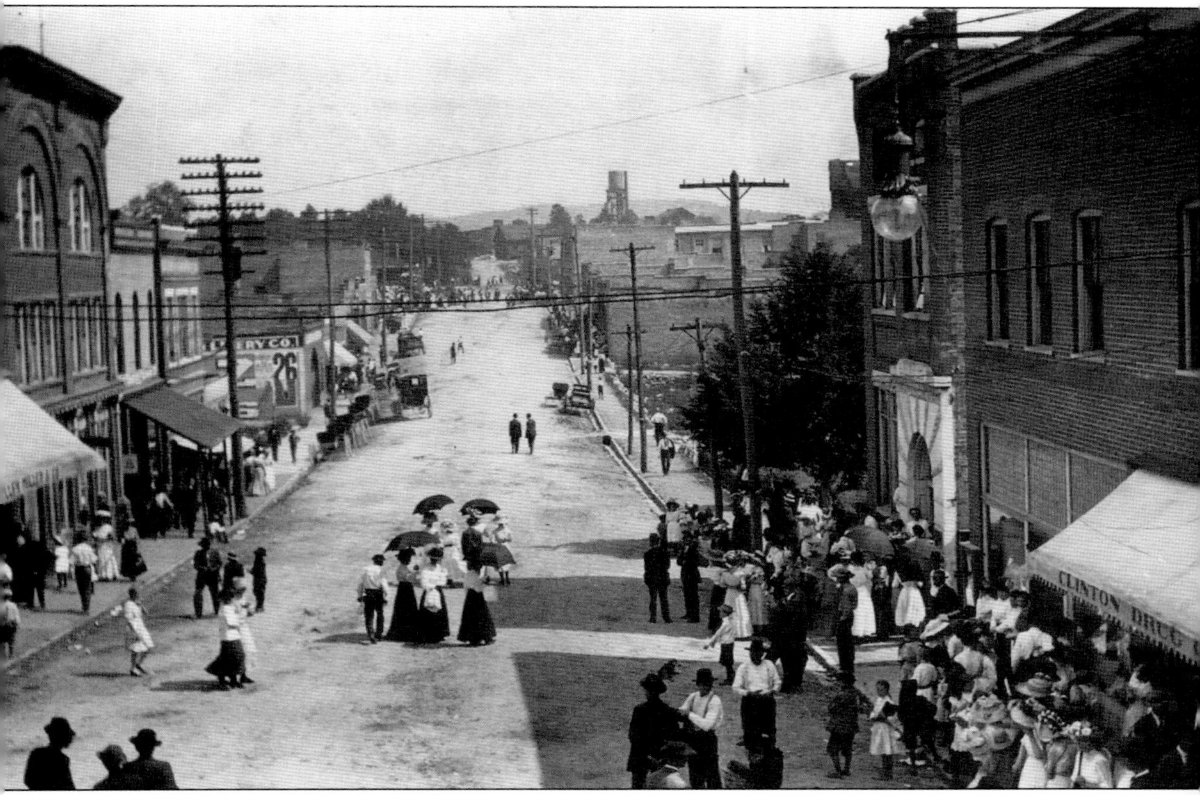

In another photograph from Labor Day, 1919, crowds line Depot (now Market) Street, looking toward the river. On the right, moving towards the middle of the picture, are the Clinton Drug Co. and the bank. On the left center is the Livery Co., with buggies parked out front. Clinton Drug Co. was started in 1895 by Dr. W.W. Medaris, who ran it until 1921, when his son took over. He sold it to Irwin Cross and Frank Margrave in 1931. They sold it to T.L. Seeber and Charles A. Haynes in 1938, and Charles Alverson joined the firm at that time. They incorporated in 1940. Alverson sold his share to Haynes in 1948, and Haynes sold the store to Paul Smith and Lon Campbell. In 1971, Campbell sold his interest to Smith. Smith brought his wife into the business, but they sold the store to Jim McBride, Fred Rowe, and Ken Smith in 1991. In 2002, McBride bought out the other interests and relocated the store to Charles Seivers Boulevard. (Courtesy of the Pellissippi Genealogical and Historical Society.)

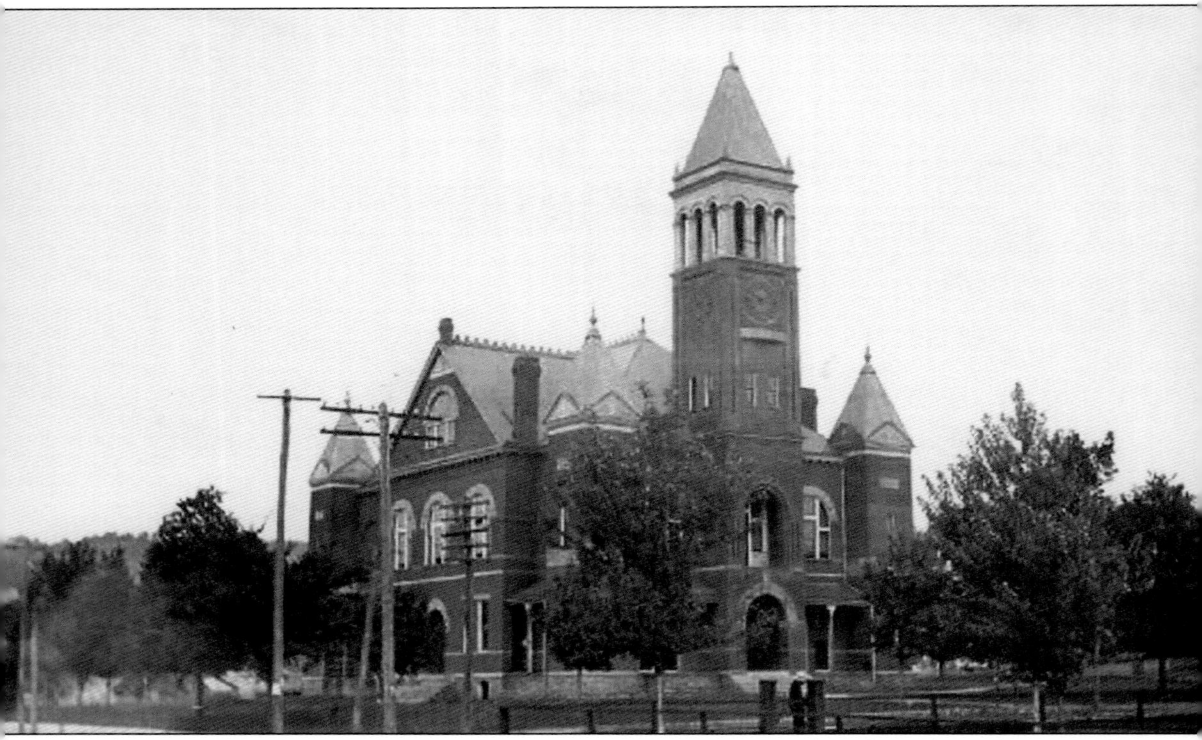

This view of the third Anderson County Courthouse shows its south and east faces along Broad (now West Broad) and Jacksboro (now Main) Streets. The fence in the lower right, with the man in the white hat passing in front of the gate, is the fence around the Jarnigan-Peak home, which stood on the corner directly across the street. This was the third courthouse to stand on the square and was built in 1893, replacing a stone two-story structure that had an outside stairway and an upstairs courtroom. This building has the classic Victorian architectural touches with stone arch eyebrows over the windows and towers with corner finials. The tower roofs are capped with finials, as is the main roof, which also has a roofline crest. This courthouse was torn down in 1965, and construction on the present courthouse began. (Courtesy of the Pellissippi Genealogical and Historical Society.)

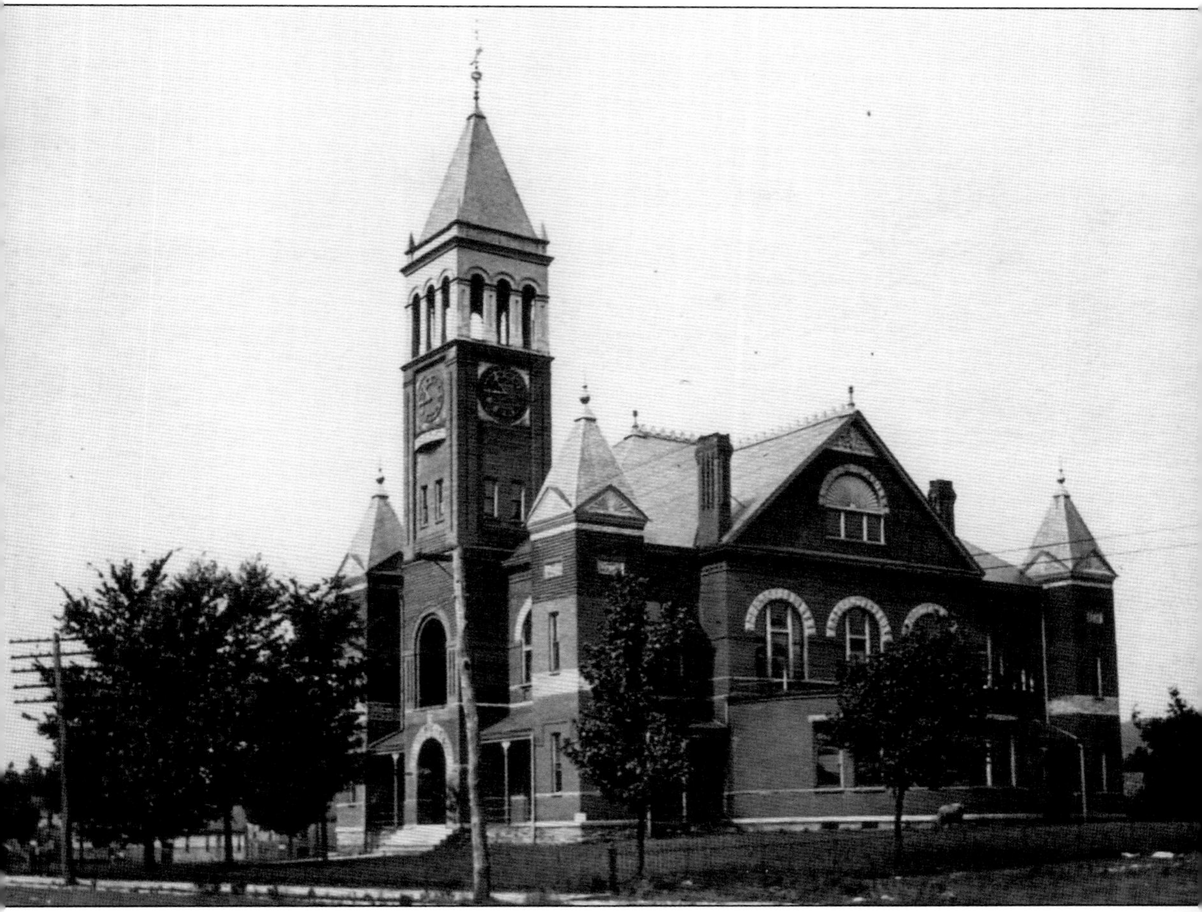

This view of the third courthouse shows its north face with the distinctive circular courtroom on the first floor. The jail was located on East Broad Street, across Jacksboro (now Main) Street from the courthouse, and was a two-story, heavy stone building. It is not visible in the photograph, as it stood on the opposite side of the street toward the old Clinch River bridge. This courthouse was built in 1893 to replace the two-story, rectangular stone building that was erected in 1820. The first courthouse to stand on the square was a log cabin built in 1803. All three courthouses had separate jails that stood nearby. The current Anderson County jail complex is located on the banks of the Clinch River, off State Highway 61. This photograph and the one on the preceding page are undated but must have been taken after 1906, when the first electrical lines were installed. (Courtesy of the Pellissippi Genealogical and Historical Society.)

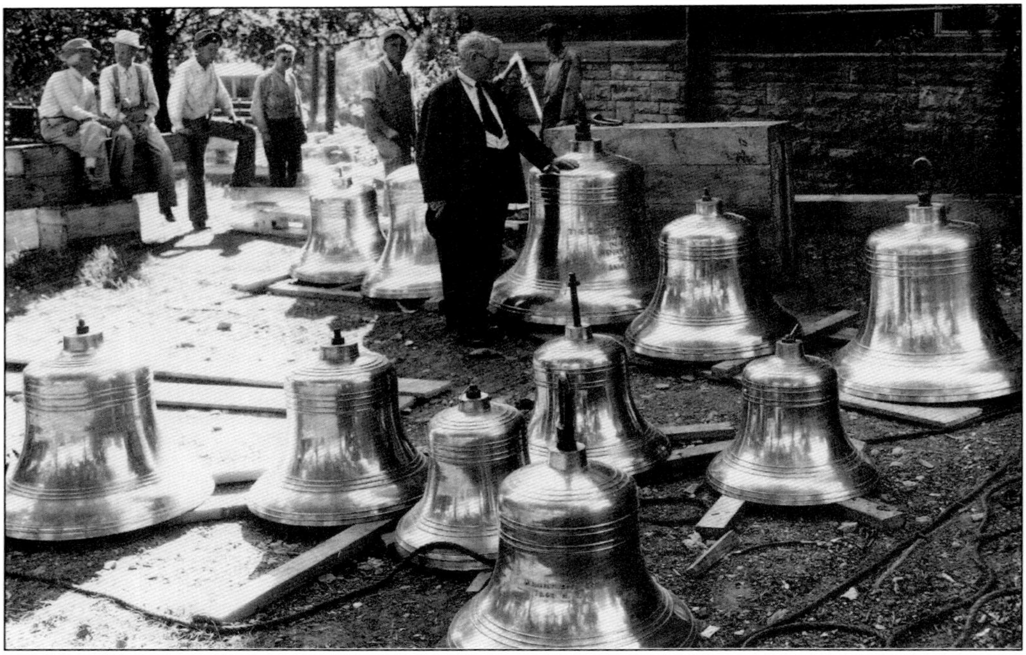

The chimes that ring from the top of the present Anderson County Courthouse were a gift from Samuel Slover in memory of his father, Henry Clay Slover. At the time they were installed in 1937, they cost $20,000. During their removal from the third courthouse, controversy arose over whether or not to save them and remount them on the new courthouse. They were reinstalled, and today, Clinton still enjoys the mellow tones of the "Slover chimes." In the photograph above, the bells are being readied for installation in 1937. The photograph below shows the bells being taken down from the bell tower of the third courthouse before it was dismantled. (Both, courtesy of Mary Harris.)

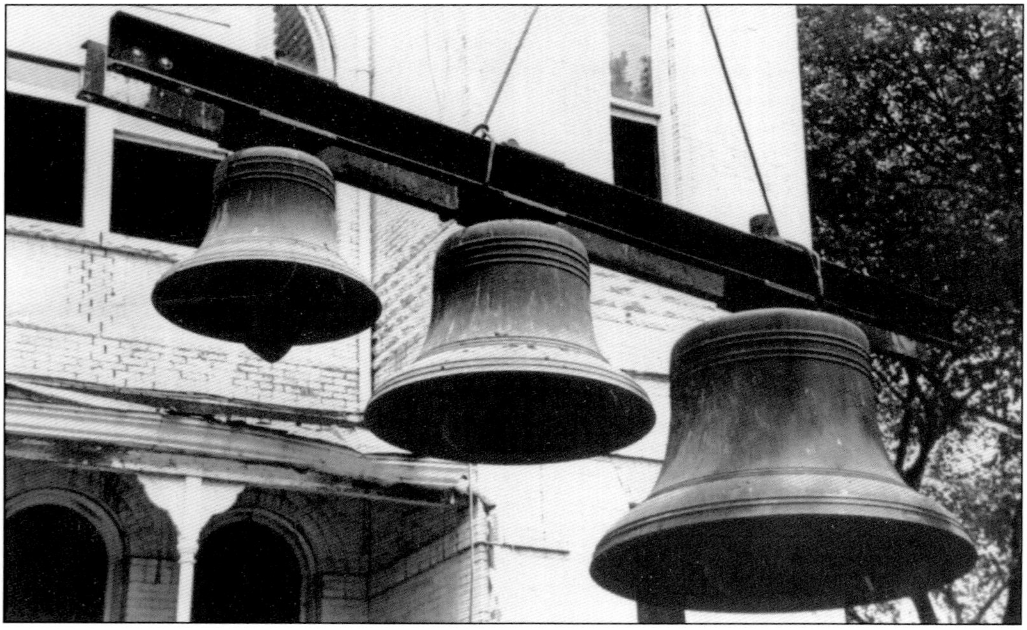

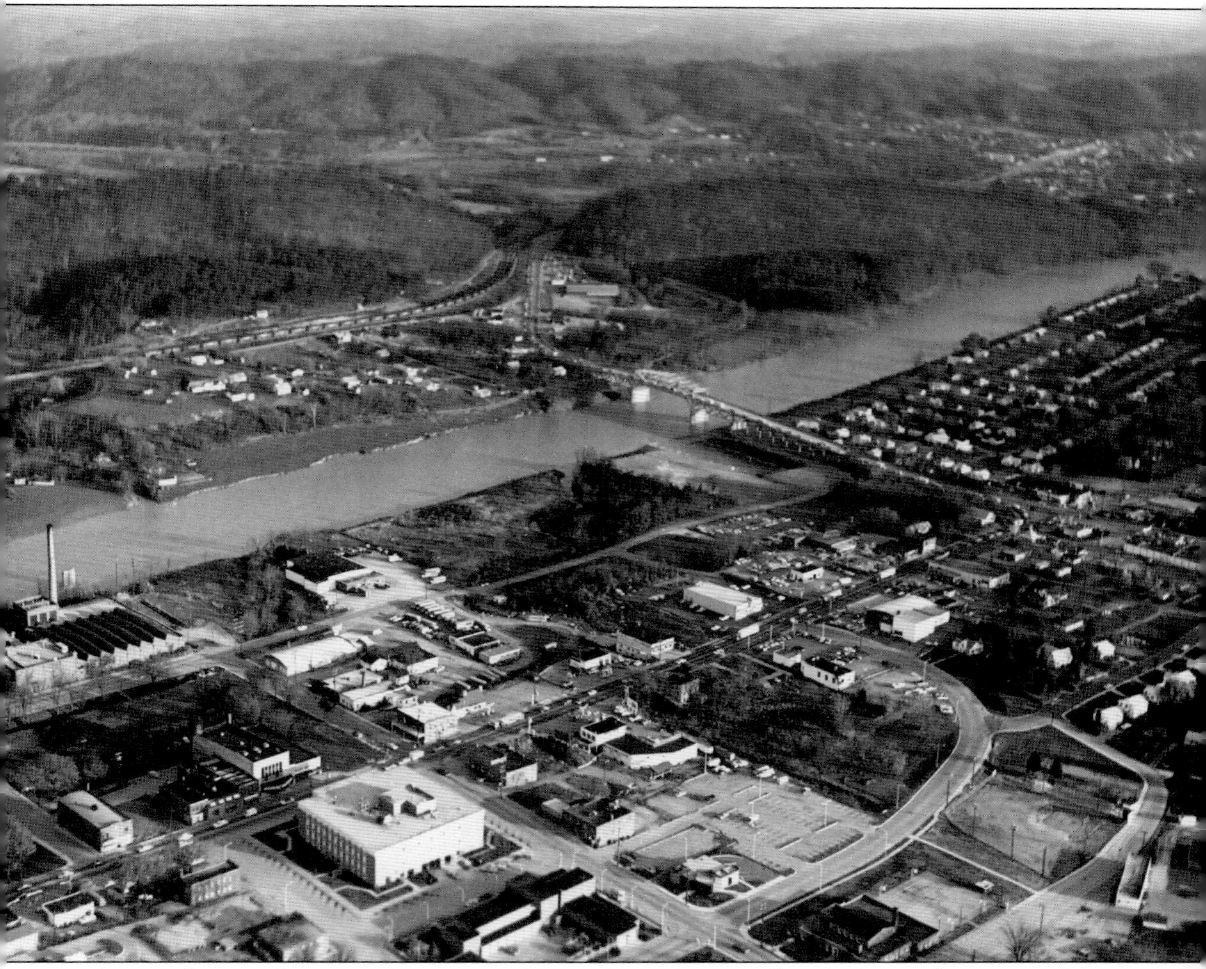

An aerial view taken over downtown Clinton shows the Lewallen Bridge in the center of the photograph. The supports for the old Clinch River bridge at the end of Broad Street are shown, still standing in the river at the extreme left above the Magnet Knitting Mills smokestack. The empty lot to the right of the mill now houses a medical office complex. The fourth courthouse, completed in 1967, is the three-story square building at the bottom left; the Ritz Theatre–Hoskins Drug Store building is directly in front of it. The empty lot directly behind the Ritz Theatre–Hoskins Drug Store building is now occupied by the Charles Seivers Towers, and the empty lot to the right of Hoskins Drug Store, the former site of the "Jarnigan Brick," is now occupied by Bank of America. The rectangular grassy lot in the curve of South Hicks Street is now occupied by the Clinton Public Library. Directly behind the courthouse is the Clinton City Hall and Police Department. (Courtesy of Maxine Meade Holbrook.)

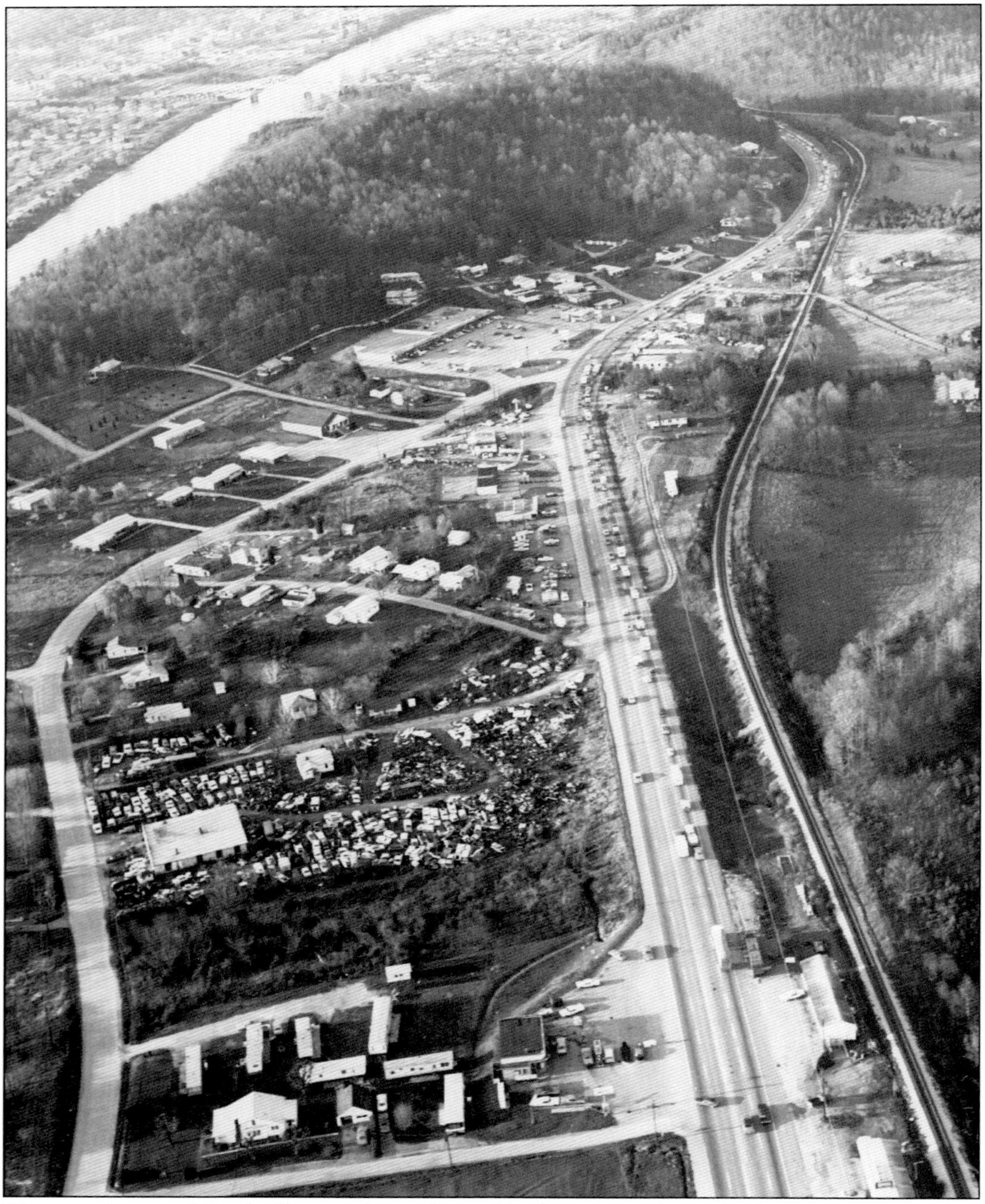

This aerial view of South Clinton shows the traffic flowing north on the four-lane US Highway 25W. Old US Highway 25W is shown running along the extreme left of the photograph and curving inward to meet the new road at the top of the image. That road is now called Hiway Drive. At the top of the photograph, where Hiway Drive meets US Highway 25W, there is a square lot with a building along the back edge of the lot. That lot is currently the shopping center where Apple Discount Drug and Save-a-Lot grocery store are located. The Clinch River is shown in the upper left corner with the Lewallen Bridge visible in the middle. (Courtesy of Maxine Meade Holbrook.)

Bibliography

"150 Members 25 Year Club at Banquet." *Clinton Courier-News*. September 29, 1956.

Anderson, Margaret and Robert Marlowe, eds. *Clinton–An Identity Rediscovered*. Clinton, TN: *Clinton Courier-News*, 1985.

"For A Decade of Service." *Clinton Courier-News*. December 23, 1948.

History of Andersonville Baptist Church and Andersonville Institute. Knoxville, TN: Coleman's Printing & Engraving, 1966.

Hoskins, Katherine B. *Anderson County Historical Sketches*. Clinton, TN: *Clinton Courier-News*, 1987.

Overholt, James. *Anderson County, Tennessee: A Pictorial History*. Norfolk, VA: The Donning Company, 1989.

Pellissippi Genealogical and Historical Society. *Tennessee 200 Bicentennial History of Anderson County, 1796–1996*. Jacksboro, TN: Action Printing, 1997.

Roberts, Snyder. *History of Clinton Senior High School, 1806–1971*. Clinton, TN: The Distributive Education Department, Clinton Senior High School, 1971.

Seeber, R. Clifford. *A History of Anderson County, Tennessee*. Master's thesis, Department of History, University of Tennessee, 1928.

"Sheriff's Staff." *Clinton Courier-News*. September 4, 1958.

Turner, Mary. *75 Years in District V*. Tennessee Extension Homemakers Council, 1989.